The Practitioner Inquiry Series

Marilyn Cochran-Smith and Susan L. Lytle, *SERIES EDITORS*

Going Public with Our Teaching:
An Anthology of Practice
 THOMAS HATCH,
 DILRUBA AHMED, ANN LIEBERMAN,
 DEBORAH FAIGENBAUM,
 MELISSA EILER WHITE, &
 DÉSIRÉE H. POINTER MACE, Editors

Teaching as Inquiry:
Asking Hard Questions to Improve
Practice and Student Achievement
 ALEXANDRA WEINBAUM,
 DAVID ALLEN, TINA BLYTHE,
 KATHERINE SIMON, STEVE SEIDEL,
 & CATHERINE RUBIN

"Is This English?" Race, Language,
and Culture in the Classroom
 BOB FECHO

Teacher Research for Better Schools
 MARIAN M. MOHR, COURTNEY
 ROGERS, BETSY SANFORD, MARY
 ANN NOCERINO, MARION S.
 MacLEAN, & SHEILA CLAWSON

Imagination and Literacy: A Teacher's
Search for the Heart of Learning
 KAREN GALLAS

Regarding Children's Words: Teacher
Research on Language and Literacy
 BROOKLINE TEACHER
 RESEARCHER SEMINAR

Rural Voices: Place-Conscious
Education and the Teaching of Writing
 ROBERT E. BROOKE, Editor

Teaching Through the Storm:
A Journal of Hope
 KAREN HALE HANKINS

Reading Families:
The Literate Lives of Urban Children
 CATHERINE COMPTON-LILLY

Narrative Inquiry in Practice:
Advancing the Knowledge of Teaching
 NONA LYONS &
 VICKI KUBLER LaBOSKEY, Editors

Learning from Teacher Research
 JOHN LOUGHRAN, IAN MITCHELL,
 & JUDIE MITCHELL, Editors

Writing to Make a Difference:
Classroom Projects for Community
Change
 CHRIS BENSON &
 SCOTT CHRISTIAN with
 DIXIE GOSWAMI &
 WALTER H. GOOCH, Editors

Starting Strong: A Different Look at
Children, Schools, and Standards
 PATRICIA F. CARINI

Because of the Kids: Facing Racial and
Cultural Differences in Schools
 JENNIFER E. OBIDAH &
 KAREN MANHEIM TEEL

Ethical Issues in Practitioner Research
 JANE ZENI, Editor

Action, Talk, and Text: Learning and
Teaching Through Inquiry
 GORDON WELLS, Editor

Teaching Mathematics to the New
Standards: Relearning the Dance
 RUTH M. HEATON

Teacher Narrative as Critical Inquiry:
Rewriting the Script
 JOY S. RITCHIE & DAVID E. WILSON

(continued)

D0916500

Practitioner Inquiry Series titles, continued

From Another Angle: Children's
Strengths and School Standards
    MARGARET HIMLEY with
    PATRICIA F. CARINI, Editors

Unplayed Tapes: A Personal History
of Collaborative Teacher Research
    STEPHEN M. FISHMAN &
    LUCILLE McCARTHY

Inside City Schools: Investigating
Literacy in the Multicultural Classroom
    SARAH WARSHAUER FREEDMAN,
    ELIZABETH RADIN SIMONS,
    JULIE SHALHOPE KALNIN, ALEX
    CASARENO, & the M-CLASS TEAMS

Class Actions: Teaching for Social
Justice in Elementary and Middle School
    JoBETH ALLEN, Editor

Teacher/Mentor:
A Dialogue for Collaborative Learning
    PEG GRAHAM, SALLY HUDSON-
    ROSS, CHANDRA ADKINS,
    PATTI McWHORTER, &
    JENNIFER McDUFFIE STEWART, Eds.

Teaching Other People's Children:
Literacy and Learning in a Bilingual
Classroom
    CYNTHIA BALLENGER

Teaching, Multimedia, and Mathematics: Investigations of Real Practice
    MAGDALENE LAMPERT &
    DEBORAH LOEWENBERG BALL

Tensions of Teaching:
Beyond Tips to Critical Reflection
    JUDITH M. NEWMAN

John Dewey and the Challenge of
Classroom Practice
    STEPHEN M. FISHMAN &
    LUCILLE McCARTHY

"Sometimes I Can Be Anything":
Power, Gender, and Identity in a
Primary Classroom
    KAREN GALLAS

Learning in Small Moments:
Life in an Urban Classroom
    DANIEL R. MEIER

Interpreting Teacher Practice:
Two Continuing Stories
    RENATE SCHULZ

Creating Democratic Classrooms:
The Struggle to Integrate Theory and
Practice
    LANDON E. BEYER, Editor

GOING PUBLIC
with OUR TEACHING

An Anthology of Practice

Edited by

Thomas Hatch, Dilruba Ahmed, Ann Lieberman,
Deborah Faigenbaum, Melissa Eiler White,
and Désirée H. Pointer Mace

in collaboration with
THE CARNEGIE FOUNDATION FOR THE
ADVANCEMENT OF TEACHING

Teachers College, Columbia University
New York and London

Published by Teachers College Press, 1234 Amsterdam Avenue, New York, NY 10027

Library of Congress Cataloging-in-Publication Data

Going public with our teaching: an anthyology of practice /
   edited by Thomas Hatch ... [et al.].
      p. cm. — (The practitioner inquiry series)
   Includes bibliographical references and index.
   ISBN 0-8077-4589-8 (pbk. : alk. paper)
      1. Teaching. 2. Teachers—Training of. I. Hatch, Thomas. II. Series.
   LB1025.G486 2005
   371.102—dc22   2004065901

ISBN 0-8077-4589-8 (paper)

Printed on acid-free paper
Manufactured in the United States of America

12 11 10 09 08 07 06 05   8 7 6 5 4 3 2 1

Contents

Acknowledgments   ix

Introduction   1
    Thomas Hatch

PART I:
THE CULTURE OF SCHOOLS AND CLASSROOMS

1. **The First Day of School: A Reflective
   Narrative Analysis**   17
   Timothy Boerst

2. **What Is a Culture of Quality?**   34
   Ron Berger

3. **Are Pullout Programs Sabotaging Classroom
   Community in Our Elementary Schools?**   57
   Lois Brandts

4. **A Narrative in Three Voices**   67
   Rebecca Akin

5. **The Mission Hill School**   70
   Heidi Lyne

6. **Circles of Influence: My Research Journey
   Into Culturally Engaged Instruction**   77
   Renee Moore

PART II:
THE CONTENT OF THE CURRICULUM:
EXPANDING CLASSROOM UNDERSTANDING

7. With an Eye on the Mathematical Horizon: Dilemmas
    of Teaching Elementary School Mathematics   95

    Deborah Loewenberg Ball

8. Messy Monk Mathematics:
    An NCTM-Standards–Inspired Class   133

    Larry Copes

9. Learning from Laramie: Urban High School Students
    Read, Research, and Reenact *The Laramie Project*   147

    Marsha R. Pincus

10. Pio Pico Student Researchers Participatory Action
    Research: From Classroom to Community,
    Transforming Teaching and Learning   166

    Emily Wolk

11. Was the American Revolution Completed Before
    the War Began?   171

    Steven Levy

12. A Friend of Their Minds: Capitalizing on the
    Oral Tradition of My African American Students   181

    Yvonne Divans Hutchinson

PART III:
ISSUES OF EQUITY, RACE, AND CULTURE

13. Helping African American Males Reach Their
    Academic Potential   189

    Marlene Carter

14. The Gap Is in Our Expectations   210

    Joan Kernan Cone

15. "And Justice for All":
    Using Writing and Literature to Confront Racism   214

    Griselle M. Diaz-Gemmati

16. Ma-Lee's Story   237

    Gerald Campano

17. Because You Like Us: The Language of Control   243

    Cynthia Ballenger

PART IV:
NEGOTIATING THE DILEMMAS OF TEACHING

18. Human Agency, Social Action, and
    Classroom Practices   257

    Vanessa Brown

19. Proposition 227, Stanford 9, and Open Court:
    Three Strikes Against English Language Learners   267

    Ramón Martínez

20. Principled Practice: New Science for the Classroom   270

    Jeffrey Maas

21. How Do Teachers Manage to Teach?: Perspectives
    on Problems in Practice   281

    Magdalene Lampert

About the Authors   305

Index   309

Acknowledgments

A book with so many editors demands a bit of explanation. From the inception of the CASTL program, we worked as a team, meeting together every week. Like the teachers in this book we differed in style, experience, knowledge, and practice. We became a team of colleagues in the best sense of the word: learning to critique, compliment, educate, and learn from one another. Among the many things we learned was how to respect our differences and acknowledge our unique strengths (and weaknesses).

In the process we have become friends and colleagues. It is our fondest hope that the teachers represented here will be read, discussed, critiqued and built upon in true scholarly and collegial fashion. And we hope that many will see these pieces as offering opportunities to learn from teachers who have thought deeply about their students, their learning, and their lives.

In developing this volume, Thomas Hatch and Ann Lieberman provided overall guidance in the design and development of the collection. Thomas Hatch developed the introduction and oversaw the editing of the selections. Kim Austin conducted the initial searches for works by teachers, and Ruba Ahmed with the help of Deborah Faigenbaum and Melissa Eiler White took responsibility for finding and reviewing numerous possible selections. Desiree Pointer Mace helped to develop the websites and multimedia contributions. Ruba Ahmed also provided the crucial leadership and tireless dedication needed to bring this volume to publication as she tracked down permissions and copyrights, corresponded with authors and publishers, edited the manuscripts, and responded to comments.

Neither the development of this book nor many of the pieces in it would have been possible without the leadership and support of Lee Shulman. Numerous colleagues at the Carnegie Foundation also contributed their time and expertise to the development of the program and the support of our work. Pat Hutchings deserves special recognition for her leadership of the development of the CASTL program in Higher Education, which served as a model for much of our work, and Toru Iiyoshi and his colleagues at the Knowledge Media Lab provided countless hours of support for the program and the CASTL scholars; led by Desiree Pointer Mace and Thomas Hatch, they played a key role in developing many of the multimedia products of the CASTL scholars.

Of course, all the work that we have been able to do reflects the hard work, dedication, and passion of the many teachers and teacher educators who have participated in the CASTL K–12 Program and enriched our personal and professional lives along the way. The program also benefited from the hard work and goodwill of a number of individuals who worked directly on the program, including original project coordinator Michele Lew, Ruby Kerawalla, Jason Raley, Kimberly Austin, Ann-Marie Wiese, and Sonia Gonzalez. Anna Richert, adding to her numerous other responsibilities at Mills College and elsewhere, served as a critical member of our team and an unflagging source of encouragement and good ideas.

The development of the K–12 CASTL program and this volume reflects the advice and support of a truly wonderful group of advisors—Marilyn Cochran-Smith, Jackie Jordan Irvine, Richard Middleton, and Richard Sterling—who gave their time and brought good ideas and good nature to our meetings. Marilyn Cochran-Smith and Susan Lytle, as the editors of this series at Teachers College Press, were instrumental in seeing that this volume was published. Ron Berger deserves special mention for the original suggestion to create a volume such as this and for his quiet and consistent encouragement throughout.

We would also like to thank the William and Flora Hewlett Foundation; Atlantic Philanthropies, Incorporated; and the Hewlett Packard Corporation for providing a significant portion of the funds to develop the K–12 CASTL Program and this book. All conclusions, however, are the responsibility of the editors and authors.

GOING PUBLIC
with OUR TEACHING

An Anthology of Practice

Introduction

Thomas Hatch

FROM PRIVATE PRACTICE TO LOCAL THEORIES

The general "problems" of teaching are well known. The difficulties of raising student achievement; inadequate pay and preparation; and a lack of time, support, and resources are often the source of public debates and the focus of research and reform efforts. These problems reflect the intractable issues of the profession and circumstances of teaching that even large-scale and systemic endeavors seem incapable of resolving. But the specific problems that teachers face every day in the classroom do not have to be seen in such a negative light. In fact, for many teachers, the "problems" they face in the classroom can lead teachers to ask serious intellectual questions about their practice that they themselves can address (Bass, 1999; Lampert, 2001): How do I help this group of fourth graders develop a robust understanding of odd and even numbers? How can I take into account the backgrounds and experiences of the Haitian students in my preschool class? How can I enable my special education students to build their academic skills and to develop as community leaders at the same time?

Teachers cannot avoid these kinds of questions: They think about them on their feet in their classrooms, while reflecting on the day's activities with their colleagues, and when lying awake at night. By pursuing these "problems of practice," teachers expand their understanding and improve their work. They begin to think about responses that cut across times, contexts, and individuals. They make inferences and develop hypotheses that suggest courses of action that may work both for their students at that moment and for the students in other classes and coming years. In short, when teachers address the "problems" and questions in their classroom, they make theory out of practice. They make local theories that they can apply in a number of related contexts and that other teachers can learn from and build upon. These local theories can serve as the basis for a powerful knowledge-base different from—but no less important than—the knowledge-base that has emerged from conventional research on teaching and learning.

GOING PUBLIC: CONFRONTING SIMPLISTIC ASSUMPTIONS AND REPRESENTING THE COMPLEXITIES OF TEACHING

Too often the sense teachers make of the real problems of practice they face—those grounded in specific contexts with real students—never gets shared beyond occasional informal conversations with colleagues. In fact, while researchers' efforts to address the general problems of teaching are presumed to be applicable to a wide audience, the responses that teachers make to the intellectual problems and questions they face in their own classroom are treated as if they have little relevance for others.

The failure to recognize and build on the knowledge that teachers develop over the course of their careers grows out of a set of assumptions about the nature of teaching and the work of teachers. Many conventional approaches to teaching and supporting teachers function as if teaching were a relatively simple process in which teachers deliver information to students and provide opportunities for them to practice and master basic skills. In such a conception, the emphasis for teachers is on delivering curriculum, not on developing it. Teachers are only seen as being "on task" when they are working with students in the classroom—not when they reflect on their practice, discuss it with their colleagues, or prepare articles about it. Consequently, teachers receive relatively little institutional support and recognition for contributing to the production of the knowledge and understandings that they need to be effective.

Despite these conventional assumptions about the simplicity of teaching, a number of individuals, groups, and organizations have long sought to support teachers interested in examining their practice and sharing the results with others (for accounts of some of these initiatives see, for example, Cochran-Smith & Lytle, 1993; Freedman et al., 1999; Lieberman & Wood, 2003). These efforts embrace an entirely different set of assumptions: Teaching is a complex intellectual endeavor that demands deep understandings of students, the appropriate disciplines, and the pedagogical principles and practices needed to bring all three together. These efforts reflect the view that the development of such understandings depends upon opportunities for teachers to examine their own practice in the company of their peers over significant periods of time. From this perspective, teachers are developing new insights and ideas and learning all the time, advancing not only their own work, but also the work of their colleagues and their disciplines.

Many of these initiatives share the belief that inquiry is central to learning. Building on John Dewey's (1904) argument that learning to teach is inseparable from learning to inquire, they see reflecting on practice—generating questions and hypotheses, exploring alternative explanations, and drawing conclusions—as one of the most effective methods for teachers to develop the deep understandings and special expertise they need to teach well. They often view inquiry as a key means for teachers to demonstrate the creativity, autonomy, and judgment of professionals (Cochran-Smith & Lytle, 1993; Darling Hammond & McLaughlin, 1995; Hargreaves, 1993; Hollingsworth & Sockett, 1994; Little, 1993; Stenhouse, 1983, 1988; Zeichner, 1998). They also reflect the idea that by inquiring into their own practice, teachers can articulate and share what they are learning in ways that can contribute to the development of a broader knowledge-base of teaching, support the learning of their colleagues, and enhance the performance of schools (Cochran-Smith & Lytle, 1999; Hiebert, Gallimore, & Stigler, 2002; Shulman, 1987).

THE PURPOSES OF *GOING PUBLIC WITH OUR TEACHING*

This volume builds on many of these long-standing efforts to support teacher inquiry and scholarship in order to draw attention to the fact that teachers are producing powerful insights and useful knowledge all the time, in many ways, and in many different contexts; not just in formal research projects that lead to publications in scholarly journals, but in a wide range of formats that can also have a powerful influence on practice. By collecting the works of a variety of teachers, we seek to illuminate many of the "problems of practice" teachers deal with every day to highlight how they come to new understandings about these problems, to show the manifold ways that they can make their teaching public, and to lend legitimacy to their efforts to do so. In the process, we hope to expand the interest in and the audience for making teaching public and to support the development of the conditions, investments, and practices that will make it possible to learn from teachers and build on their knowledge and expertise.

The works in this volume are not intended to be viewed as a "best of" collection, but rather as a representative sample of the kinds of work that teachers today produce. We selected works that we hope will function as an "ensemble" that stimulates discussions of the nature and variety of teachers' work and facilitates the recognition and support for the development of new methods, forms, and directions for their work in the future.

THE ORIGINS OF *GOING PUBLIC WITH OUR TEACHING*

This collection grows out of our experiences in designing and leading the K–12 program of the Carnegie Academy for the Scholarship of Teaching (CASTL). Under the auspices of the Carnegie Foundation for the Advancement of Teaching, the K–12 program of CASTL, along with the CASTL higher education program, launched in 1997, was established in order to enhance the practice and profession of teaching and to bring to teaching the recognition and reward afforded to other forms of scholarly work. As Lee Shulman, the president of the Carnegie Foundation, argues, teachers make their examinations public and subject them to critical review by peers, and when others are able to build upon those examinations to advance their own work, teachers are meeting many of the same criteria that are used to distinguish scholarly work in many other disciplines (Hutchings & Shulman, 1999).

The Carnegie Academy for the Scholarship of Teaching and Learning

The CASTL program has been designed to enable teachers to document what they are learning and to make their teaching public; to foster the development of the language and standards that permit their work to be reviewed critically; and to contribute to the creation of new forms and forums of publication through which teachers can exchange and build upon one another's work. In order to accomplish these goals, the K–12 CASTL program provides fellowships that include a small honorarium and opportunities for small groups of teachers to come together with colleagues several times over a one- to two-year period while they carry out an inquiry into their own teaching. The program initially supported two groups of CASTL scholars: The first cohort (1999–2001) included 14 K–12 teachers and 6 teacher educators, and the second cohort (2001–2002) included 18 K–12 teachers. A third group that includes 19 new teachers and teacher educators was launched in 2003.[1]

Scanning the Field:
Searching for Models of the Scholarship of Teaching

When we began our work with the first cohort of K-12 CASTL scholars in the summer of 1999, we experienced a problem that confronts many of those who seek to make teaching public: Although many teachers are actively inquiring into their own practice and many are sharing that work within their own schools and organizations, it is still difficult to get quick access to a wide variety of that work. Much of their work remains unpublished and that which is published is spread out in books, journals, and publications of various networks and organizations.

We encountered this problem when we asked the CASTL scholars to propose and pursue a project related to their teaching that would be of interest and of use to a wide audience. Hoping to provide as much freedom as possible for the teachers to represent what they were learning, we simply asked them to develop a "final product" but did not specify what that might entail. Many of the scholars still wanted to know what kinds of "final products" we had in mind—what might "count" and what might not. In response, we sought to find a diverse set of examples that could serve as models for their work.

Our search turned up a small number of well-known and previously published pieces that many of our colleagues refer to again and again. However, many of these articles reflected a somewhat similar "research" or narrative format, and we found it hard to find examples that used other genres or multimedia. In order to find a more diverse collection of works, we contacted teacher networks, educational reform organizations, disciplinary associations, and editors of educational journals and newspapers. We also consulted with teacher educators and colleagues and asked them to send us pieces by teachers that they used in their own classes. Ultimately, for our own purposes, we put together an informal ensemble of sample products that included some research articles, book chapters, op-ed pieces, early teaching portfolios, and rough videotapes. Subsequently, we expanded our group of examples by adding works produced and sometimes published by the first and second cohorts of CASTL scholars.

SELECTION AND ORGANIZATION OF THIS VOLUME

This volume brings many of the pieces in our informal collection to a wider audience. We selected pieces that address key problems of practice across diverse contexts; reflect the diversity of styles and genres in which teachers present their work; link to new forms of representation that use video, audio, and the Internet to make teaching public; and bring together work from some of the many groups and individuals who have long made teacher inquiry and research a focus of their work.

Representing Different Styles and Genres

In the volume, we purposely include works that represent different styles and genres of writing. Some pieces reflect the rigors and demands of writing for academic audiences while others offer the kinds of opinions and reflections that might be found in newspapers or dairies. Deborah Ball's research originally published in *The Elementary School Journal* sits alongside the narratives of Vanessa Brown and Emily Wolk, the personal reflections of Heidi Lyne and Yvonne Hutchinson, and the editorial and opinion pieces of Joan Kernan Cone and Ramón Martínez.

Also, the pieces vary substantially in length and substance. Some pieces are printed in their entirety, but others, such as the excerpts from Ron Berger's monograph, from Heidi Lyne's reflections, and from the narratives on Rebecca Akin and Emily Wolk's website, are meant to provide readers with a glimpse into the kinds of issues and ideas presented in other forms of representation such as books, videos, and websites.

Representing Published and Unpublished Work

The differences in style and substance also reflect our desire to include both published and unpublished works. This decision grows from a commitment to recognize the many avenues through which teachers can make their work public and to embrace the possibility and the power of pieces that may convey expertise, experiences, emotions, practices, ideas, and results in nontraditional ways.

We selected the previously published pieces because both we and our colleagues continue to draw on these pieces in teacher education courses and professional development work, and because they reveal some of the history of the work teachers have carried out. These pieces raise issues that are as important today as they were when they were written.

Some of the unpublished pieces have been presented at conferences or submitted for publication, but others, such as the written excerpts from the videos and websites, remain largely unknown because appropriate channels for distribution and dissemination have yet to be developed.

Representing Teaching Beyond Traditional Texts

We have chosen to include writing from several multimedia works in this collection, because we believe that they reflect new and potentially powerful ways to show the complexities of teaching and to enable people to learn from the experiences of teachers.

In our own work, simply seeing what a colleague's website looks like, hearing what a narrative can sound like, or seeing what a video can represent, has inspired CASTL scholars to experiment with entirely new forms of conveying their ideas to others. For example, several members of the first cohort of CASTL scholars who had written extensively about their research changed their approach after viewing the first page of a website by Elizabeth Barkley, a professor of music at Foothill Community College in California (see Figure I.1). The scholars immediately envisioned the potential for using the web to share their own writing as well as their curriculum materials, student work, and video and audio recordings of their classrooms.

In that spirit, we have included written texts or written excerpts that go along with an audio performance developed by Rebecca Akin, a video and website created by Heidi Lyne, and websites produced by Yvonne Hutchin-

---

Figure I.1. The work on Barkley's website, *From Catastrophe to Celebration: An Analysis of a Curricular Transformation*, incorporates musical video clips to underscore the transformations she made in her music courses. See http://www.gallery.carnegiefoundation.org/ebarkley/

son and Emily Wolk in order to open a small window into the kinds of multimedia representations that we hope will inspire teachers in the future. One of our biggest challenges in including these materials remains that the power and possibilities of websites, videos, and other multimedia materials cannot be contained in printed text. The writings from the websites include quotes and descriptions of the sites, as well as some longer excerpts.

If we could, we would include the websites and videos themselves alongside the written excerpts and more conventional texts that appear in this volume. Ideally, we would create a hybrid product that embraces the challenge of inventing new forms for conveying teachers' work. Of course, such an effort presents a number of problems, not the least of which is how to refer to such a collection (is this a book? a volume? a transmedia collection?) and the pieces it cannot completely contain. From our perspective the only way to begin to deal with the problems of language, "reading," and distribution that come with such a venture into a new frontier is to invite others to come along. To that end, we encourage readers to view a special exhibition of teaching and learning on the public website of the Carnegie Foundation for the Advancement of Teaching (see Figure I.2). That site contains the websites, videos, and

Figure I.2. The *Going Public* online exhibition includes related websites, videos, and audio recordings. See http://goingpublicwithteaching.org

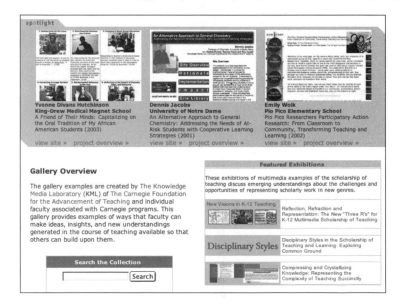

audio recordings referred to here as well as a number of other works, including websites that represent the work of several other authors in the book, among them Vanessa Brown, Joan Kernan Cone, Renee Moore, and Marsha Pincus.

Clustering Work Around Central Issues of Teaching

For the teachers and others we have worked with, the power of the pieces collected here comes from their ability to represent the complexity of teaching in a variety of guises. For the most part, these works do not relate investigations that focus on a single problem or question and try to provide a definitive "solution" or explanation. Some pieces, for example, Magdalene Lampert's, focus directly on the complexity of teaching. Others—among them the work of Rebecca Akin, Gerald Campano and Emily Wolk—explicitly try to capture many of the different issues that teachers have to deal with all at once. As a result, simply by reading through these pieces one finds that any number of important issues come to the forefront. However, each of these pieces also reflects some of the fundamental issues and dilemmas that teachers face, and we have tried to organize the volume around them, as seen in the part titles: "The Culture of Schools and Classrooms"; "The Content of the Curriculum: Expanding Classroom Understanding"; "Issues of Equity, Race, and Culture"; and "Negotiating the Dilemmas of Teaching." Each Part is described in the book.

Highlighting "Leitmotifs" That Cut Across the Parts

Although we have placed each of the chapters into what seems to be the most appropriate part, most—if not all—of these pieces belong in more than one place. In order to capitalize on the common issues and themes that arise across different pieces, within each section we chose to juxtapose pieces, rather than group them by level, style, or methodological approach. In this manner, the pieces also raise a number of issues that function almost as themes or leitmotifs that come and go, providing harmonies and counterpoints to the major topics.

In fact, if you read these pieces in another sequence, different issues may arise, including how teachers can hold fast to their own beliefs and standards when facing increasing demands from all sides; the importance of the "second look"—the hard, critical look—at initial assumptions about the nature of "success"; the difficulty of bridging the cultures and languages of home and the academic discourse of school; and the roles of students and teachers in creating meaningful or "authentic" educational experiences.

Many of the pieces collected here deal with controversial issues of race and ethnicity. Some of them are included in the Part "Issues of Equity, Race, and Culture." However, issues of race and ethnicity lie beneath the surface of many educational debates, and they cannot be confined to a single topic or section. As a result, controversial topics and language are spread throughout the volume. The issues addressed in these chapters include how to work with students from many different backgrounds, but they also raise such concerns as like how to represent students and their work. Is it possible to describe the struggles and family circumstances of students who are experiencing problems without stereotyping them or others like them? Is it appropriate and necessary to use offensive language and describe troubling scenes that many involved might prefer to keep private? These kinds of questions and many others were discussed and debated among those in the CASTL program and others who reviewed many of the works in this collection. The conversations were not always easy to have, but we felt it was important to include controversial works in this volume because teachers have to face these issues every day, often without the benefit of the distance and careful examination that these pieces help to provide.

MAKING TEACHING
PUBLIC AND PROFESSIONAL

A single collection such as this cannot resolve the challenges of making teaching public or suddenly render the work of teachers accessible to a wide audience, but we hope that it can draw attention to the power and value of teachers' work and reinforce the need for other collections, outlets, and organizations that can make that work more accessible. In order to ensure that the works collected here and produced by teachers in many other groups and settings contribute to a larger movement to improve teaching, not just the advancement of the work and ideas of a few groups or individuals, several critical issues have to be addressed.

Teachers cannot be expected to do the kind of work represented in this volume alone and in isolation; they need opportunities to reflect on their practice with others, and they need the support of the social and intellectual infrastructure that is essential to scholarship in so many other disciplines. To begin expanding opportunities for teachers, we can build on the support that already exists in the activities and norms of some teacher networks, professional development groups, and academic institutions. For example, the deadlines, conversations, and feedback that come with opportunities for teachers to present their own work in meetings of teacher networks and school reform organizations can be powerful motivators and supports for teachers like the authors in this collection. At these meetings, teachers can test out their hypotheses, give and receive feedback, come into contact with real audiences, and develop the connections that can help them gain new information and resources as well as find further presentation and publication opportunities. Even informal meetings among teachers at a particular school or in a district can provide some support for the scholarship of teaching. But these kinds of informal conversations and presentations need to be connected to more formal and public opportunities that can make teachers' work available for debate and discussion outside their own contexts and networks.

While we hope that the works collected here will support the recognition of the many ways that teachers can make their practice, their "problems," and the theories they produce available for others to build upon, the use of a wide range of formats, media, and technologies in representing teachers' work does not necessarily transform teachers into scholars or turn personal reflections into scholarship. Websites, videos, and other media afford opportunities to produce different kinds of work and reach different audiences, but only the critical and collaborative examination of that work can determine whether it is useful for others. To that end, the mechanisms and forums for exchanging and reviewing teachers' work across groups, organizations, and contexts also have to be developed.

Finally, we have to go beyond lip service to the notion that teachers are professionals. Too often, teachers are treated as if they cannot be trusted to make decisions about teaching and learning—as if their classroom practice has to be monitored and controlled. Guidance, support, and direction can be valuable assets that help teachers deal with the complexity and unpredictability of their classrooms. But to advance their own practice and the practice of the profession as whole, teachers have to be able to engage in professional activities—examining problems, raising questions, evaluating alternatives, making judgments, and sharing their conclusions with others—as a regular part of their work.

NOTE

1. To learn more about the scholarship of teaching and the CASTL program that led to the development of this book, see the CASTL website at www.carnegiefoundation.org/castl/k-12/

REFERENCES

Bass, R. (1999, February). The scholarship of teaching: What's the problem? *inventio, 1*(1). Retrieved January 28, 2004, from http://www.doiiit.gmu.edu/Archives/feb98/randybass.htm.

Cochran-Smith, M., & Lytle, S. L. (1993). *Inside/outside: Teacher research and knowledge.* New York: Teachers College Press.

Cochran-Smith, M., & Lytle, S. L. (1999). Relationships of knowledge and practice: Teacher learning in communities. In A. Iran-Nejad & C. D. Pearson (Eds.), *Review of research in education* (Vol. 24; pp. 249–305). Washington, DC: American Educational Research Association.

Darling Hammond, L., & McLaughlin, M. (1995). Policies that support professional development in an era of reform. *Phi Delta Kappan, 76*(8), 597–604.

Dewey, J. (1904). The relation of theory to practice in education. In C. A. Murray (Ed.), *The relation of theory to practice in the education of teachers* (Third Yearbook of the National Society for the Scientific Study of Education, Part I, pp. 9–30). Chicago: University of Chicago Press.

Freedman, S. W., Simons, E. R., Kalnin, J. S., Casareno, A., & the M-Class Teams. (1999). *Inside city schools: Investigating literacy in multicultural classrooms.* New York: Teachers College Press.

Hargreaves, A. (1993). *Changing teachers, changing times: Teachers' work and culture in the postmodern age.* New York: Teachers College Press.

Hargreaves, A. (1996). Revisiting voice. *Educational Researcher, 25*(1), 12–19.

Hiebert, J., Gallimore, R., & Stigler, J. W. (2002). A knowledge base for the teaching profession: What would it look like and how can we get one? *Educational Researcher, 31*(5), 3–15.

Hollingsworth, S., & Sockett, H. (1994). *Ninety-third yearbook of the National Society for the Study of Education, Part 1: Teacher research and educational reform.* Chicago: University of Chicago Press.

Hutchings, P., & Shulman, L. S. (1999). The scholarship of teaching: New elaborations, new developments. *Change, 31*(5), 10–15.

Lampert, M. (2001). *Teaching problems and the problems of teaching.* New Haven: Yale University Press.

Lieberman, A., & Wood, D. (2003). *Inside the National Writing Project: Connecting network learning and classroom teaching.* New York: Teachers College Press.

Little, J. W. (1993). Teachers' professional development in a climate of reform. *Educational Evaluation and Policy Analysis, 15*(2), 129–151.

Rose, M. (1996). *Possible lives: The promise of public education in America*. New York: Penguin.

Shulman, L. S. (1987). Knowledge and teaching: Foundations of the new reform. *Harvard Educational Review, 57*(1), 1–22.

Stenhouse, L. (1983). The relevance of practice to theory. *Theory into Practice, 22*(3), 211–215.

Stenhouse, L. (1988). Artistry and teaching: The teacher as focus of research and development. *Journal of Curriculum and Supervision, 4*(1), 43–51.

Zeichner, K. M. (1998). *The nature and impact of teacher research as a professional development activity for P–12 educators*. Unpublished manuscript.

PART I

The Culture of Schools and Classrooms

In this section of the book, teachers write about both the problems and the possibilities of creating rich learning cultures in their classrooms and schools. The pieces cover a wide range of interests and styles, beginning with Boerst's thoughts about the first day of school in a fifth-grade classroom in Michigan. Berger's sixth-grade students build a culture of quality by working in their rural Massachusetts community, learning to critique one another's work, and pressuring one another. Brandts illustrates how well-intentioned "pullout" programs in one southern California school disrupt learning and deny students opportunities to participate fully in the dynamics of their elementary classrooms. Akin's narrative explores complex and sometimes contradictory perceptions of one student in an early childhood classroom in the San Francisco Bay Area. Lyne—through a website and video documentary—provides a glimpse of how the development of standards and exhibitions contributes to the culture of a K–8 pilot school in Boston. High school language arts teacher Moore chronicles how her struggle with teaching Standard English in the Mississippi Delta becomes the impetus to develop "culturally engaged instruction" for African American students.

CHAPTER 1

The First Day of School: A Reflective Narrative Analysis

Tim Boerst

New Fifth Grader,

When you get to fifth grade you find your desk and then Mr. Boerst starts to talk about himself . . . Since this is your first day you'll listen to Mr. Boerst talk and talk, about how he's really happy to have you in his class and that he hopes you all have a great year. Be prepared to be bored! . . . Then you'll probably go outside for recess. You'll find out he's got a couple easy rules so be sure to follow them. . . . In the middle of the week you will probably start easy fifth grade work. . . . The totally best thing about the first day is that it's a half-day of school!

—Merged excerpts from multiple texts/fifth-grade students, June 1996

Sometimes the thought of teaching 30 students makes me nervous, turns my stomach, and makes my heart beat a bit faster. This phenomenon happens within many different time frames. Each morning as I drive to work I think through my day. At some point on Highway 23 North, M14 West, traveling through Plymouth or seeing the Inkster Road exit, I think of something new or newly remembered that begins that mixed feeling of unease and anticipation. I get the same feeling often enough on Sunday nights that my wife and I have dubbed it the "Sunday Troubles." After roughly considering the week ahead and plotting out what I hope to accomplish I become unnerved at the thought of teaching. Aside from the daily and weekly battles with this feeling there is one particular time the thought of teaching causes emotional turmoil, the start of the new school year. (8/25/97 Teaching Journal)

To everything there is a beginning, and the school year is no exception. If possible, the first day of school takes the normally complex act of teaching to even greater levels of difficulty. The first day of school marks a time when teachers and students must begin to undertake work that cannot be accomplished in one day. In fact, much of what is undertaken on the first day of school will continue to be a work in progress, never fully finished even by the end of the year. On the first day of school, anxious groups of students and teachers need to strike out on an ambitious learning adventure without a shared understanding of destinations, maps, basic knowledge of one another, or how they might work together to reach their goals. Each group has its own account of the first day of school, as you can see from the excerpts that begin this chapter. The intersection of my students' narratives, filled with boredom and inactivity (aside from recess); my own nervous unfulfilling narrative; and my peers' quirky, often incompatible narratives indicated that critical examination of the first day of school was in order. Could I design and enact an approach to the first day of school that might yield more satisfactory narratives?

Aside from a personal desire to begin the school year in a positive way and student concern about what transpires on the first day, is there any foundation for believing that success on the first day of the school is critical? Relevant literature on this topic, while scarce, is primarily found in journals and books written for and marketed to practicing teachers. Messages such as those of Wong and Wong (1991) help to create a sense of urgency about the first day of school: "The first days of school can make or break you. What you do on the first days of school will determine your success or failure for the rest of the school year. You will either win or lose your class on the first days of school" (p. 3). It is not enough to be prepared with content or rules on the first days of school. Teachers are encouraged to be passionate and personable so that they can make positive impressions on those they wish to lead. "Students don't just want someone who is nice. They want someone with personality. Put yourself in your students' squeaky new shoes. While they're anxiously asking themselves, 'Who am I going to get?', ask yourself, 'How am I going to be me?' (Amato, 1995). Perhaps another indication of the importance of the first day of school in practitioner literature is the sheer volume of space devoted to sharing of "surefire" first-day-of-school activities. With the varied content and goals of these activities, there appear to be many essential tasks to accomplish on the first day. While there are many different views about what it means to have a successful first day of school, practitioner literature underscores its importance.

With the importance of the first day of school confirmed by practitioner literature (albeit scantly available), there are four reasons to study the event carefully. The first two concern me personally, the third concerns practitioners, and the last concerns educational research. First, by making the first day of school a focus of study I hoped to more carefully construct what I planned to do on the first day and better understand what happened on that day through structured reflection. The combination of these undertakings would better inform me for subsequent first days of school. Second, I honestly wondered what factors might contribute to the feelings of worry and anxiety that I feel each year before and during the first day of school. If I examined events and factors leading up to the first day, I might be able to think about future first days in a more enlightened way, reducing to some degree the emotional stress of that initial day of teaching. Third, the first day of school is a phenomenon in which other teachers take strong interest. Since little research has focused on this event, research could spur other practitioners to more carefully consider what they do during the first day of school, why they do these things, and how they feel about the day. My thinking about this issue in the context of my own teaching may provide practitioners with a familiar frame of reference from which to glean useful ideas, even if their own teaching circumstances are not identical. Fourth, most educational research frames inquiry in ways that tend to omit or strongly downplay temporal considerations. Most practitioners realize that teaching Monday morning is far different from teaching on Friday afternoons, teaching in mid-October is different from teaching the day before Halloween, teaching on the first day of school is much different from teaching near the end of the year. By researching the first day of school I will contribute a different frame to educational research. With all these considerations in mind, I undertake the research of my own teaching in hopes that it will bring me closer to a different narrative for my students and myself, one filled with participation, learning, and excitement (but with less stress).

CONTEXTUALIZING AND FRAMING
THE FIRST-DAY-OF-SCHOOL NARRATIVES

The particular first day of school that is the focus of this chapter occurred on September 2, 1997, in a small metropolitan suburb of Detroit, Michigan. The school day started at 8:45 A.M., a new school-start time mandated by state changes in school-year requirements, and ended at 11:50

A.M. The class was composed of 30 students of varied economic and racial backgrounds. I was assigned 15 boys and 15 girls, in a self-contained fifth-grade classroom. This would be my fourth year teaching Grade 5 in a building with two sections of each grade and a student population of nearly 350. Only one student in the class was new to the school, and the majority of students came from blue-collar, two-parent families. This is as much as I knew about the class when the school year began, not counting the hallway encounters, teacher gossip, and sibling insights that would undoubtedly color my perceptions.

In this chapter I will analyze several narratives, only one of which was constructed in the context just described. Other narratives that will be analyzed include one developed from collective experiences of first days of the past, one developed in planning for this particular first day; and one that anticipates future first days of school. Each of these narratives has its own unique context, but they are inextricably tied together in my mind because they all affect and are affected by this year's first day of school. The narratives are of my own construction, but they are flavored and influenced by the narratives of peers and students. I will frame my investigation of the first-day-of-school phenomenon through analysis of a chain of temporally ordered stories. Initially I will share an analysis of a "historical narrative" that is cobbled together from pre-1997 first days of school. Following this, I will analyze a "scripted narrative" that describes the story I hoped/planned to enact on the first day of school in 1997. Then I unfold an analysis of a "spontaneous narrative" in which I attempt to capture what happened and my thinking about the first day of school of 1997. The set of narratives cannot end here. One of my purposes in this research was to use deep reflection to construct an improved "future narrative" of subsequent first days of school. I end with my ideas about themes that I hope to embed in next year's first-day-of-school narrative.

A NOTE ABOUT METHOD AND DATA

Before delving into the narrative analysis, I should briefly share some relevant features of my approach to data collection and analysis. To aid my construction and analysis of narratives I employed Brown's (1996) use of multiple texts to reflect on teaching. In this method, "chains of stories" that document classroom practice are compared over time to scaffold reflection. The act of constructing new text based on previous writings deepens the researcher's perspective on practice, thereby enhancing possibilities for future action in that setting. I created a chain of stories through my teaching journal and used these writings to construct my "historical narrative" and "scripted narrative."

I compiled the detailed teacher journal through August and September 1997 with my thoughts about the first day of school, preparations for that day, and interactions with others before and during the day. I developed and analyzed my "spontaneous narrative," using several data sources, including an audiotape of the entire first day of school, student work samples from the first day, and my teaching journal. These records of practice can been viewed as a collage of historical markers that document the first day of school. Each source has its own texture and unique dimensions, but it is through the sources' overlapping and through the spaces between components that I could create a more critical narrative of experience. Finally, I created ideas for a "future narrative" of subsequent first days of school. To do this I critically conflated my past and present first-day-of-school narratives, to envision the following first-day narrative.

HISTORICAL NARRATIVE: *PRECURSOR*

Across my 5 previous years of teaching, I had developed a first-day-of-school narrative that entwined personal plans, actions, and rationale, with memorable occurrences from past first days and ideas from peers and students. The basic elements of this narrative, each of which I will address in more detail later, include appearances (personal and the classroom); composition of students in class; helping students get to know me; learning classroom procedures and rules; and portraying what fifth grade is "really" like. These elements are influenced by the instructional setting, events that happen in it, protagonists, and outcomes of the first-day narrative. When coalesced into one story, they illustrate the difficulties I faced in creating a first-day-of-school story with a personally satisfactory solution. A satisfactory solution would be a first day that provided a "good start" to the year in light of multiple instructional goals and a workable yet thoughtful template for future first days of school. My teaching during previous first days of school was inevitably disappointing and yet exhilarating, frenzied in pace but seemingly null in content. My peers contributed ideas to this narrative that revealed excitement about new beginnings tempered by summer regrets. Some half jokingly doubted personal skill, while others were concerned about what to wear or how to decorate inviting bulletin boards. My own thoughts were focused on ideas I had not heard from my peers, but my thinking was flavored by their comments. Any peer consensus about the first day of school or personal knowledge of the first day must be considered all the more tentative and situational when 30 fresh, relatively unknown students enter the picture. The actions and comments of my students regarding the first day of school tempered the construction of my narrative. A major theme that dominates this historical narrative and made my thinking about the upcoming first day of school most troubling was that thoughtful planning and well-founded concerns prior to the first day often seemed ill-suited to the actual dilemmas occurring that day. In other words, this narrative has a foreboding moral: Planning (or practice, for that matter) doesn't necessarily make perfect.

HISTORICAL NARRATIVE: *REFLECTIVE ANALYSIS*

A colleague of mine said that she needed to get a new outfit for the start of the year. Not an outfit with slacks, but a dress. I asked her why this was important, implying that I didn't think it mattered. She said that if she could find the right outfit, it would make her look more professional and send a message to students that she meant business. (Teaching journal, 8/25/97)

Many of my peers were preoccupied with concerns about setting the right tone for learning on the first day of school. This could be done in many ways and mean many different things. For the teacher referred to here, looking competent and businesslike would encourage students to respect her and know that she expected them to work hard. Dressing more casually might have courted familiarity, making teacher authority more difficult to establish. For other teachers, setting the right tone meant discussing the rules and consequences for following and disobeying those rules. This conception often includes the idea that the first few weeks of school and especially the first day is the best time to rigidly enforce these rules. Failure to do so may set a course for classroom anarchy later in the year. Whether a businesslike tone or an orderly rule–following tone is the "right tone" for a particular teacher, it appears that one theme in contemplating the first day concerns establishing an appropriate learning atmosphere and facilitating its creation from the very start of the year. Setting the tone on the first day is a high-stakes venture, not only because incorrectly setting the tone could conceivably have significant long-term repercussions, but also because there is an incredibly limited window of opportunity, one half day of school, in which successful execution needs to occur.

> In the course of the in-service days leading up to the first day of school teachers invariably inquire about the students in my new class. Depending on the teacher I may be asked to share some names to help with remembering the group as a whole, after which comments are made regarding the general behavior, intelligence, and parental involvement of "that group." In other cases teachers ask to see the list of students and make the same sorts of comments about individual students. (Teaching journal, 8/26/97)

While there is debate among teachers about the appropriateness or necessity of this type of interaction, it is difficult to avoid prior to the first day of school. For better or worse, peers accentuate the challenges and possibilities presented by each new group of students. The clairvoyance of their perceptions often cannot be easily challenged before the start of the year, leaving me to attempt to ignore negative comments while comforting myself with their positive insights. Hearing these ideas prior to the first day of school runs contrary to my predisposition to avoid clouding my thinking about new students with their documented past. I consciously avoid "learning" more about my students through the files kept in the office. Ironically, a theme of the historical narrative that causes much consternation before the first day of school is this lack of knowledge about new students. So much of what needs to be done as a teacher depends upon knowledge of them—their personalities and understandings. Knowing them cannot be replicated through peer comments or office files. The first day initiates the gargantuan process of learning about students, which needs to be augmented throughout the year, but also needs to start as quickly as possible. On the first day of school, I will seat students next to one another and may require them to work together, with either wonderful or disastrous consequences, which result from my lack of knowledge.

Other themes of the historical first-day narrative were more personal in nature. It occurred to me that I was as unknown to students as they were to me. They might have heard of me through peers, siblings, or parents. Exposure to the "folklore" about Mr. Boerst could work to my advantage or disadvantage, depending upon which stories were remembered and shared. At the start of the year, and particularly on the first day, I wanted to convey to students what I was about as a teacher and, in some sense, what I was about as a person. I did not think that my first-day attire would do enough to establish this. My new students would come in with vague ideas about me and better formed ideas about school in general. I wanted to do things the very first day that let the students know that I was worthy of being trusted, worked for, and maybe even liked a little. I realize that these things are time-consuming ventures and cannot be accomplished easily. It was difficult to know what I could do to help students learn about me or if this was something that students would find out naturally over time. It was stressful to consider that students might get a possibly long-lasting impression of me that first day, so I wanted to make it an accurate and, hopefully, positive one.

Another theme that dominates my narrative is concern about quickly establishing classroom procedures, possibly including a message about rule enforcement. Well-formed procedural patterns could help students efficiently manage their time and foster productive classroom interactions. While many of the procedures of classroom life become second nature as the year progresses, those very same routines need to be taught to students at the start of the year. Poorly establishing routines on the first day of school could be a costly mistake. Determining which procedures were worth teaching, what rationale supported their use, and how to teach them was a nerve-rattling experience.

> It is not as if I know the exact way to start these patterns of classroom life, but there are certainly ways not to. Last year I remember I tried to get many routines going the very first day. One was lining up and walking to specials. It is not as if kids hadn't walked in line before, but I've seen some classes get pretty rowdy going through the halls. I talked about this procedure and even stopped the students once or twice on the way down to Music to insist upon quiet and order for fear that slack at this point would promote greater disorder later. Well, we arrived at the music room to discover that we didn't have specials on the first day! Trying to salvage some routine, I decided that we'd just practice walking our fire escape route. (Teaching journal, 8/26/97)

Here the establishment of multiple procedures on the first day caused some apprehension, but it also illuminated a few of the potential factors that make mistakes a very real possibility on the first day of school.

A final theme of this historical narrative was contributed through the letters that my previous fifth-grade students had written at the end of school the preceding year. In creating comments to be read by future fifth-grade students on the first day of school, many children wrote about how boring the first day of school was and how I had talked the entire day. This could be an amalgamation of their experiences on first days of school throughout their school careers, but I felt that it spoke pretty accurately about the first day in my classroom. However, many students went on to write glowingly about their fifth-grade experiences in the classroom over the course of the year. It seemed that the students saw a discrepancy between the start of the year and the rest of it.

> I began to wonder how the way I taught on the first day of school compared with how I regularly managed, planned, and interacted with students during the year. I don't think that my first-day teaching matches well with the kind of teaching I tried to do on a regular basis during the year. The fact that the two may be markedly different is one thing, but the necessity of it is another. Does the dichotomy need to occur? Could I avoid it and still develop the many first-day ideas I want to?" (Teaching journal, 8/27/97)

The question here was how to compose the day and my teaching so that they would not be as markedly different from the teaching and learning occurring in the room during the remainder of the year. This relates back to presenting students an accurate impression of what learning in fifth grade would be like. This spurred me to consider what else was missing from the first day of school.

My historical narrative operates under the assumption that it would be best on the very first day to establish classroom procedures and rules, to dress and decorate the room appropriately, to tell students about myself as a teacher, and to speak about what fifth grade was like. In isolation, any of these goals may plausibly help students and myself begin a productive year together. In concert, these first-day components would place students in a decidedly receptive role. While they could make conjectures based on previous grades, they would know little about the direction of the fifth-grade curriculum. Since they also knew little about what I'm like as a teacher or what procedures were particular to this classroom, student participation would amount to guessing and listening. No wonder former fifth-grade students were thankful that the first day was a half day! This is an even greater concern, since a key point I would be making throughout the year was that students in my class have a critical role in discourse and planning. By filling the first day with topics they couldn't contribute to in powerful ways, I had set up the first day at odds with what I wanted the students to learn that day. I was trying to tell them things that they might more powerfully learn, possibly in some small way on the first day, through engagement. By having students sit and listen, I was also delaying the important process of learning about my students. On their own and in concert, the themes described in this section contributed to making my historical first day of school narrative a problematic one.

SCRIPTED NARRATIVE: *PRECURSOR*

In thinking about the first day, I see that a curious absence from the agenda was subject matter. It seemed that everything done on the first day revolves around getting ready to learn at some point about the content matter of fifth grade, but that the first day had no hint of it. Since my usual teaching centered strongly on teaching subject matter, it is no wonder that the first day felt out of the ordinary, adding to all the other reasons mentioned earlier. Also, by incorporating subject matter into the first day I could begin to build notions about students' content knowledge and how they were able to use that knowledge. However, there were many things to be accomplished the first day, so adding subject matter would be a tricky, but justifiable, proposition. Even if I did find a way to incorporate subject matter into the first day, there was no telling how students would receive it. I also did not have an idea about how the intent to teach subject matter could be feasibly translated into actual practice that first day of school.

SCRIPTED NARRATIVE: *REFLECTIVE ANALYSIS*

The room was decorated and arranged, meetings with teachers and administrators had been completed, and school supplies were dispersed to still-studentless desks. I was ready to plan the first day. It being only a half day, there was no question that it would be easy to fill. The goal I started with was to plan a first day in which students could experience what fifth grade would really be like during the year, even if only in a small way, while also laying the foundation upon which the rest of the year could productively be built.

One possible way to both lessen my anxiety about the first day and to represent what I'm like as a teacher/what it's like to be a fifth-grade student, would be to include some meaningful yet reasonable amount of subject matter in the first day of school. I can't close my eyes to the necessity of other components of the first day, but I need to find some way of including subject matter in a first day of school way (whatever that means). The question then becomes what subject matter and in what guise. (Teaching journal, 8/28/97)

After much consideration I decided to structure the subject matter learning of the first day of school around the topic of "school." So school is the theme of this scripted narrative. Since the rest of the day would be spent doing many school-centered things, such as creating rules and learning procedures, it seemed that I could incorporate subject matter applications most naturally around this topic as well. I also wanted to do something that integrated subject matter areas so as not to send a message to students that there would be one subject that mattered the most in fifth grade. Brainstorming and scanning many sources, I decided to have the students read some excerpts from the letters of Laura Ingalls Wilder (1991) that discussed what schools of the early 1900s were like and how people viewed the role of schools. In this way I could listen to students read. I could engage them in historical comparison of past and present schools and use some components of the stories to solve math problems about the cost of textbooks and the amount of work it would take to buy them now as opposed to then. This plan was integrated and connected to the topic of schooling, would involve students in several ways with subject matter, and hopefully would allow me to vacate center stage on the first day of school.

In addition to this, I planned to accomplish several other things in our half day of learning time. Students would make desk name tags as they entered until everyone had arrived. I would briefly introduce myself, using my professional portfolio. Then, students would get to know one another through a brief cooperative learning activity. We would also discuss the classroom rules and consequences, as well as determine assignments for school-related jobs known as "safety duties," which our class was responsible for performing the very next day. Throughout the morning would be smatterings of procedures necessary to complete the various tasks. It would be a more-than-busy first day, but I was determined to give this plan a try. However, I knew from my historical narrative that this script was for a story that would never come to pass, no matter how thoughtful or well intentioned its outline.

SPONTANEOUS NARRATIVE: *REFLECTIVE ANALYSIS*

My day started with an ironic twist. I looked at the shirts I had ironed for the week and realized that I did not own a tie to match any of them. It would be the first time in my career that I had not worn a tie for the first day of school. The importance of the first-day-of-school wardrobe came to mind again. I chose not to wear a tie, hoping that doing so would not haunt me by the day's end. I do not mean to make light of what had been shared as a very real concern for others. Each teacher has beliefs, just as I do, that may cause anxiety about the first day of school. For some it is wardrobe, for others it is the necessity of an immaculate classroom, and for me it was a worry that students would form false impressions about what fifth grade would be like in my room. I am not trying to establish particular teacher beliefs as legitimate first-day narrative themes, but rather to call attention to the fact that teacher beliefs complicate the first day.

Wary of being center stage the entire first day, I structured my plans in hopes of better involving students, thus better mirroring what the rest of fifth grade would be like. The plans included interaction between students, involvement in whole-class discourse, and integrated subject matter. Each of these planning decisions had been made with great care, and I felt relatively comfortable that the plan would indeed involve students more strongly in the first day activities. However, in examining the tapes of the first day, I found that I still occupied a large amount of the discussion space. Since students had few ideas about components such as school safety jobs and information about myself, they understandably participated less. I was troubled by the blank stares that greeted my requests that they discuss ideas with their new classmates. They roamed the room to learn about one another's interests for approximately 20 minutes. What follows is the extent of the whole-group discussion that ensued:

> *Teacher*: Did anyone find out something interesting about someone that they didn't know before? (long pause) So two people didn't know everything about the people they talked to, but everyone else knew everything about everyone?
> *Max*: That Kareen wants to go to Disneyland.
> *Teacher*: Anything else?
> *Bart*: That Jake's dream car is a Slingshot.
> *Jasmine*: Albert's favorite color is blue.
> *Teacher*: All right. Did anybody find out anything interesting? Kurt? No? Did you change your mind about it being interesting? (Class transcript, 9/2/97)

This discussion is not what I would characterize as highly engaging or student centered. After this, I talked a bit more about the task and then started the next planned task. There were two notable exceptions when students did participate more: I will discuss one of these here and explore the other later. At times, in the morning students would contribute ideas—which I hadn't anticipated—that appeared to spur greater student involvement. The first time this occurred was when I was sharing information about myself using my portfolio.

> *Teacher*: I used to live in Iowa before teaching here. I taught fourth grade there for 2 years in Cedar Rapids, which is [pulling down map] right here. I taught third grade in Wausau, Wisconsin, which is right about here. Now I teach in a place called South Redford. Have you heard of it?
>
> *Students*: (Laughter)
>
> *Teacher*: This is my 3rd year here and I think I have it figured out. *Ha*!
>
> *Albert*: Can I come up and show you something on the map?
>
> Teacher: Sure
>
> *Albert*: During the summer I, um, we started right here, we went down from Michigan into India [he meant Indiana] through Illinois, Nebraska into South Dakota. Then we went . . . [the story of his trip continued]
>
> *Teacher*: Wow! How many of you went on trips this summer? OK, let's see here. I went on trips, but I didn't go anywhere exciting, just to Wisconsin and back to Michigan. How many of you went to Maine? Some of you and, oh, Albert too. Imagine that! How many of you went to New York? Oh, Albert again. How many of you went to Pennsylvania?
>
> *Students*: (Laughter [Albert is the only student to raise his hand again.])
>
> *Teacher*: OK, now that we know where Albert has been, did anyone travel over here? [pointing to the Midwest]. How about over here . . . (Class transcript, 9/2/97)

After this exchange students asked questions about me. It may at first seem trivial, but this move, initiated by students, changed my thinking about how I would use my plans. Seemingly a more effective way to involve students in the first day was to allow them to help determine the direction of our discourse and even the content of our work. In other words, I would not rigidly stick to the ways I had planned to involve students. Many times during the day students interjected comments that called issues to my attention that would be useful or interesting to discuss on the first day of school. I still could guide the discourse and tasks toward what I thought needed to be accomplished, but capitalizing on these opportunities and leaving other tasks I had planned unfinished did markedly improve student involvement. It encouraged the kinds of interactions more typical of what students could expect during the school year, thus helping me realize my goal in a way I hadn't considered. This type of interaction also encouraged me to be more spontaneous, inquisitive, and even humorous at times. This is the kind of person I wanted to portray to the students on the first day of school, instead of the hot-air bag that made students long for the bell at noon. I could more easily show students what I was like as a teacher and a person, instead of trying to tell them using my portfolio.

A second source that fostered active student participation and discourse was the subject matter included in the first day of school. The subject matter was also affected by student interest. In fact, the grandiose integrated subject matter idea that I had constructed in my plans was only afforded 25 minutes of class time right before the bell that ended the day. Instead, a mathematical problem arose early in the day when students swooned upon hearing when I was born.

> *Teacher*: My birthday is October 21, 1968.
> *Students*: Ooooooo!
> *Teacher*: That means I will, I'll let you figure that out.
> *Student*: You're 30.
> *Teacher*: That's pretty close.
> *Jackson*: 32.
> *Teacher*: Well let's figure it out. If you want to figure it out we'll
> figure it out.
> *Albert*: 39
> *Students*: (Laughter)
> *Student*: 32!
> *Teacher*: Whoa, now hang on a second. If you do have a comment to
> make in our classroom you're going to need to raise your hand.
> Now that is a first-grade rule and we will keep following that in
> here. So if I was born in 1968, about how old am I? Why don't
> you talk it over with someone you're sitting next to?
> *Teacher*: (After excited discussions in small groups) Do you have an
> idea? How did you figure that out? Raise your hand and tell us
> about it.
> *Loni*: Um, I counted up 6, 7, 8, 9 and I noticed 9. The 9 . . .

Teacher: So you counted up from this (6) to this number (9)?

Loni: You need to add one year because it is an 8 and not a 9.

Teacher: Uh, ha. So you went up 3 tens and then add one to that 3 tens because it's 1999. Then 31 is what you got. OK, that is one way to do it. Other ideas? How did you do it?

Kurt: It was 37.

Teacher: You thought it was 37. How did you get that?

Kurt: I don't know.

Students: (Laughter)

Teacher: One thing we will talk about or the thing you will learn about being in fifth grade is that when we talk about stuff in class . . . It's great that you have ideas and I want to encourage you to share those as much as possible but I will also be asking you, whether you're right, wrong, or in between or whatever, how you got that. How did you think of that? Does that make sense? So when you share something I want you to kind of be thinking in those ways and you can think about other peoples' answers in those ways too. (Class transcript, 9/2/97)

There are several points that can be made from this excerpt. Since the content of the first day included learning about others, the "How old is Mr. Boerst" problem was a natural way to delve into subject matter thinking. In fact, this was much more natural than a later transition to work on the subject matter tasks I had planned. Building upon student contributions helped generate discourse earlier, so I had more reason to believe that an impromptu chance to do subject matter work based on student interest would be productive. Interestingly enough, mathematical work on this problem set the stage for work later in the day about the age of Laura Ingalls Wilder's writings.

Even within this brief excerpt, I can also see the opportunity that subject matter afforded me to teach procedures that would be useful in creating a smoothly running classroom. Instead of trying to teach procedures as discrete topics on the first day of school, I could teach students the procedures when they needed to know them, in order for them to participate in a meaningful discussion. Students were learning about two important types of procedures in this situation. They were learning the necessary components and format of sharing answers, an important subject matter procedure. They were also learning more mundane procedures such as how to be recognized in the room when they wanted to share their thinking. So the introduction of subject matter on the first day of the year not only helped me to engage students in discourse, it also helped me to conduct the first day in a way that more realistically captured what fifth grade would be like. In addition, it helped me to address classroom procedures, which was another stressful factor involved in starting the school year.

I had hoped that use of subject matter, even at this early point, would help facilitate a quick start in compiling the information I needed about each student's knowledge and skills. Based on what I now know about these students, transcripts of classroom discourse on the first day provided sketchy information that easily could have lead to incorrect impressions about my students' academic prowess or lack thereof. Students I have since found to be highly effective critical thinkers and engaged classroom participants were either absent from the recording of the first day or were unwilling or unable to share much in the way of reasoning to support their ideas. Students with reading difficulties, typically silent in reading class during the year, were answering reading questions with accuracy. However, retrospectively considering the class as the unit, I see that already on the first day there were accurate foreshadowings of the overall demeanor and work style of the class that I came to know over the year. Of course, any meaningful impression of students cannot be formulated in one day. The process is invariably made murky by scattered performances and the diversity of classroom tasks. Collecting information about students on the first day related to a bit of subject matter work, be it well aligned with typical performance or an outlier, it at least allowed me to be hazily proactive as I planned the subsequent days of instruction to meet student needs.

FUTURE NARRATIVE: *PRECURSOR*

> I heard that a principal encouraged his staff to really get to know their kids during the first weeks of school. To facilitate this, he actively instructs teachers to avoid teaching subject matter the entire first few weeks of school. (Teaching journal, 8/28/97)

This puzzling statement has new meaning for me following my research into the 1997 first day of school. I wholeheartedly agree that I need to learn about my students, but I now believe more strongly than before that subject matter is an important medium through which I can learn about my students and they can more accurately learn about me as a teacher and person. While it is unlikely that the first day of school highly reflects what learning will typically be like for fifth-grade students in my classroom, the inclusion of small, student-centered or timely subject matter topics helped to make the first day less of the troublesome outlier it had been in the past. I can use subject matter as a tool through which to meaningfully teach about various procedures and rules of my classroom that are necessary for a successful school year. Through the events of the first day of 1997 I have come to realize the possibility of coordinating, instead of juxtaposing, themes from my historical narrative. There are pedagogical strategies that could assist in lessening the tensions between numerous legitimate aims for the first day of school, including establishing classroom procedures and rules, telling students about myself as a teacher, and showing what fifth grade would be like. The first day will probably never be an event about which teachers are calm or self-assured, but the process of researching the event can strengthen awareness of why it is so often a troublesome occurrence. While there are no definitive answers, because of the personal beliefs or goals of individual teachers and the ever changing contexts in which they work, teachers empowered through critical reflection can take action to improve the first day of school for themselves and their students. While I have not been able to construct a "dream story" of the first day of school, I am moving toward facilitating more satisfying first days of school for myself and, hopefully, for my students.

NOTE

To learn more about Tim Boerst's teaching, see *Exploring the Rule of 3 in Elementary School Mathematics*, at his website, http://www.goingpublicwithteaching. org/tboerst/

REFERENCES

Amato, M. (1995). Be yourself. *Learning, 24*(2), 1.

Brown, T. (1996). Creating data in practitioner research. *Educational Studies in Mathematics, 27*, 260–270.

Wilder, L. (1991). *Little house in the Ozarks: The rediscovered writings.* Nashville, TN: Nelson.

Wong, H., & Wong, R. (1991). *The first days of school: How to be an effective teacher.* Sunnyvale, CA: Wong.

CHAPTER 2

What Is a Culture of Quality?

Ron Berger

There is a common perception that today's schools are in crisis. People are grasping for solutions—longer days, new management structures, alternative assessments, fresh curriculum, even a return to curriculum from the past. Though I support many of the initiatives being proposed, I think there is a real danger in assuming there is any quick fix or single strategy that will "save" schools.

The quality of a school lies in its culture. Particular aspects of the school—budget, curriculum, teaching roles, decision making, assessment, physical layout—are elements of this culture but do not in themselves define it. The only way to understand a school culture is to understand what students experience in being part of it. Not just the motivated, mainstream students, but also the students who look or feel different. How safe do students feel, physically and emotionally? What kind of pride and intensity is encouraged for work? What values, what sense of courtesy and responsibility, are modeled? A school culture of quality connotes a culture of high standards for *all* students in *all* domains: standards for academic achievement, arts, physical fitness, critical thinking, and creativity, but also standards for kindness, integrity, industriousness, and responsibility. Some schools renowned for high test scores sustain a culture where students carry an air of entitlement and are disrespectful or cruel to each other, where students who don't "fit," due to race, class, or physical differences, are alienated and mistreated.

I would like to offer here a vision of a positive school culture based on a real-life model–this is the vision that I and my colleagues hold for the school in which we teach. The premises and strategies underlying the culture are not our invention. Although I try to describe them in practice here, I take no credit for them and I acknowledge that they derive from many sources. Because I am a teacher, the illustrations that follow are often from my own classroom, but they reflect the wider school culture that sustains them.

Reprinted with permission from "What Is a Culture of Quality?" in *A Culture of Quality: A Reflection on Practice* by Ron Berger, Occasional Paper Series, No. 1, September 1996, pp. 21–46.

If what follows runs counter to the ideas of today's educators and re-formers, whether "progressive" or "traditional," it is because I feel that people in general are not looking deeply enough at schools and children.

WHAT GOES ON IN THE HALLWAYS IS AS IMPORTANT AS WHAT GOES ON IN THE CLASSROOM

To understand how a school culture shapes the attitudes of children, one must understand that elements having nothing to do with curriculum often have the most profound effect on the lives of children. The aspects of a school that most clearly engrave the school experience on children are often in the "other stuff" category: the physical appearance of the school building, outside and in; the manner in which school property and personal property are respected and cared for in the school; the levels of physical safety and emotional safety that children and adults in the building feel; the way routines of arrival, class transitions, lunch times, and dismissal are handled; the ways authority is exercised; the tone of courtesy, kindness, and acceptance in peer culture; the ways in which student achievements are shared within the school community and outside of it; the aspects of the school that define it in the larger community. These things are every bit as important as curriculum.

"Oh, yeah, those things," people may say. "Well, of course, those are important; those go without thinking." The problem is, those things *don't* go well without thinking, and they don't go well in many of the schools in this country. To keep a school clean and in good repair, filled with displays of beautiful student work, to maintain an environment where students feel safe from physical danger, exclusion, or ridicule, where people are polite and patient and helpful, and where all the students have forums in which they can succeed and take pride in their work—this is no easy job. It re-quires a school culture that takes real time in the day—time *away from* curriculum, time "off task"—to sustain such a culture.

My sixth-grade students are assistants to the school cooks in the caf-eteria and to the custodian in the lunchroom. They set up the library for assemblies and the gym for events. When the school secretary is absent, they run the office. They are responsible for cleaning and caring for the classroom, and caring for classroom animals. They each have kindergarten advisees whom they tutor and help in school and on the bus. If there is a problem on the playground or in the hallways with my students not treat-ing others kindly, they know that nothing in the curriculum is going to take precedence over a group discussion and consequences regarding that behavior. None of this is *curriculum*, as we usually define the term.

Part of maintaining a culture of quality is taking the time as a school staff to build and sustain structures, traditions, and rituals to make sure these realms of school are positive. Most schools have "school codes" that remind students to "treat others well." If, however, these same schools ignore exclusion and mean behavior in the lunchroom and hallways or tolerate disrespect for student belongings or feelings in the school yard, the code means little. Schools that strictly enforce and celebrate polite and kind behavior, that regularly use staff meetings to discuss behavioral issues, that actively use community meetings, peer mediation, peer tutoring, mentor programs, community service work, and community exhibitions of excellence, must take a lot of time planning things that aren't purely curricular. It is time well spent, because quality in one area supports quality throughout the system.

There are no short cuts to building and maintaining a school community of courtesy and kindness, of integrity and responsibility. Some families, in exasperation, remove their children from public schools and place them in parochial or military schools, looking for a strict environment. I think strictness is essential, and I credit many of these schools with taking issues of character and physical environment seriously. But strict rules alone are not the answer: They maintain order but do not guarantee that children will treat each other well or feel good about themselves. Prisons have plenty of strict rules. What is necessary is a school community that not only demands the best of its students in terms of character but that models that character through school tone, routines, and practices.

In the end, I would be surprised if anyone really thinks that these things are less important than curriculum. I would be surprised, too, if anyone who really took the time to think about these issues could conclude that they could be attended to with little effort, in the margins of the school day, rather than as a primary and explicit priority and commitment of time, all day, every day.

LESS CAN BE BETTER

More hours, more days, more assignments, more homework—there is an obsession with quantity these days. I believe the obsession should be with quality instead. I have no problem with sweat, hard work, and challenge; I relish it and demand it. But I am concerned with the quality of what such hard work produces.

Schools can sometimes take on the feel of a production shop, students cranking out an endless flow of final products without much personal investment or care. The emphasis is on keeping up with production, on not falling behind in class work or homework, rather than on producing something of lasting value. As in a fast-food restaurant, the products are neither creative nor memorable. Teachers create and perpetuate this situation, even though they grow tired of repetitive, trivial assignments and dread correcting piles of such work.

Turning in final draft work every day, often many times in one day, forces even the most ambitious of students to compromise standards continually, simply to keep up the pace. Internalized high standards are no antidote to a system that demands final draft work at this rate. If an adult writer, scientist, historian, or artist were asked to turn in a stack of finished pieces of work every day, how much care could he or she put into each? The same phenomenon occurs with "getting through" textbooks. Textbooks rule curriculum and time; in-depth critical discussion, thought, and original research must be cut short, or cut altogether, because there are always more pages, more exercises to get through, and the year is only so long.

One alternative is a project-centered approach, in which students still work hard very day, but each day's work is a small but meaningful part of a long-range, significant project. Daily work entails the creation or revision of early drafts of a piece or the continued research of a topic or the management of an experiment or the perfection of one component of a large piece of work. Final drafts or presentations of completed projects are no longer trivial events occurring every day but special events, moments of individual and class pride and celebration.

This longer process allows time for students to produce work of real personal value and of substantial depth and quality. It allows time for multiple drafts, rehearsals, or experimental trials. It allows time for serious critique of unfinished work—teacher critique, peer critique, and self-critique. It allows the teacher and the class community to set rigorous standards for final drafts and presentations and requires that they be met.

Qualities of a Good Project

There is no one good model of such projects. I've seen a range of successful ideas and structures in different schools, from first graders publishing novels for their school library to fourth graders creating field guides to local ponds to eighth graders preparing development plans for vacant lots based on surveys of neighborhood residents. Across the range, though, there are common features to the successful projects I've seen. All allow, indeed require, students to be creative, to make decisions, and to take real responsibility for their own work. All include a substantial focus on learning new academic and artistic skills and perfecting those skills in practice. All use the project as a framework in which skills are acquired and polished. And, importantly, all provide a forum for sharing finished work with a wider audience.

These projects are different from the project model that I call the "science fair" model. When I was a student in elementary school, the only substantial projects we worked on were science projects. The structure was as follows: The teacher would say to the class, "Next month is our science fair. I'd like you all to submit a project. They are due May 9. Good luck." These projects were completed entirely out of school, which meant that students who came from privileged homes (and I use *privilege* not just in terms of wealth but in terms of emotional and organizational stability) had a tremendous advantage over students who did not. In fact, we students could never tell how much of the work of others was done by parents (and I'm not sure the teachers could either).

These science fair projects were not a culmination of classroom learning, but topics chosen at random, pursued without critical assistance from peers or teachers. We were not taught the importance of breaking down the project into manageable steps nor were we required to do so; we were not even taught time management. Some kids always started early, but I was one of the last-minute kids and I made life miserable for my family the night before due date. (People say that you learn from the consequences of your mistakes, but I didn't seem to: I went through same painful panic every year.) Moreover, we were not taught standards for assessing these projects. We couldn't aim for quality because we had no real sense of what quality was.

On the day of the fair, some students brought in impressive-looking work, some students (I among them) brought in last-minute work. Many students brought in awful work or no work at all; for them, the project was a total failure. Then, ribbons magically appeared on some projects, but it was never the ones we thought should win. Not understanding the criteria for judging nor having any background in the subjects explored by others, we were always more taken with the visually impressive posters than the experiments that represented good science.

Quality Entails Universal Success

In contrast, the project model I propose is predicated on every single student succeeding. And this doesn't mean every student finishing, but rather every student finishing something that represents the *best* of his or her talents. This model does not preclude work at home, but it uses the school as the hub of creation, as a project workshop. The *overall* quality of work to emerge from this workshop, not just *individual* quality, is a vital and explicit concern. If *any* student is failing to succeed, if *any* student is producing work without effort or care, it is a problem for the whole workshop.

The project must therefore be structured to make it impossible for individuals to fail or fall far behind. Through continual conferences, critique sessions, and peer and teacher support, student progress is sustained and assessed at all points during the creation process. Projects are planned with distinct checkpoints through which each student passes on the road to completion, with explicit methods and procedures that must be followed at each stage. The resulting display of completed projects from such a workshop, such a class, is characterized by universal success and whole-class pride.

Universal success does not mean uniformity. Although the structure that braces and guides student progress is common to every project, each student's project is unique. The structure provides a frame for common learning and critique, as well as for appraisal of progress, but it also leaves room for significant creative expression and direction by individual students. If every student in a classroom prepares a guidebook to a different local building, the steps and skills involved may be somewhat prescribed—conducting interviews, researching local history, consulting city records, trying to obtain blueprints, doing sketches, taking photographs, preparing diagrams, writing and proofreading drafts of text, preparing illustrations, composing book layout, learning bookbinding. Within this frame, however, individual students have substantial latitude for artistic choices—the selection of building, the decision of whom to interview, the use of research and interviews, the nature of text and illustrations, the balance of text and illustrations, the use of photographs or diagrams, the tone of presentation, the layout of the finished book.

As much as possible, these projects should represent "real work," work that is original and offers something of value to a wide community. When my students interviewed senior citizens to prepare biographies of their lives, they were doing something much more than a classroom exercise. They were building relationships and working to provide an artifact that might be treasured by that senior and his or her family for the rest of their lives. The reason for high standards of research, organization, written language, and visual presentation in these biographies was clear to the students: This was real, important work. There was a clear reason for the students to learn 20th-century history, interview techniques, shorthand, tape transcription, photography, illustration, and research skills. And they applied what they learned immediately.

Such projects represent more than just a mastery of skills; they demonstrate an internalized dedication and competence in planning and crafting high-quality work. Once a student leaves school, she is judged for the rest of her life on her ability to produce such work, not on her ability to take tests or answer questions at the end of a chapter. To structure learning around the creation of quality work, rather than around the ability to memorize facts, seems not only sensible but vital in preparing students for life.

THE MOST IMPORTANT ASSESSMENT
IN SCHOOLS IS DONE BY STUDENTS, NOT TEACHERS

When the word *assessment* is used, the first thing that comes to mind for most people is testing. Schools in this country administer annually over a hundred million mandated tests at a cost of over a billion dollars. American students are tested far more than the students of other countries, and to what end? Rather than focusing on creating environments that breed healthy learners, our schools treat all students as sick patients, taking their temperatures constantly and even publishing them in the local paper.

I think assessment has been confused with ranking. I will admit that it is difficult to rank students without numerical results of tests or performance assessments, and I will admit that there are times when it may be important to rank students. But I believe these times are rare. I use tests in my classroom occasionally, though not to rank. I teach test-taking as a life skill: Because the academic world, unlike the real world, judges personal merit so much by test-taking ability, it would be a terrible disservice not to help my students learn to take tests effectively.

But in our school, assessment means much more than testing. Every time a student produces a piece of work in our school, he or she *assesses* it while it is in process, and *assesses* it again before turning it in. If it is to be redrafted, it has been *assessed* yet again when returned with comments, and later the new draft is *assessed* for quality. The quality of what is produced depends upon the assessment skills the individual student has developed. If schools feel a need to obsess about assessment, it is this level of assessment on which the obsession should dwell—this is the level of assessment that determines quality.

Every student carries around with him or her a picture of acceptable standards, a notion of what his or her work should look like before it is handed in or before it is a finished piece. This picture is a vision of how accurate, neat, thorough, thoughtful, original, and elegant a piece of work should be. This should be a vital concern of every school: What is the picture of quality in the heads of our students? Not our "gifted" students or our "motivated" students, but what is it in *all* our students? What is it in a student chosen at random in the hallway? And, most important, how can we get into the heads of our students and sharpen that picture as needed?

The Language of Critique

A vision of quality can be learned, and it can continually develop. If schools can step off the treadmill of work production and decide to focus on fewer pieces of work, refining these thoughtfully, there are many strategies they can adopt to this end. One is to set a realistic time frame for high-quality, finished work, setting out in advance for students the idea that they are embarking on a serious commitment to produce something powerful, and that time and multiple drafts will be required.

Self-assessment is only as strong as the vocabulary and conceptual depth of the student doing the assessment. Teachers must model assessment by taking exemplary pieces of work and flawed pieces of work and dissecting them with students, building the vocabulary of critique in the process. These examples can be taken from well-known resources; but it is often more helpful to use actual work of current or past students, as long as the feelings of students are protected. For most projects, I produce a sample piece of work that is very strong in many ways, flawed in others, and spend a great deal of time pulling it apart with students and building vocabulary and vision as we do so. With the permission of students, I often save particularly strong examples of student projects from past years and keep them in a portfolio at school. I use these samples to set a high base level of expectation for the current class (which they try to exceed) when I introduce a project. My students are so enamored of this portfolio that they constantly finger through it, admire it, ask questions about it, and critique the work within it.

We have regular critique sessions in my classroom. The work critiqued may be writing, drafting, experimental design, even a mathematical solution. Sometimes the work of every child is pinned up for review and feedback. Sometimes only a single piece of work is the critique focus, and it is done in real depth. In either case, we have a strict set of rules that governs critique etiquette. The rules exist to establish an environment safe from ridicule or sarcasm but equally to prevent wasting time on vague compliments. One particular rule is that statements such as "I like it" or "It's good" are not allowed: If the statements are not specific enough to assist the creator of the work or to enlighten the critique audience, we don't want to hear them. Critique is like surgery, cutting into a piece to find out what is working and what is not. The vocabulary of the domain is the kit of surgical tools. Using only words like "I like it" or "I don't like it" is like trying to do surgery with a butter knife.

The vocabulary of our critique sessions is basically the working vocabulary of practitioners in that field. For this reason, we like to have "experts," professionals or craftspeople in a field, visit the school and teach us this vocabulary. To highlight an unusual example: One year, we hosted a nationally ranked collegiate women's soccer team. When my students began to model the language of the soccer players and the strategies they defined, both the style of play in the students' games and the level of their postgame analysis changed dramatically. They now had precise terms to describe particular passes, defenses, shots, movements, and they reveled in this new vocabulary on the field, shouting directions and ideas during games, even seeing options that wouldn't have occurred to them before, and playing quite differently.

There is never enough time to critique the work of every child in a group setting or even in individual teacher conferences. For this reason, group critiques, formal peer critiques, and formal teacher conferences merely build the skills and set the tone for the most significant critique— informal peer critique that is ubiquitous. I have no desks in my classroom; students work in small groups at tables. Whenever it is not a silent work time, the room is filled with students asking each other for suggestions, assistance, editing. Students wander around the room and offer critique and encouragement to each other continually.

The Role of Portfolios

The culture of critique in my classroom changed dramatically when I began to use portfolios. Although I had always saved student work for parent conferences, I hadn't realized the power of having comprehensive portfolios in supporting student reflection, investment, and pride. I learned that the key to portfolios wasn't in *saving* work; it was in *using* the work that was saved. My students these days have portfolios that weigh about eight pounds. (I know this because whenever I borrow a few to share with teachers in another school, my arms are sore before I get there!) We use these fat collections of work constantly. Students are required to tune up portfolios regularly, to do regular portfolio searches for work that exhibits certain criteria, and to present parts or all of their portfolios regularly to a range of critical eyes—students, parents, teachers, community members.

When students present their portfolios to parents, it is a formal presentation and requires that parents fill out and return a reflection form to me, noting their reactions, thoughts, and concerns. At the end of each year, students prepare—with much discussion, critique, and rehearsal—a formal portfolio presentation for a panel, highlighting their accomplishments and profiling their strengths and weaknesses as learners. The panel consists of teachers from the junior high they will be entering, community members, and outside educators. Each presentation is videotaped by a student camera operator.

When I sat down to write out report cards this year, which in my school have narrative assessments rather than grades, I brought home four boxes of portfolios. I don't know how I ever did these progress reports without the portfolios to guide me. I get to know my students well, and 5 years ago I simply trusted my memory, my conference notes, and my account book of work turned in. Now I sit down with the collected work of each student, revisiting the small victories and leaps of understanding, recollecting the nagging problems in accuracy in a particular domain. I read the many self-evaluations my students write, evaluations of particular projects and holistic evaluations of strengths and weaknesses in life, and I weigh my judgment against their own.

The written descriptions I now send home to parents in report cards are stronger than those of past years in myriad ways. I can present a full and balanced picture, citing specific examples of work to celebrate strengths or key moments of growth and can give specific examples of areas needing growth, even quoting from a student's own reflection to make this clear. "Your son mentions in his self-evaluation that he feels he is 'kind of rude sometimes, . . . not in regular class but in music and in the lunchroom and stuff.' I think he is accurate here, and it's something we need to work on."

You will understand most clearly why I have become a portfolio advocate if you pay a visit to my school. A pair of students will give you what we call a curriculum tour of the building and end up in the classroom. There they will look at you with great expectation and pride and ask, "Would you be interested in seeing our portfolios?" And if you agree, they will smile and ask if you have an hour or two free to sit with them!

PEER PRESSURE SHOULD BE DIRECTED,
NOT DISCOURAGED

All of my life I was told to avoid peer pressure. Peer pressure meant kids trying to talk you into smoking in the bathroom or ganging up to tease someone; always it meant being coerced into violating one's inner ethical wisdom and responsible nature. A few years ago it became clear to me, however, that our school is successful to a great extent *because of* peer pressure. Peer pressure can be a force for right as well as wrong. It is one of the strongest forces that govern the actions and attitudes of students at all ages, and it will be there whether schools and parents want it to be or not. It makes sense to me that schools recognize this power and actively shape it and direct it as a force for positive development.

When Quality Is Cool

Imagine a school in which to be cool, to fit in and be regarded as popular, you have to do quality work and treat others well. How do you build such an environment? If the school itself sanctions exclusion and hierarchy by supporting only the academic "stars" with awards, opportunities, exhibitions, and privileges, then quality work is regarded as the exception, not the norm. If the work of every child is going to be shared in an exhibition or presentation, and the merit of the school as a whole or the classroom as a whole will be judged by the *overall quality of the entire exhibition*, there is a reason for students to work together and push each other. It would be letting the class down, or letting the school down, to do less than quality work or to behave in a less than exemplary manner. Peer pressure would compel students to do a good job.

This dynamic, which may at first seem unlikely, is actually not hard to picture in some contexts. If a class were painting a mural on the wall of a city building, the work of every child would reflect on the class as a whole. It is easy to envision students being very concerned with high standards for each other's work. If a class is putting on a play or is engaged in a sporting event with another group, any student who does not know his or her lines or does not know how to play his or her position hurts the entire group. Students may need guidance in making their critique of others sensitive and constructive, but the pressure to do a good job will be unquestionable. This same pressure exists in my classroom as we build for a presentation of work—which, to varying degrees, we are always doing.

Pressures Has Its Rewards

A few years ago, I received a new student in the middle of the fall. This student was a seriously troubled young man, and his experiences had left him unwilling to trust adults, myself included. He had no reason even to assume I would be in his life very long, so investing me with authority and trust made no sense to him. I believe he would have had little success in my class if the peer culture had not shaped his development. He wanted to fit into the group, to be popular with the girls in the classroom, with the guys on the playground, and he found to his surprise that such acceptance required putting real effort into his work and behavior.

On one of his first days at the school, he saw a girl on the playground with a physical disability and began to mimic her. At his old school, this might have brought him some laughs and some positive attention from some of the boys. At our school, he found himself surrounded by a group of angry students. I had to speak sternly to the group and remind them that they shouldn't threaten someone, even to protect a person's feelings. In my heart, however, I found it difficult to be too angry with them. In fact, they were teaching the culture of their school, and the boy learned the lesson. That was the last time he tried something like that. To fit in this school culture meant treating others well.

The first time he dashed off a piece of work, a student sitting next to him asked, "You're not going to turn that in, are you?" To which he responded, "Yeah! What does it matter to you?" Difficult words and disciplinary issues were often the result of my efforts to tune up his manner, but he did come to see that the other students regarded him as strange for his careless work and attitude. And on those occasions when he experimented with putting more time and care into something, he got very positive critique and encouragement from classmates, attention which he welcomed. Over the course of a few months, he began to produce his first work that, in his words, "was worth something." He said, "You know, I don't think I ever did something in school that I really cared about. This character file book is pretty cool. I can't believe I did this."

My sixth-grade students walk through a school library filled with novels written by first graders and fifth graders, maps of local ponds and amphibian field guides drafted by third and fourth graders, models of futuristic homes built by second graders. This is their school's heritage—impressive, meaningful projects—and as the oldest kids in the school, they feel compelled to show that their work is among the most striking and sophisticated. This is pressure, and it is positive pressure. Conversely, first graders look at the blueprints of homes designed by my students, drawn to scale with professional drafting equipment, and they wonder if they will be ready someday for that level of work. This too is pressure, also positive. In the peer culture of our school, to be cool means to contribute to this heritage of elegant and powerful work.

ART IS FUNDAMENTAL

It is possible to attend an educational conference on high standards in learning and never hear art mentioned. During times of crisis or crunch, art is the first subject schools discard. But in the teaching approach I espouse, art is at the core of standards. It is not decoration but rather the primary context for work.

To understand what I mean requires a shift both in the adult conception of art as something for museums and concert halls and in the student conception of art as something that happens between 1:45 and 2:30 on Thursday afternoons (barring budget cuts). It means seeing art as inextricably a part of all that we produce and share, which is how many kindergartners naturally view it.

All student project work in our school is shared with others through some expressive medium. It may be expository writing, fiction, or poetry; drama, dance, or music; illustrations, diagrams, models, maps, photographs, or video; formal presentations or lessons; or, most commonly, some combination of these media. Moreover, every classroom project is viewed through aesthetic eyes, and viewers and producers both strive for aesthetic mastery.

An unspoken commandment in this classroom is that if you're going to share a final draft, a final presentation of a project, *you do it well*. You make it impressive, exciting, memorable. If it's a project in history or science, you not only research it with rigor, you also try to share it in a persuasive, elegant, and compelling manner. If it's a presentation, make it powerful! Use drama, music, slides, graphics, illustrations; refine and rehearse it. If it's a written project, include maps and diagrams, make a provocative cover, lay it out clearly and instructively; make it look good! All of these concerns, and the skills involved in addressing them, are part of this concept of art.

Setting Standards

I feel that standards for artistic expression must be central and passionate, not pushed aside. This doesn't mean adopting a traditional perspective of Western art, where the work of "masters" defines all standards. It does mean that art is a world of skills and knowledge, just like sports; and to learn to practice art well, one must look for and celebrate mastery in others.

It is not enough to ask students to make their work aesthetically powerful; they also must learn to understand and control aesthetic media. For this reason, a great deal of time in our school is spent learning and practicing artistic skills. When students are engaged in scientific projects, they learn drafting skills to create impressive charts and diagrams. When they are documenting a family history, they learn and perfect skills of ethnographic narrative in writing, of clarity and sensitivity in interviewing, and sometimes skills in photography or illustration. Some art lessons are planned outside the context of specific projects, because they are foundational and can empower students to approach projects with more sophistication. Occasional projects, such as plays, murals, or musical performances, are connected to themes of study but are also an opportunity to gain knowledge and mastery in a particular artistic domain.

Concepts of art, and artistic forms of learning and knowing, are treated with the same respect as all other disciplines of learning. Artistic aspects of project work are showered with time, attention, and quality materials. The use and care of quality materials—the kind that adult professionals use—contribute much to what might be called an elite sense of classroom standards. I encourage parents to use holiday and birthday gifts as opportunities to provide art supplies for their children. Using school funds, student-raised funds, and personal funds, I try to keep the classroom stocked so that no student is denied access to good materials.

Is This Really Art?

What constitutes "real art"? If illustration is regarded as an unimportant decoration for a report, if a fictional historical journal is judged simply for its historic content and not its aesthetic power, then I'm not sure. But that is not the case in our classrooms. The aesthetic components of work are given as much attention and critical guidance as any part of content.

Let me give a specific example: A few years back, several students of mine made a presentation to the whole school explaining the geological formation of the valley in which the school is situated. The content of their lesson was carefully prepared, critiqued by the class, and revised. Much time, however, was spent on the quality of their delivery. The information they needed to share wasn't difficult to gather, but the question of how to make that information clear and exciting to students as young as kindergartners was a different story.

My students spent many days preparing carefully drafted and lettered charts and maps on large posterboard, getting critical feedback from individual students and the class as a whole. The quality of illustration, the choice of lettering, the layout and composition, were discussed in the type of detail one might expect in the art department of an advertising firm. Their vocal presentation, even their physical movements during the presentation, were rehearsed and critiqued in front of the class. The result was remarkably different from the common experience of students nervously reading a report in front of a group. The difference, I think, was art.

The idea that the line between what is art and what is not art should be hard to draw is not as strange as it first sounds. In the Japanese culture, for example, almost everything is viewed aesthetically. The way food is arranged on a plate, the way cleaning is done in a home, the way apologies are given to a friend—even the manner in which one dies—may be viewed in aesthetic terms. Elegant samurai deaths were often planned far in advance and critiqued aesthetically for generations afterward. A Japanese friend of mine, preparing her résumé to send to prospective employers, told me that she drafted two copies: one typewritten, for American employers, and one done by hand in careful calligraphy, for Japanese employers. "They would never accept a typed version," she explained. "They judge my character by my calligraphy."

The concept that even the most mundane events and products may be crafted and executed with aesthetic care describes precisely my goal in the classroom. Rough drafts can be messy and confused; that's their purpose. But final drafts should be impressive, even on the smallest level. I know things are succeeding in this regard when math papers are turned in with elegant layouts and lettering, and when I find student notes on the floor done in calligraphy.

This concept of art cultivates a school and classroom culture where there are high standards for just about everything. There's no escaping them. Students even debate aesthetic arrangements for our giant turtle tank and stay in at recess to rearrange it.

DETAILS ARE IMPORTANT

For years, I have read that teaching and learning should be process-centered, not product-centered. Or perhaps person-centered—*anything* other than product-centered. For some time, I carried with guilt my passion for the beautiful artifacts my students created: They were only products; I shouldn't be so attached to them. But eventually I emerged from that educational closet to declare my love for the physical products that are the result of our studies. These products—books, maps, blueprints, models, sculptures, scientific reports, paintings, product designs—are treated with almost religious significance in my classroom. The tools we use to create them are treated with utmost respect and are generally professional quality, rather than junior versions of tools ordered from a school supply firm. If all of our architectural templates are not returned in perfect condition, there is a price to pay.

An Obsession with Detail

We are obsessive about detail in my classroom and proud of it. If that means we are small-minded, so be it. To create beautiful fiction without concern for spelling and grammar makes a lot of sense to me. When that fictional piece reaches final draft, however, and is bound as a book and put on display for the community, spelling and grammar make a big difference, and obsessing about it is crucial. When students show me a technical diagram they've drawn that has graphic balance and artistic flair but is inaccurate in some of its technical detail, I don't accept it on effort. It goes back for another draft. Perhaps it can be traced (we built a light table in my room to make tracing easy and accurate) or perhaps it can be xeroxed and pasted up to save redrafting of key sections. But leaving it wrong sends a poor message about the integrity of our work.

The strange thing about obsessing over technical detail is that it is often so much fun for students. Introducing a project, I typically describe with precision the tools we are about to use—where they were made, how they were made, where they were purchased, how much they cost, and where they fit in the hierarchy of quality. When we visit professionals in the field, my students' first questions are often about the brands and qualities of tools and materials the professionals use. I have taken my students to an art supply store where they could peruse and purchase all levels of architecture tools and materials. I will often specify exactly which tools need to be used at which steps of a project—which paper for this draft, which pen for that draft—and it gives a tone of importance and clear structure to the process.

Unexpected Benefits

Details make a difference. In a study of geology, my students made polished stones at school using rock tumblers. At 5 weeks per batch, the process took a lot of patience and work. We bought jewelry-making supplies and made jewelry from the stones we had tumbled and from crystals we had collected during fieldwork. The jewelry was sold at a store set up for the town, and the profits financed a multiday field trip to New York City. We wanted the jewelry to be of good quality, even if the components were low-budget, so we got advice from professional jewelry designers and we set up a quality-control system to ensure that anything going into the store was without flaw. In addition, students wanted workmanship to be guaranteed; all repairs would be free of charge. This was a kids' store, but it was vital to the kids that the merchandise be adult-quality.

After months of work making necklaces, earrings, rings, pins, and key chains, we were $600 in debt (my money), but rich in merchandise. Students were handling all the finances of the store, and at a certain point, they were faced with an important decision—pricing each item. This is the kind of detail that might have occupied 10 minutes. Instead, it took 3 days, and I'm not sorry it did. The first 2 days were spent in discussions and calculations of how to maximize profit. The higher the price, the higher our profit margin; but at high prices we might sell fewer items. What was the perfect balance? Through surveys of students and parents, the class finally came up with what seemed a reasonable markup. Then, on the 3rd day, the discussion took a different turn. What was a reasonable amount to ask for items when our shoppers were often low-income children? How would kids from poor families feel if they were priced out of our store? To what extent was this a profit venture and to what extent was it a friendly outreach to the community? This was getting interesting.

At that point, prices were lowered, but it still didn't resolve everyone's concerns. Could we give discounts to families with less money? If so, which families should be eligible? Could they have access to the school's free-lunch list? (They couldn't.) If discounts were given, how could they be done in a manner so as not to embarrass the child or family?

The pricing policy that the class eventually came up with was quite different from what one would find in a typical store; any clerk working in the store was to be trusted to make the call on whom to give discounts to and what the discount should be. If there was a crowd at the store, the customer would be asked privately to return at a later time, when the discount could be given discreetly. In addition, a whole category of 1-cent and 5-cent items were added, especially for kindergartners who had no chance of buying a necklace for $3.50. The store grossed about $1,500, and there was no worry about loss of profit.

This jewelry store project is as much an example of deep thinking about substance as of obsession over detail. But my point is that the two are highly interdependent. My students could not have attained the same level of learning and of pride if they had failed to attend with great care to the many details of this work.

HIGH STANDARDS REQUIRE NEGOTIATION

People may assume that high standards must be rigid and unquestionable. Negotiation could only undermine them. For some aspects of school culture, such as safety, behavior, and respect, this is indeed the case. But what about best work? What represents the best effort and best work of each child, and how do we elicit it? If we hold to one rigid standard for all students when it comes to work, some students will achieve it with minimal effort and others may struggle earnestly and still fail.

Teachers in my school spend their evenings and weekends appraising the work of each student to determine just what level of effort that work represents. Is it acceptable at this level, or should it be returned for another draft? Like good teachers everywhere, we aspire to push each student to his or her maximum potential by refusing to accept work of poor effort.

Students know we do this. There is no secret teacher magic in our appraisals. When we return work, we conference with those students whom we feel need support or instruction, while others continue on project work. Students can choose to conference with us, and they can choose to contest our opinion. More than once this year, a student has approached me, often with eyes a bit teary, to explain that the work I would not accept represented much more effort than I had guessed. Often they provided explanations or evidence that were quite convincing. I applauded their self-advocacy.

What Is Negotiable?

With a class of all levels of ability, including substantial special needs, how do I hold everyone to the same high standard for final products? What is negotiable is not the quality of work, but the types of support needed to produce this quality work. Perhaps a student will need teacher or computer assistance for one part of a project, or an extended deadline or a waiver from certain components of the project. Quality is not negotiable, but scope can be. Students learn to self-advocate, not to avoid work but to ensure that they can realistically complete work with integrity. Almost every project we complete has mandatory components, which all students do, and optional components, which are clearly negotiable. This way students can work at different paces and still finish at the deadline.

This year a student with fine-motor problems ran into real difficulty: She had designed an enormous house as part of an architectural project and now was struggling with her drafting. Moreover, she had problems with the fragile paper we were using for blueprint work—all of her drafts were quickly torn. The solution she negotiated was to scale down the size of her house, which we agreed to, and to have her work taped down to a large drafting board, which she took home each night for homework.

During the course of projects or studies, the class as a whole often negotiates changes or additions in the project requirements or even whole new directions for the study. For example, I had intended to end our study of Deaf culture midyear. My students simply refused. "How can you stop us in the middle of our learning?!" Too many of the aspects of the study represented ongoing relationships and ongoing language studies they were unwilling to give up. Not only did we decide to continue aspects of the study throughout the year, but this year a number of those students, now attending junior high school, are returning to my classroom in the evening for classes in American Sign Language taught by a Deaf woman with whom we established a friendship last year.

Another realm of negotiation for me is use of class time. I make plans for each day and plans for the week; but in project work, as in real life, things aren't always predictable. Time allotments for certain work must be lengthened, cut short, or changed entirely. Most often, I make these changes, but students learn that if they are polite and constructive in suggesting changes, their wishes will be given serious consideration. There may be a schedule full of different activities, but with an exhibition approaching, students plead for extended time to work on writing or drafting. If they can remain responsible, quiet, and focused, we often agree to this. There have been days in my classroom when students worked on blueprints for 4 or 5 hours straight, staying in the room for recess and only leaving briefly for lunch.

This negotiation of class-time use can also be individual. While it is initially clear what is class work and what is homework and what a particular silent work time is set aside for, students learn that there is some room for individual negotiation here. If a certain draft of a piece of work is due Friday, a student may approach me and ask if she can work on this during the evening, as homework, and use the class time allocated for it to work on another aspect of the project. If she has proven herself responsible in this regard in the past, then she has good negotiating currency with me, and there is a good chance I will agree. Students watch this process and strive to be responsible enough to be allowed to plan parts of their own time also.

Earned Power

Clearly, this is a scary process for a teacher: It's hard enough to get kids to do work on time when deadlines and tasks are clear and rigid. What a mess it would be if students could negotiate these things! Strangely, teaching in the way I suggest isn't really as hard as it seems. Students are given power over their time and work only as they earn it, by showing that they can make responsible choices, that they can follow through on promises, and that they can plan their time wisely. These habits come quickly to some children, slowly to others. The level of teacher-imposed time structure that each student needs—and, indeed, wants—varies from student to student, and the teacher can adjust this accordingly, being frank in negotiations with the student.

I can't say that this is an easy process for me, or that I don't make mistakes in negotiating work with students. I sometimes find myself disappointed. Yet every student wants to be trusted and respected, and even students I've taught with serious problems in emotional stability, behavior, or academic skills have worked very hard to earn the responsibility for managing their own time. Students often work twice as hard as normal during extra time they have negotiated; they want to prove their level of responsibility.

SCHOOL CULTURE MUST EXTEND
BEYOND THE SCHOOL WALLS

At my school, we do all we can to bring the outside world in, in the form of local experts for our studies and community members to view and critique our work. And we also do all we can to get our students out into the community for fieldwork, exploration, and service. The town support that my school enjoys could never have been built without this two-way outreach.

Field trips are an integral part of all major studies. Classes visit caves, mountains, sawmills, factories, laboratories, artist studios, retail stores, farms, hospitals, private homes, colleges, other elementary schools, and all kinds of sites. These trips are a chore to plan and often exhausting to manage. The payback, though, in student and teacher excitement and investment is well worth the trouble. Because we have no money for buses, all trips are accomplished with parent drivers. Almost all families have two working parents, so arranging field trips takes early and ongoing effort to persuade parents to take a day off work to help with their child's education.

This tiring task has its hidden benefits. Students are prepared well for field trips—already possessing an impressive knowledge of the area under study—and parents accompanying us on trips are invariably delighted to see the students shine in this way, asking perceptive questions and exhibiting real interest. Parent loyalty to the classroom, the school, and its methods is forged during these occasions, and parents begin to feel an ownership of the school's goals. Parents, teachers, and students are all learners together. Most of all, these trips serve to put learning and knowledge clearly in the sphere of life, rather than simply in books and classroom studies.

Similarly, outside experts are brought into the classroom to speak with students whenever possible. These experts may be professionals in a field, sharing information in an area we're studying. They may be individuals coming in to critique or assist with artistic or academic skills. Or they may be people just coming in to share firsthand stories from their lives that bear on our work. Some of these "experts" are professors, craftspeople, or businesspeople; some are parents or siblings of students; some are even ex-students or students from other classrooms.

Once again, students are prepared thoroughly for each visitor so that they are not only polite but sophisticated and astute in listening and responding. Some experts are hard to line up for the first visit, but most are so pleased and excited by the level of interest and knowledge in the students that subsequent visits are easy to schedule. One professional Egyptologist, who I think had never presented to students below the college level, lowered her fee to visit us and planned to give a one-hour talk. She was so astonished at the students' passion for ancient Egypt and their knowledge of history and hieroglyphics that she stayed all morning, sharing stories and knowledge and helping students to translate hieroglyphics. She offered to guide us free of charge on an upcoming museum trip and stayed in touch all year. These outside experts serve to keep me fresh and excited as a teacher, and serve as models for students. They provide us with the vocabulary and concepts we need to critique our work in their field. They interest students in careers. And they allow students to watch me, as teacher, learn along with them.

We try to involve parents and families in school projects and studies as much as possible. Aside from field trips and giving presentations, parents, relatives, and neighbors are also invited to school regularly to listen to presentations by students or outsiders and to see exhibitions of student work. Families are encouraged to take an interest in projects, and their help is welcomed. Some projects are specifically designed to be community projects.

Bringing the community into our school builds for us the foundation of support we need in our town. We are a strange and newfangled school in a small, conservative town; we have no textbooks, no grades, and, in some rooms, no desks. We have won over the hearts of much of the town not because we talk a good line, but because the students do well in real-life measures of learning. They are capable and confident readers, writers, and users of math. They are strong thinkers and workers. They are polite and treat others well. We want people to see this, and we achieve it both by bringing the community in and by sending out of school each day students whose excitement in learning doesn't end at the school door.

TEACHERS NEED SUPPORT
FOR GROWTH AS MUCH AS STUDENTS DO

In addition to working as a teacher, I also work as a carpenter. This has been a financial necessity for my family, given the salary limits of my primary career. In carpentry, the process of learning skills and expertise follows a sensible course. Carpenters do not learn their skill from a book, spend a monthlong "internship" on a crew, then get certified as master builders ready to build a whole house by themselves. You wouldn't want someone with such training building your house. Carpenters spend years acquiring skills on the job, being given successively greater levels of responsibility, and they serve an extended apprenticeship to experienced builders before they are considered experts.

Now, consider the teaching profession: Teachers study education theory in books, typically spend a few months in a classroom (frequently with only one week of being in charge), and are then considered finished products of "teacher training." Following this training, they may immediately be placed in total charge of a classroom, with as much responsibility as they will have for the rest of their teaching careers. Whoever dreamed up this notion of teacher preparation must have been crazy.

In the absence of true apprenticeships, models, and on-the-job critique and support, most young teachers fall back on the memories of the teachers they had when they were in school themselves, not long before. They copy from memory and eventually build a repertoire of strategies to survive in that devastatingly scary and isolated first year. Most teachers cling insecurely to these early strategies for the next few years and even the next 40 years. They make a fortress of their classroom, hoping to be left alone. They take pride in the success of individual students but feel always insecure about the success of the class as a whole, and react with inner terror when an observer enters their classroom.

Staff development is the cornerstone of building a culture of quality in schools. But such staff development cannot be purchased with a single mandate or structure imposed from above. Because it is ultimately a way of thinking, good staff development can only be purchased with respect for what teachers can accomplish together. There must be a wide range of opportunities and structures that allow and compel staff members to emerge from the fortresses of their classrooms and take responsibility to learn in different ways. Staff members must begin to work in teams to make important decisions; they must forge changes in school culture together. They must visit other classrooms and other sites and begin to see themselves as learners who are willing to give and accept critique. They must become reflective practitioners—teaching, learning, and researching in concert.

The same applies to administrators. Roland Barth points out in *Improving Schools from Within* (Jossey-Bass, 1990) that when the Harvard Principal's Center was founded as a place for school principals to share ideas and become active learners, 1,500 local principals were invited to attend the opening. Three showed up. Although interest picked up enormously later, it remains hard for principals everywhere to find the time and commitment necessary to learn and grow within the profession.

It is a common thing to read in newspapers these days that students in Japan do well on tests, despite large class sizes. It is less common to read how well respected and well paid teachers in Japan are, how important education is in Japanese culture and families (to the point that mothers will come to school and take notes when their children are absent). And most significantly, it is less common to read that teachers in Japan only teach for 60% of their workday; the other 40% is given to the vital tasks of lesson preparation, meetings, critique, and staff development. Sometimes I dream about what kind of teacher I could be if I had a third of my day to plan and prepare, and not just nights and weekends.

CHAPTER 3

Are Pullout Programs Sabotaging Classroom Community in Our Elementary Schools?

Lois Brandts

Raising the front legs of his chair well off the floor, second grader Ronnie leaned back in his seat. Just before he fell, he managed to catch not only himself but also Jorge's attention at the same time. Together they looked up at the clock and then back at each other, and then they began mouthing words across the room to two other children. Alternately looking at the clock and pointing, the four children spent the next 7 minutes surreptitiously watching the hands make slow revolutions and trying to look engaged in the assignment. They were concentrating on keeping track of the minutes. Just before the sweep hand touched the 12, Ronnie stood up and headed for the door. The other three followed while the rest of the class continued with the task at hand. Just outside the door, the four broke into a sprint and disappeared around the side of the building.

These three boys and one girl were part of a pullout reading program provided at their elementary school to help children who are struggling in reading. By the time they left my room, Ronnie and Jorge had been off task for 8½ minutes. Or had they? Might not a better question be, Which task were Ronnie and Jorge earnestly attending to? And which was more important to them? That of the classroom instruction or that of being sure to be on time for their remedial reading class?

Traditionally, and in increasing numbers, children in our schools are assessed, labeled, and declared eligible for pullout programs which require them to leave the home classroom and travel to a smaller room to receive specialized instruction. Although pre/post tests determine individual student growth in each particular program, pullout programs are based on a set of assumptions that seldom come under scrutiny for their ultimate effectiveness. More often than not, teachers and administrators—and to some extent the children themselves—assume that adequate reading instruction for all children cannot be provided in the regular classroom. As a teacher, I began to examine those assumptions and now suggest that there may be better ways to deliver specialized instruction. Further, I argue that pullout programs may have a negative effect on the community of learners which is not always visible but may critically affect learning.

WHY PULLOUT PROGRAMS
POSED PROBLEMS FOR ME

Since 1983, I have been a teacher of first- and second-grade children in a California school where over a third of the primary children qualify for specialized instruction in at least one pullout program and sometimes in a combination of several pullout programs. After struggling repeatedly to schedule pullout times when children would not miss important events in our room, I began increasingly to question the accepted assumption that pulling a child out for instruction was necessarily maximizing that child's opportunity to learn. Further, as I began to believe that the way children learn how to learn is through the culture of the classroom, it became apparent to me that many children were being deprived of marked periods of time to practice ways to be members of a learning community. Since important things were happening all the time in our classroom, there was no way that I could schedule a time for the children to be out without missing something crucial to their understanding of themselves as learners.

A decade ago, the teaching time slots in a primary classroom were more easily delineated. Reading instruction might have been scheduled for 9:00–9:30 and a child might not have been affected adversely by simply substituting pullout reading for the classroom instruction. Fewer classrooms function like this today. With the implementation of writing and reading workshops, reading and writing across content areas, long-term integrated projects, inquiry studies, and flexible groupings, classroom schedules cannot be precisely clock-bound day by day. Rather, these practices combine to create a dynamic learning environment where instruction is largely seamless, integrated, and overlapping (Langer & Applebee, 1998). Thus the concept of pullout programs makes assumptions about the structure of the classroom day—and about our beliefs regarding how children learn—which are radically different from and more static than what is practiced in many of today's classrooms.

WHAT HAPPENS TO THE CLASS
WHEN CHILDREN LEAVE?

Time for remedial reading instruction in the official pullout program is customarily set aside in half-hour blocks. Most teachers prefer that children leave during the regular language arts time rather than during social studies, math, PE, or art. The prevailing thought is that it would not be fair to have too much "fun" while certain children are gone. Instead of getting a double dose of reading, pullout children are often offered a substitute for the reading instruction in the homeroom. Further scheduling complications arise when a single classroom includes a sizable number of children who qualify and are reading at many different ability levels. Thus, grouping children across classrooms often is the solution to scheduling, but it means that several groups may be watching the clock. Since some of the same children go to other specialists in speech, special education, ESL (English as a Second Language), or counseling, the revolving door becomes the way school is "done" for these students. An important attitude about the rhythms of learning is established when the rhythm of the classroom culture becomes fragmented. One can begin to see how the classroom teacher must struggle to build, maintain, and nurture a sense of classroom continuity that can give rise to a risk-free environment where students can construct their learning through social interaction.

At our school, planning lessons and keeping track of who goes where and when becomes a logistical nightmare for the teacher. In one first-grade class, 12 out of my 28 children were pulled out at various times of the day and week. Because of complicated scheduling, some went for the same special help at different times on different days. In order to help all of us remember, I posted a very large chart indicating days of the week, with each day broken down in half-hour increments with children's names marked in the appropriate times. Children would often be halfway out the door before someone would check the chart and shout that today wasn't the day. Again, disruption affected not only the pullout children but the rest of the class, as well.

Preparing to leave, leaving, and then reentering a classroom constitutes a major disruption in a young child's continuity of thought. If we document only the time lost, we can conservatively say there are 15 minutes lost every day just in relocating and readjusting. For those children who qualify for more than one program, the process begins all over again upon their return from one pullout as they begin to watch the clock for their next exit. There are times when the revolving door becomes the pattern for some children as they struggle to recall who goes where on what day and at what time, marching in and out of different learning situations and changing communities. It becomes a little like the old comedy routine of Bud Abbott and Lou Costello, whose joke keeps circling back to the same predictable and frustrating punch line: "Yes, but who's on first?"

Even the most well intentioned veteran teacher is often at a loss when attempting to fill in the gaps for the absentee. At first, I was concerned about the sheer loss of time—travel time and time spent in the pullout program rather than in class—but later I became alarmed over some students' sense of disengagement, their lack of connection and their feeling disheartened at not understanding what was going on when they reentered the classroom. For although the tasks, activities, and projects may be explained by a teacher, parent, or aide, little can be done to reconstruct the culture of the classroom events—both planned and spontaneous—which may have taken place and which show children ways to learn and how to be a member of the community culture. Often, the way children positioned themselves on the edges of the group when they reentered a room in progress gave a clue to their sense of insecurity. Occasionally, homeroom children quietly offered help without being asked, seeming to intuit their classmates' sense of confusion and insecurity. If a classroom discussion was in progress, seldom would the pullout children be called on by their peers because others seemed to recognize that they had not been privy to the entire discussion and therefore might either be embarrassed or give unclear or incorrect answers.

Consider, for example, Ronnie's experiences with a pullout program. On a Tuesday in November, Ronnie, Jorge, and the other two reentered the classroom where, for the last 30 minutes, students had been steadily practicing their skills. In this instance, the class was engaged in reading workshop, practicing how to select a book at their independent reading level. Reading workshop daily followed mini-lessons, oral language, and daily news but preceded flexible guided reading groups. In addition to missing these kinds of experiences, pullout children also missed a number of other learning opportunities that were an important part of our classroom culture. In only one week, Ronnie's group missed, among other things, messages over the intercom telling about school events and contests, a visit from Scott's golden retriever, the teacher's husband bringing her lunch and giving an impromptu art lesson, and a grandparent storyteller.

Messages over the Intercom
- School events
- School contests

Classroom Visits
- Scott's golden retriever
- Talk about the dog and the visit
- Teacher's husband bringing lunch
- Farmer Bob reading a poem
- An impromptu art lesson from an artist
- A grandparent doing storytelling
- A guest reading a book of tales

Mini-lessons for Reading and Writing
- Connections between authors
- Connections between subjects and themes
- Writing letters to grandparents
- Mail coming from grandparents

These important events in a classroom provide connections and links for the children to help them make sense of how to interpret their world and what their place is in it. Often, these conversations and interests were reflected in their writing and the types of stories they chose to read. If a guest read a book of tales, children often sought that type of story during independent reading time. These events were fruitful distractions which expanded a child's sense of place within the larger community.

LEARNING TO SEE THE PATTERNS OF REENTRY

The pullout children began the year by all returning through the same door, but as time went on they began to divide and use both classroom doors to come into the room. As their teacher, I didn't think of the significance of this until I began to focus on everything they did for purposes of researching the effectiveness of the program. Their reentry into the class consistently caused more discussion among their classmates than did their departure. Often, they returned with evidence of rewards, that is, stickers or candy. Although it was much later in the year when they began to flaunt their prizes, some of the children took careful note of them from the beginning and asked leading questions: "Where did you get it?" "Can I have some?"

Next, I began to keep track of the way Ronnie and Jorge positioned themselves in the room when they returned. No matter what we were doing, the boys consistently sat down together, placing themselves on the fringes of any group. If we were on the rug, then they sat in the back row; if we were all still at our desks, then they sat at the back or side tables. They were, I concluded, purposely staying together and out of the way, trying their best not to call attention to themselves. By talking to them, I came to understand that neither boy made any connection between what he was doing in the reading pullout class and "real reading." Selecting a book of choice—sitting down and reading it for pleasure—was something they did only in the classroom. Both saw the pullout program as an incentive program where they were rewarded for "good work."

Students' Views of a Pullout Program

Teacher: Tell me what you do when you go to Mrs. ———.
Ronnie: We play games—
Jorge: —and cards.
Ronnie: No, not cards. We don't play cards.
Jorge: I mean, we look at cards, you know, like *buh* and *ssssss*.
Teacher: Oh, learning the letters and sounds.
Ronnie and Jorge: Yeah, like that.
Teacher: Anything else?
Ronnie: Uh, yeah. If we do good work, we get a sticker.
Teacher: What is "good work"?
Jorge: Like saying all the sounds and getting a lot of cards—
Ronnie: —and finishing everything
Teacher: Why do you think you go there each day?
Ronnie: To learn to read?
Teacher: Um, hmm. To work on reading. When you come back to the room, what do you do?
Jorge: We come in and get to work.
Teacher: What does that mean, "get to work."
Ronnie: We see what everybody is doing and then we do that too.
Teacher: Sometimes, what is everyone doing?
Ronnie and Jorge: Reading, talking.
Teacher: Is it ever hard to figure out what to do.
Ronnie: Sometimes.
Jorge: Yeah, sometimes.

On average, 10 minutes passed each day after the group returned and before they became engaged participants. At times, Ronnie seemed confused and unable to concentrate, literally shaking his head from side to side as he tried to figure out what he should do. Over time Jorge slowly began to develop mannerisms which reminded me of a politician. He learned how to work the room, broadly smiling and on at least one occasion offering his prize to a boy who was admired by many and feared by some. I was curious about what the other children thought about the groups of children marching in and out of the room at various times during the day and what, if anything, they believed this had to do with the learning in our classroom. Early in the school year they seemed to know only that some children were singled out to leave on a regular basis to go to another teacher and return at the end, sometimes smelling like candy or carrying stickers. However, before long, signs of subtle, pejorative labeling surfaced. During art time, which generates informal talk, Allison once referred to the pullout group as "the dumb guys." Increasingly, as the year progressed, several athletic boys who had formed a tight bond in class purposely ignored Ronnie, refusing to play with him at recess. We teachers, I concluded, had failed to inform the students about the purpose of the pullout program. This issue became of great importance to me because it established an attitude that particular children have about their classmates and which the pullout children had about themselves and their own ability and right to learn.

HOW UNDERSTANDING WHAT HAPPENED
TO RONNIE CHANGED THE PROGRAM

What was Ronnie learning during this time? Based on the data I had collected, my assessment was that he was learning very little. I shared my data with my talented and innovative team teacher, the school principal, and the reading specialist, and we agreed to shift to a "no-pullout" classroom in the middle of the year. The reading specialist cooperated fully by agreeing to work each day with the children in the context of the classroom. By the end of the year, Ronnie had gained 2 years in reading. His progress elicited the comment "Amazing growth!" from the reading specialist. She recommended that he be dropped from her program in the following year. Jorge's growth, while less dramatic, was steady.

I cannot say for sure that the elimination of a pullout program was the cause for Ronnie's growth as a reader. What I can say is our insistence that he receive his support within the rich classroom setting definitely did not impede his growth as a reader and thinker, and it certainly did enhance his self-confidence. According to the reading specialist, he had often been stubborn, resistant, and even belligerent in his reading class, but his attitude changed markedly when the specialist became part of the classroom culture. In my opinion, learners need numerous and varied encounters in reading, writing, listening, speaking, and viewing in their endeavors in literacy. The richness of the opportunities increases children's sense of engagement, constantly contributes to their linguistic data pool, and enables their learning (Cambourne, 1996). Formal and informal events shape children's thinking about learning, and these events occur constantly in an elementary classroom.

My work as a teacher-researcher with the Santa Barbara Classroom Discourse Group caused me to focus on what was happening to the pullout segment of my classroom population. Then, in 1996, when California instituted class-size reduction in grades K–3, I had the time to document my concerns about the children's actions and attitudes by keeping field notes, videotaping, and conducting interviews both with students and with other teachers. Gathered evidence suggested to me that children progress just as rapidly, and far more comfortably, when they remain in the classroom, so long as they and the teacher are given the support they need from the principal, specialists, fellow teachers, and parents.

WHAT TO DO WITH WHAT WE LEARN
FROM OUR RESEARCH

As an experienced teacher, I would be irresponsible to advocate doing away with all specialized programs. I do not. However, I strongly suggest that school districts need to review seriously the way that specialized instruction is delivered. Support from a specialist in a "pull-aside" program within the classroom, where the two teachers work as a team to support and clarify a struggling child's thinking, may have as much effectiveness as, or more than, the traditional pullout program. However, radical change in classroom practices is complex and demanding. Not all desired changes are easily made (Barr, in press).

Furthermore, I now think that pullout programs may retard the social interaction not only inside the classroom, but on the playground and outside of school as well. I firmly believe that we can do better for our children as we approach the millennium. In my opinion,

- remedial reading instruction time can and should be reconfigured so that the learner remains within the community of the classroom;
- it is critical for specialists and classroom teachers to align their approach to teaching reading based on assessment and the child's needs rather than relying solely on a reading series or program;
- classroom teachers must themselves be competent, vigorous, and rigorous teachers of reading.

Lingering Questions

I offer these genuine questions to help us challenge our assumptions about pullout programs.

1. What are we doing to teach children to read?
2. Why are we doing it this way?
3. Is what we are doing working in the best interest of the learner?
4. Can we do it better?

CLASSROOM CONNECTIONS:
BRINGING ABOUT CHANGE IN PULLOUT PROGRAMS

Preparing for Change

1. Classroom teacher should observe pullout children over time, noting departure and return times, what they missed while they were gone, and exit/entry behaviors.
2. Schedule conferences with children to discuss their learning in the pullout class and assess what their attitudes are about leaving the regular classroom.
3. If possible, arrange a time for both teachers to observe in each other's class.
4. Schedule times when both teachers can discuss ways to align their philosophy about teaching and learning.
5. Make an appointment with the principal to discuss the changes you propose.
6. Inform other teachers who may be affected by changes.
7. Telephone or write to parents to make sure they understand that services are continuing but in a different way.

Implementing Change

Teacher's Role
1. The teacher plans and shares the lessons with the specialist well in advance.
2. The teacher gives direct instruction to the whole class or small groups depending on the lesson.

Specialist's Role
1. The specialist is on the lookout for materials which support existing classroom lessons and which will help teach the necessary skills.
2. The specialist supports the child's learning within the classroom environment.

Student's Role
1. The student works at his or her ability level on the concept or task presented by the teacher.
2. The student works collaboratively with the specialist when he or she needs support or clarification.

Evaluation

1. Both teacher and specialist will keep informal, anecdotal notes to share at regular intervals.
2. Formal assessments will be regularly administered by the specialist using an action plan drawn up by both teacher and specialist based on the findings of the assessment.
3. Surveys will be given at the beginning, middle, and end of the year to determine if the student is showing positive changes in his or her attitude regarding him- or herself as a learner.

REFERENCES

Barr, R. (in press). Research on the teaching of reading. In V. Richardson (Ed.), *Handbook for research on teaching* (4th ed.). New York: Macmillan.

Cambourne, B. (1996). *Coming to grips with reading . . . the whole learning way!* Torrance, CA: The California Elementary Education Association.

Langer, J., & Applebee, A. (1998). *English update*. Albany: Center on English Learning and Achievement, State University of New York, Albany.

CHAPTER 4

A Narrative in Three Voices

Rebecca Akin

Figure 4.1. Home page of Akin's website

A Narrative
in Three Voices

A Narrative in
Three Voices

A Narrative in
Three Voices

"A Narrative in Three Voices" was written halfway through a year in which I was exploring with my first-grade students how we construct our understanding of academic literacy in our classroom. Frustrated with my inability to articulate what I was seeing going on in our daily reading-group conversations, I experimented with representing both the data and the varied interpretations of them in a form that reflected the nature of classroom experiences more broadly, which entail relationship, a nonlinearity, context, and conflict.

The classroom itself was situated in a large elementary school in an urban district in Northern California. The children who participated with me in the study were 5- and 6-year-old African American students and English-language learners. I am a White woman who had at this point taught at this school for 6 years. Although the narrative itself was a complete piece of writing, it was not meant to stand alone. It was rather an attempt to help make some sense of our inquiry that year. The narrative was also not meant to be read independently, but to be performed in a group and then engaged through conversation.

The intent in using multiple voices is to attempt to represent the fact that in teaching, data are often conflicting and that multiple interpretations can be made of the same event. The boundaries between these voices are murky, seeming at times to overlap. Part of what is being represented here is the complex and often contradictory nature of teaching. Holding conflicting emotions, interpretations, data, understandings, and perceptions is part of the nature of teaching.

Were I forced to explain the differences in specific voices represented, I might call upon categories such as "observational," "reflective," and "exasperated." Yet while the purpose here is to illuminate the complexity of teaching, the idea that we might strive to either reconcile these perspectives or make neat and definitive boundaries between these voices is not the purpose. Rather, this illustration of conflicting perceptions is intended to illuminate the difficulty of a teacher's coming to know and understand her students. The intention is not for the audience to name the different voices, but rather to experience some of the complexity and disonnance teachers feel as a normal part of their practice.

EXCERPT FROM "A NARRATIVE IN THREE VOICES"

Voice 3: I chose four children to be the focus of my study of students' use of language in the context of academic discussion. One of the reasons Nadji was among this group was because he challenged me. Nothing about him was predictable, and few of the things I perceived about him were reconcilable with one another.

Voice 2: He couldn't keep still.

Voice 1: He always got his work done.

Voice 3: He had few friends.

Voice 2: He was kind and caring.

Voice 3: He talked incessantly.

Voice 1: He spoke with crystal clarity.

Voice 3: He hummed as he withdrew inside himself.

Voice 2: His gender expression was nonconforming.

Voice 1: He listened intently.

Voice 3: He often didn't know what question was being asked.

Voice 1: He had original ideas.

Voice 2: The work space around him was always in disarray.

Voice 1: His work was fluid.

Voice 2: His work was often indecipherable to all but him.

Voice 3: Jerome Bruner reminds us that one can love and hate at the same moment and not find it a contradiction. Although I certainly have only ever felt love for Nadji, it was what Bruner was getting at—the coexistence of seemingly contrary characteristics—that Nadji so visibly embodied.

Voice 1: We sit in our small discussion group, video camera on. Nadji lifts his gaze to speak, meeting my eyes with tilted head. The sun illuminates the right side of this delicate face, while the other half falls into shadow. His braided hair, loose from days of wind and play, draws the morning rays like a halo. Had Vermeer painted angels they might have looked like Nadji at this moment of responding. Yet just as the light and shadow played themselves off his face, so too does his participation play itself off the poles of my understanding. Speaking to us all singularly focused and still, he displays a presence rare in such a young child.

Voice 3: The next moment he flies off into what I perceive as fits of disengagement, into a detached world of physicality. His actions cycle through waves. First his hand writes circles on the desk in front of him, head swaying in motion with the movement of his fluid strokes. Then he drums violently, hands in fists banging on the table in unison four or five times. Those same fists then find themselves on his eyes, rolling gently around his sockets, growing to include his cheekbones, then temples. That motion expands to include his whole face, one hand dropping and the other opening to stroke first his forehead, then cheek, chin, cheek, and back up to his forehead again, around and around, head moving in gentle rhythm with his touch, followed conversely with quick, slapping motions. A brief still interlude foreshadows the severe jutting out of his chin, the mouthing of sharp words, the jerking back of his shoulders—the visible manifestation of a private drama playing itself out in his head.

Voice 1: Just as quickly as he falls into these actions, back but he comes, gaze again intent upon the speaker, or he is drawn back into focused conversation.

Voice 2: Within my various data sources I find I've described Nadji thus: engaged, disconnected, silent, articulate, expressive, calm, unable to keep still, mature, off task, brilliant, lost, intuitive, deep, invisible.

NOTE

To hear an audio version of one performance of "A Narrative in Three Voices" and to read a downloadable, full-text version, visit http://www.goingpublicwithteaching.org/rakin

CHAPTER 5

The Mission Hill School

Heidi Lyne

I am strongly committed to the idea that it is the habits of mind that are most important in teaching, rather than a certain set curriculum, and that portfolio assessments must demonstrate these habits, whatever the subject matter. I hope my school's work around habits of mind will stimulate others to think about both what kinds of portfolio assessments might work in their schools, and what is important to teach. Through my work, I have found hope and a new belief that it is possible to change teaching and learning for the better, given the right conditions.

My website, *The Mission Hill School*,[1] is designed for an audience of teachers, administrators, teacher educators, policy makers and others. The site (see Figure 5.1) captures the challenges and opportunities in the development of a portfolio graduation process at our small Boston middle school. The centerpiece of the website is a documentary video that, through four major sections, depicts both the yearlong development of the students' portfolio presentations in history and the efforts of our school faculty to implement a rigorous and authentic approach to assessment. The students present their portfolios to a committee composed of faculty, family members, school staff, and fellow students, to whom they provide work samples and evidence demonstrating their mastery of Mission Hill School's "habits of mind": conjecture, connections, viewpoint, evidence, and relevance.

The website and documentary are oriented around four sections:

- "Overview," a description of the portfolio process and an interview with Deborah Meier, the founder and principal of Mission Hill School;

Figure 5.1. Home page of Lyne's website

- "Preparing," interviews with students and teachers as we prepared for the portfolio presentations;
- "Presenting," videos of students sharing and reflecting on their portfolios; and
- "Reflecting," thoughts on the process from students, myself, and my colleagues.

These sections of video are juxtaposed with related resources, such as a library of student writing drafts and revisions, a text overview of the portfolio review process and other documents developed by the school, additional footage of student portfolio presentations and reflections, and my reflections on the year. The rest of this chapter is an excerpt from my reflective narrative, "Redemption," which is available on the home page of my website.

EXCERPT FROM "REDEMPTION"

There is a lot of self-assessment and self-directed learning in portfolios and performance tasks that allow students to experience a process of revision and redemption. I call it redemption because both high-achieving and low-achieving kids, if they have the opportunity to continually revise their work, will make huge gains. And when the work is publicly exhibited, it says to the students that their work is what the school is about. They're proud of it, and it gives them the motivation to want to do this very tough work. (Darling-Hammond, 1999).

Re-Presenting

The students returned to school this year as eighth graders, older, more serious, prepared to work. As a staff we had decided that their mornings this year would mainly be spent on portfolio work; they would be exempt from the whole-school designated curriculum but would be expected to spend some of that time learning to become media literate (which would be reflected in one of their portfolios) and some of the time learning some new science. Science and Beyond the Classroom portfolios would be presented in February. Those who needed to present again for History, Literature, or both would do so in November and December.

This work time impressed me even more than the spring had. The students worked independently, coming to me only when they could not figure something out or had an editing question. Whereas in the spring I had felt there was not enough of me, and not enough time, I now felt almost useless. I watched as students researched deeply into subjects they had skimmed the year before, made connections to other things they had studied, explored varying viewpoints, and thought about how things might have been different in other circumstances. (See Figure 5.2 for an example of student work.) I handed back the weekly homework essay assignments with editing comments and questions and watched as more than half the class, unasked, redid them and handed them in again.

Figure 5.2. Links to an example of student work on Lyne's website

**Example of Student Work
from Mission Hill High School**

Fifty-One Stars?
By Rebecca

I wrote the essay "Fifty-One Stars?" about a response that I read in a magazine. I was in shock about what I read. I thought Puerto Ricans were happy being a Commonwealth country. I was a little mad about the column I read. I was shocked because, how could the Puerto Ricans want to be part of the United States of America (U.S.A)? . . .

One student had been asked to add another historical piece to his portfolio—I watched him become deeply immersed in the Tudors and Queen Elizabeth—something we had never touched on and I had never suspected he had any interest in. I saw a student who had done a perfunctory report on Josephine Baker when we studied the Harlem Renaissance become so intrigued by her that she could not stop researching both her and the time period and adding to her paper. She said, "I would like to meet her. I wish I had lived back then to meet her. I think that she was one of the greatest people to have lived. She showed people that being different is good."

I listened as one boy, whom I was deeply worried about because he could not seem to come up with any ideas of his own, say to me, "I don't think I can rewrite this piece on the death penalty—I've been thinking a lot about it, and about racial profiling, and about how most of the people on death row are Black, and I've changed my opinion. I don't believe in the death penalty no more."

There are many more stories. All the students were successful in their presentations. All proudly passed. One community committee member summed up the feelings of many: "I was really a critical voice in our last meeting and I was pleasantly surprised. I read this [piece of student work] with a lot of happiness to see that she really had taken the comments to heart and worked on it. This piece is so much more full and rich."

All the students are now working on their next portfolios. Several of them still have the persuasive essay-on-demand to do again and are going to try it in the spring, when they have more writing experience. Several need to produce further proof of reading. But they all passed, and rightfully, on their portfolios and their presentations. Their work is in the school, available for anyone to see. To quote Deborah again, "You want to make standards explicit, public, available to everybody to show what they mean—and to disagree—people disagree about standards."

I am confident that this is all work to be proud of, work that proves that our eighth graders will be ready for ninth grade in these domains. I am incredibly proud of these students and the progress they have made over the past year. The school will be honored by having them as our first graduates.

Thoughts as I Take This Work Forward

Looking back on this experience, I feel that there are several things I would change, or would recommend that others do differently. Ideally, students would have input in creating the graduation requirements (as a brand-new school we did not feel able to do this). We have decided as a staff that we need to add self-reflection to the portfolio presentation—we are discussing ways to do this. We also realize that we need to develop a handbook containing all of the steps in these presentations for parents, advisors and sixth-grade helpers.

Another thing we as a staff need to look at is the enormous amount of work and time spent by adults in the school helping these 14 students get ready. The staff believes that this will be less intensive each year, as the entire school adjusts to the demands of the graduation standards and begins to align curriculum to these standards. Already this year's sixth graders are in excellent shape for their presentations next year, as they have been doing many of the same assignments as the seventh graders and have been immersed in the work ethic engendered this year (See Figure 5.3). As one sixth grader said of his seventh-grade presenter, "I'm going to work harder than she did. I'm going to try to get most of the stuff out of the way this year." These students will have finished pieces to use as portfolio work, which this year's students did not. However, even with less to get ready, extra time will always be demanded from advisors and teachers. Our staff has been extraordinary in its commitment to these students. We need to talk as a school about what this means to our lives and our classrooms.

We have decided to change the order of presentations. History and Literature/Writing portfolios both rely heavily on writing. This year we

Figure 5.3. Image from Mission Hill School in Lyne's documentary

will ask our seventh graders to attempt History and either Art or Beyond the Classroom, depending on what they are most ready for. We hope this works; we want to be flexible as we design these requirements but do not want to continually put the students and the community through a lot of change.

I expect that this year will bring a new set of problems and joys. The preparation and presentations for next year's domains will, I am sure, have the same kinds of difficulties we had with these domains; though we will be better at the actual presentations we will have the same confusions about the material required. Again, advisors, teachers, and students will all be living this for the first time, creating what until now has only been a group vision represented on a piece of paper. What is created will probably not be exactly what any of us envisioned when we wrote the graduation standards 2 years ago, but it will be something unique and, I am now sure, something wonderful.

The main thing I have come away from this experience with is an enormous respect for these particular students, and I marvel at the people they have become. They began the year as an average group of seventh-grade students. By the end of the year, I saw a group of hardworking, self-motivated students, each of whom showed enormous self-possession in presenting her or his work to a committee, and each of whom felt great pride in her or his work (See Figure 5.4). Though I have not yet finished documenting the evidence and plan to continue following these students this

Figure 5.4. Image from video clips of students discussing portfolios

year, I have no doubt that the students' standards for their own work and work habits have greatly changed through this process.

There are several possible reasons for this, and all of them are intertwined. Clearly these students received a great deal of attention and help. Many of the adults and children in the school were invested in their success; most members of the staff were advisors, and each sixth grader was a helper. The standards set were rigorous; work was edited and reedited by students working alone or with a teacher, with a lot of one–on–one conferencing. Also, it was clear to the students that everybody at the school took these standards very seriously.

But for whatever reasons, these students were outstanding—not necessarily in the skill level they finally reached but in their rate of improvement and in their development as thinkers, workers, and human beings. When I first read Linda Darling-Hammond, I felt she was using a very strong term to describe the effect of portfolio presentations. Now I believe her. This has been a process of "redemption."

NOTE

1. Lyne, H., Pointer Mace, D., Hatch. T., & Iiyoshi, T. (2001). *The Mission Hill School.* Retrieved April 1, 2004, from http://www.goingpublicwithteaching.org/hlyne/

REFERENCE

Darling-Hammond, L. (1999, November). *Making Relationships Between Standards, Frameworks, Assessment, Evaluation, Instruction, and Accountability* (Asilomar Restructuring Brief, Monograph No. 21). Santa Rosa, CA: California Professional Development Consortia.

CHAPTER 6

Circles of Influence:
My Research Journey into
Culturally Engaged Instruction

Renee Moore

When I began teaching English at a rural all-Black high school in 1990, I enjoyed a genuine fellowship with my students, many of whom I worked with outside school in church and community activities. Lessons in literature and writing went reasonably well (for a beginner), but then I started to teach grammar. Pardon the cliché, but it was like hitting a brick wall. Whenever I tried to teach grammar or usage, my students put up a fearful, sometimes hostile, resistance. Yet in my class surveys and course evaluations, the students and their parents have consistently asked that I teach more grammar. At first, I tried to account for these contradictions with various excuses ("Grammar is just boring to them; I need to make it more interesting!"). Still, the tension and the fear were real. Looking back, I realize that I shared their uneasiness with the topics; however, I felt it was my duty to help them become proficient in "standard" usage.

I had two simultaneous responses to the wall. On the one hand, I immediately started searching for and experimenting with methodologies. How could I teach them grammar more effectively? On the other hand, I began what would become a career-long action-research study on the issues surrounding the teaching of Standard American English to African American students.

SELF-TALK:
THE BEGINNING OF RESEARCH

My teacher-research experience began with a frustrated outburst in my teaching journal during my 2nd year in the classroom:

> The first semester is over and it is time for serious reflection and preparation. We [the English department] have decided to launch the new grading scale. We will use it to penalize students uniformly for the most common grammatical errors after we distribute the departmental grammar handbook. . . . I approach this with a good deal of anxiety. Will it achieve the desired results, or will we simply frustrate the students and make life miserable for everyone? One grim omen has been the grammar diagnostic that I used at the start of the school year. This past week, I had my accelerated ninth-grade class take the same test again as a posttest. I've only made it about halfway through the scoring, but the results so far are depressing; most of the students' scores improved only slightly, several stayed the same, and some dropped! This is after a solid semester—two grading periods—of intense grammar instruction! So what now? (12/23/91)

Since that time, I have been investigating the teaching of Standard English with my students, all of whom are African American. I have boxes and bags of raw data: tapes and transcripts of individual interviews and group discussions; notes from interviews with parents; teacher and student surveys, teaching logs, and observation journals. Making some sense of all this as I continue teaching every day has been challenging. I have learned, however, that teacher research is not about looking for some great new way to teach: It is the prima ballerina at the bar; it is the concert pianist playing scales; it is the basketball star practicing layups; it is digging for treasure deep in one's own backyard.

Later, that same year, I was writing in my teaching log about our work on part of a *Romeo and Juliet* unit. I found myself spiraling off into reflections that led to the first coherent formation of what would become my research question. I repeated this process of observing my work, writing about it, reflecting on what I was doing and seeing, then posing more questions over the following months. These self-talks became the first and most critical circle of dialogue for my action research.

UP AND DOWN THE HALL: TALK WITH OTHERS

Although I was working on the research alone, there were some important dialogues with my coworkers. The topic of grammar instruction came up frequently within our English department. This is the one area on which most of us disagreed with the state curriculum framework. All topics related to grammar and usage are lumped together under one competency; and above Grade 8, the framework simply says students will "maintain proficiency" in standard usage and conventions. However, as my former department head loved to point out, "Everybody likes this teaching grammar through writing stuff because all it requires is doing a little 5-minute review of something we assume the students already know, then showing them how they can use it to improve a particular piece of writing. But somebody has to do the dirty work of teaching the concepts the first time, and that's the job nobody wants."

In truth, most of us were teaching grammar skills as if every time was the students' first time being exposed to the topic. After these generally unsuccessful lessons, we would commiserate over how little the students knew or remembered from the last time they had studied the topic.

From one of these discussions, I decided that one of my goals the following school year would be to look at how I go about teaching grammar and what combination of factors created the context in which I did it. The word *context,* however, gave me trouble. What counted as context? Everything? How would I describe or measure the influence of context on my teaching?

Friends and Mentors

It was my Bread Loaf [Graduate School of English] teacher and friend Jackie Jones Royster who first suggested that I might need to examine how I was defining culture and how others were defining it. Jerri Cobb Scott, of the National Council of Teachers of English (NCTE), now at the University of Memphis, was helpful in this area also. The two of them drove down to the delta and visited my school. They commented repeatedly on the distinctive "southerness" of the school—"southern" in the sense of the traditions of the African American communities of the old rural South and how those were evident throughout the school. For example, students deferred to the two female visitors, calling them "ma'am," and they watched as our parent volunteer hung elaborate Christmas decorations on each classroom door. These things, they pointed out to me, were part of our cultural context.

I began to understand that the particulars of a child's community help define what is important and acceptable in a child's education. I became convinced, moreover, that I needed to gather such information and analysis in conjunction with the students and with their respective communities in order for any real teaching to occur. The most effective teachers I knew accomplished this by getting to know each student and at least attempting to know his or her family or family situation. This process could be a major undertaking for the typical secondary teacher who has to work with upward of 100 (more commonly 120–150) students per day. What does it take on the part of a teacher to even begin to "get to know" this many students and their circumstances well enough to teach them something as intimate and complex as language arts? I was about to find out as I prepared to carefully document the journey.

Reading

I also had to broaden my circle of critical conversation. I started a review of the professional literature, which I sometimes think of as dialogue with an extended network of colleagues and mentors. I was both thrilled and dismayed to find that the questions I was raising had in fact been asked many times by an array of experts. I refamiliarized myself with the work of Geneva Smitherman, Michele Foster, and Asa Hilliard, while opening new "conversations" with Keith Gilyard, Lisa Delpit, and Emilie Siddle-Walker. All together, I read more than 75 reputable studies. The review was helpful, but it was not enough to answer the questions my classroom situation presented. I found it difficult during class time or even after school trying to make connections between all the reading I had done of the academic research and what I was dealing with daily in the classroom.

One important lesson I did take away from the research was that there was not any one especially effective method of grammar instruction with Black students. I realized that simply analyzing the *methods* of successful English teachers would not be enough.

The review later became a paper for one of my graduate courses at Bread Loaf School of English, at Middlebury College, Vermont. My Bread Loaf mentors and colleagues encouraged me to pursue the research, so I applied for a teacher research grant from the Spencer Foundation. As I wrote the grant proposal, I in turn found I had a long list of questions for my mentors and network colleagues, including

1. What are teacher-researcher groups and how do they function?
2. What is the difference between qualitative and quantitative analysis?
3. What is ethnography, and how does it apply to what I'm trying to do?
4. What do I, as a teacher-researcher, need to know, if anything, about standard educational research methods?
5. What kind of data would I need? How would I go about collecting it?
6. How do I know whether I have a good research question?
7. How do I ensure that my data is valid and reliable?
8. How many different ways are there to analyze data? How do I decide which is best suited for this project?

One day as I was wrestling with these questions, I wandered into Dixie Goswami's living room at her summer house on the Bread Loaf campus. As I sat on the floor bouncing ideas off Dixie and other BL friends, we got a surprise visit from Ann Berthoff, a great scholar of composition and rhetoric. She launched into a discussion of writing, the power of language, and why we should reclaim practical criticism. In the midst of her amazing remarks that afternoon, Berthoff made the following observation: "We are born into history. The relation between individual and society should not be a dichotomy, but a plurality."

About this same time, I discovered Gloria Ladson-Billings's work, summarized in her wonderful book *The DreamKeepers: Successful Teachers of African American Students*. With Berthoff's observation still ringing in my ears, Ladson-Billings's words seemed amplified: "There is a stubborn refusal in American education to recognize African Americans as a distinct cultural group. While it is recognized that African Americans make up a distinct *racial* group, the acknowledgement that this racial group has a distinct *culture* is still not recognized. It is presumed that African American children are exactly like white children but just need a little extra help. . . . Thus the reason for their academic failure continues to be seen as wholly environmental and social" (1997, p. 9).

BACK TO ME: REDEFINING THE QUESTION

After much discussion and painstaking revision, I came to a working definition of culturally engaged instruction (CEI):

Empowering language arts instruction is a dynamic practice shaped by informed and collaborative analysis of the particular cultural experiences, strengths, and learning goals of a specific group of students within a particular community.

These words, first written in the idyllic setting of Bread Loaf's Vermont mountain campus, took on an entirely different character once I was back in the throes of a typically chaotic school year. By Christmas break, I was rereading my own research paper and asking myself, Which points still mattered? Out of 30 pages, I found 10 thoughts that still resonated:

1. Language arts instruction among African American students must take into account the specific historical and cultural features of language use and abuse within and upon the African American community.
2. Helping African American students reach their full potential as literate citizens . . .
3. Black students learned better when (and where) Black teachers had more control over the curriculum and classroom practices.
4. Value of studying Black schools and teachers especially in the South that retain the earlier traditions . . .
5. We should not perpetuate the myth that acquiring proper usage is a guarantee of social or professional success.
6. The key factor becomes not language but the contextual use of that language.
7. Social behaviors are learned along with language by native speakers that are not easily duplicated for those who learn the language as a second tongue.
8. Many things in standard American English are inherently racist.
9. Why do we teach SAE and will that knowledge and how we teach it empower the students and their communities?
10. Black teachers' attitudes and expectations of their students were an important part of their methodology.

THE WHOLE VILLAGE: WIDENING THE CIRCLE

One of the dangers of doing the classroom research alone was not having anyone around to contradict me when I was wrong or to check me when I started to get, as Black folks say, "beside myself." My circle of online mentors and colleagues performed this very important function for me. For example, one Sunday afternoon, I received an e-mail from another Bread Loaf teacher and mentor, Andrea Lunsford, in response to a question I had posed a few days earlier about using surveys to measure teacher attitudes toward student language use. She reminded me: "I think you'll have to find a way to at least fully acknowledge the 'halo' effect likely to accompany applying your own measures to yourself."

A day later, a message from Jackie Royster brought me even closer to reality. My question was whether I needed to compare some "objective" measures of my students' performance in grammar with those of students from classes that did not meet the criteria for CEI. She cautioned:

> You could use pre/post data for your class and another teacher's class who is not consciously using the pedagogies that you're talking about. I wouldn't put too much weight to this data though. My concern is that you would need to be clear in articulating this culturally conscious approach in the specific terms of intervention strategies to make it meaningful. Otherwise, it seems awfully messy to try to tie performance to classroom culture rather than changes in attitude, etc.

Students

If I were right that a teacher needed to develop a cultural engagement with his or her students in order to be effective in language arts instruction, then the student's perception of their English teacher mattered a great deal. That spring, I selected the first group of students and parents who would work with me in the research process, and another circle was born.

My research assistant was Sheila (not her real name), a high school senior whom I had taught for the 2 previous years. She was familiar with my work on BreadNet (our online exchange network). In fact, she had taken great interest in the work of a professional researcher from the Philadelphia-based group Research for Action who came to study my classroom. Sheila was delighted to learn that a person could make a career of doing that sort of research and vowed that she would someday be such a researcher. Her enthusiasm for research and her strong language skills made her of invaluable help to me. I used part of the grant money to pay her a small stipend. Her perspective added yet another circle of influence to my expanding research dialogue.

Choosing the students who would make up the focus group for my research interviews was difficult. I wanted a mix of males and females and of ability levels in grammar and usage. Also important were their parents or significant adults, who would make up the adult focus group. I deliberately chose students whose parents I knew would be more cooperative and likely to participate in the project all the way through, although I did try to diversify the group in terms of economic status.

With the help of my online partners from Bread Loaf Teacher Network, I engaged my students and parents in discussions of the question, "What makes a good English teacher?" I knew from previous experience that students from our small, closely knit community often expressed themselves more freely to distant online peers than they would to me or to their classmates. I was surprised at the commonality in opinions among my rural students and their more urbane, online counterparts in East Orange, New Jersey. These comments were typical:

> *CA (Mississippi):* A good English teacher is a teacher that has a good relationship with their students. Not only do they teach their students but they talk to the students about things other than the things that are supposed to be taught. Good teachers take time out and speak to students like they are your friends. They never give up on any student no matter how much a student does not understand the work, the teacher always keeps their patience and tries to help the student no matter what.

> *KL (Mississippi):* I believe a good English teacher is a teacher that teaches and explains a lesson and not just assigns the work.

> *PW (New Jersey):* A good teacher is understanding and supportive. They never give up on you.

A spontaneous discussion with one of my senior English classes about learning English grammar at school proved to be another rich dialogue. Some of the student remarks included "When some teachers explain about grammar, I'm embarrassed to ask a question"; "English is more embarrassing than math"; "You don't want people to know that you can't talk"; and "When I asked [Mrs. X] to explain something, she'd just wave her hands. She doesn't help us."

Parents and Community Members

The next logical and essential circle was parents and other members of the larger school community. A Saturday-morning conversation with one of the parents taught me much about our community's view of the study of

English grammar. A friendly, college-educated father, he looked straight at me and said:

> English has a way of degrading you. Talkin' is s'posed to be natural.
> I feel angry. I'm angry about this. This deals with my self-esteem.
> They always tell us we're shiftless; we're lazy. I passed ENG 101
> class at junior college, but the teacher flunked me and wrote on my
> last paper that it was because I "talked funny." English is a weapon of
> oppression. Just another tool to keep me in my place. Even if I master
> the language . . . [trails off].

He was one of the five I had invited to participate in my parents group that year. His comments were typical of the group's response to my question, Why are our students so resistant to learning and using Standard English?

Only a few weeks later, at a reception for a retiring colleague, another retiree who had taught for more than 40 years in our school system, reminisced about the period during which the schools here were first integrated. Black teachers, she said, were paired with White teachers in the White schools because the prevailing opinion among many Whites was that they [Black teachers] could not teach. I made a mental (and later a journal) note to interview her. Her comments had sparked a round of indignant response from the retirees that, in fact, Black students had been better taught in the old segregated schools than they were now.

What I noticed in these conversations with the parents and other community members was a sense of loss; a grudging resignation that the price of bringing African American students into the mainstream of academic success meant giving up some very important cultural ground. I found myself going back to my paper, especially my original thesis. Using what I had learned from the many discussions and from my classroom experiences, I began to unpack and expand the terms I had used almost 6 years earlier. Something akin to the delivery of my first child occurred as I watched what had begun as an academic exercise come alive.

FULL CIRCLE:
THE IMPLICATIONS FOR TEACHERS

The next summer, back at Bread Loaf, I returned to my notes from all these discussions to further unpack the key parts of my original thesis:

1. "Empowering language arts instruction" is teaching information
   or skills in such a way as to help students become effective
   communicators. I now preferred the term *language arts* to *English*,
   even though I am a secondary teacher, because it is more accurate
   and comprehensive.
2. "Dynamic practice" means changing teaching practices;
   varying them according to the makeup and needs of the student
   population.
3. Such practice is "shaped by informed collaborative analysis"; in
   other words, the teacher is actively seeking knowledge about the
   nature and goals of the student population, including evaluating
   and assessing the information gathered. Indeed, the information-
   gathering process itself should be shared with other professional
   colleagues, but most important, with the students.
4. The focus of this information gathering should be on "the unique
   cultural experiences, strengths, and learning goals of a specific
   group of students." This suggests an ethnographic profile of this
   community of learners: their values, beliefs, language patterns,
   literacy habits, family patterns, and attitudes toward education.
   This can be done formally and informally.

Of the items listed above, which may be most helpful in facilitating
language study? What interests and talents are available to be shared? I
use the term *learning goals* rather than *needs,* since the latter implies a
deficit. It is not necessary to annually reteach everything in the grammar
workbook to everybody. It is necessary, however, to keep the students'
goals focused within the social context in which they must live and succeed—what are the goals and expectations of the community that produced these students and with whom they must primarily communicate?
Based on a collaborative analysis, I believe that I should be able to set
individual and class goals in language arts. To be a truly effective language arts teacher, I must limit and tailor assessments and instruction
for each group of students and resist the pressure to overgeneralize and
stereotype.

As I continued to weave my findings and my thinking about culturally
engaged instruction through my various discussion circles, I began to see
more clearly the patterns that lay beneath the surface of my classroom
routines. I could begin to discern where and how the real teaching and
learning were occurring (or not occurring) specifically in regard to grammar instruction.

MAKING IT REAL: BACK TO THE CLASSROOM

I put this new understanding to work the following fall as I refined my preassessment process and developed individualized communications-skills portfolios for each student, which required the participation of a significant-adult member of the community. I have always used some kind of preassessment, but that was the first year I used the specific process that grew out of my research on culturally engaged instruction. I was very meticulous about recording the results. Looking back, I also realize that my earlier preassessments had been too long and had too many separate parts, making the analysis very time consuming. I had learned it was more important that the students and I be able to draw some immediate conclusions from this early assessment, so we could begin working in a more personalized way sooner in the school year. Based on my hypothesis, an early, accurate, and detailed knowledge of the students is vital for culturally engaged instruction. Certainly, such knowledge is important for all good teaching; culturally engaged instruction is simply good teaching for this particular population of students.

Early Assessment Process

The preassessments do several things at once. First, they help me learn about my students' strengths and weaknesses in key areas of language arts instruction. Second, they help my students learn my classroom procedures and give the class a preview of the type of work we will be doing during the year. Third, the process of doing the assessments provides every student an opportunity to begin the school year with a successful assignment and the same grade (an A for following the directions). With the fear of failure removed, I eliminate the need to cheat or to impress. (Contrary to my earlier misgivings, the students do give an honest effort on these assessments). Fourth, I get to give the students information on how to be successful the rest of the year and some academic motivation that, hopefully, they will remember through the year. Finally, I get students, and ideally their parents, involved right at the beginning in collaboratively setting learning goals for the year.

My preassessment process revolves around having students demonstrate through performance their abilities in reading, writing, listening, and speaking. Only reading and writing are tested in the district or statewide assessments; however, I include oral skills, not only because they are part of the state framework, but also because they are highly valued communication skills within the local African American community and the ones in which the students tend to be strongest.

We begin with a short, carefully chosen reading passage. It is almost always by or about an African American (preferably someone with whom they may not be familiar). First, we do a timed reading to determine their speed. Then, they are allowed to read the article in full, set it aside, and free write what they remember from the article (this tests recall and ability to pick up on main ideas and key details). Next, I'll have them listen to an audiotape of a professional speaker on a motivational or inspirational topic (such as how to be a better reader or how to be a successful student in high school). They are required to take notes during the tape. Scanning these later gives me an idea of their skill at listening comprehension. Finally, they may use their notes from both exercises to draft a essay. I make sure to give the essay an I-Search twist, such as "What, if anything, did you get from the reading or the lecture that might help you this school year? What goals would you personally like to accomplish this year in English class?" These essays become my writing and grammar samples. All this usually takes a few days.

Personal Learning Plans

By the end of the first full week of school, we are ready to begin analyzing the results together and developing personal learning plans (PEPs). The PEP is the first requirement in the communications-skills portfolio for my class. I spend at least one full class period introducing the portfolio. There are several points in the portfolio that are negotiable, both initially and as the school year progresses. The final step is for them to take the PEP and the portfolio checklist home. Each student must identify a significant adult of his or her choice (parent, relative, neighbor, teacher, church member, Scout leader) who is willing to act as a mentor for the duration of the school year. The mentor's role is to encourage the student to keep up with the class and complete his or her portfolio. Students must explain the portfolio to the mentors and get them to sign a contract. As soon as I know who they are, I contact the mentors to introduce myself, answer questions, take suggestions for adjustments in the PEP or portfolio, and open the door for communication throughout the year. All these steps help us create a culturally engaged learning environment.

THREE KEY LESSONS

Applying what I have learned from my research specifically to the teaching of grammar instruction has led to several meaningful changes in my classroom practice. First, I made a decision to talk with my students honestly about why we are required to study and master Standard American English. Second, I use what I have learned about the students, starting with the extensive preassessment.

Over time, I realized I was searching for a more empowering approach to language arts instruction. I wanted to teach the language arts in such a way that each student not only became technically proficient or skillful, but also became cognizant of the effects of language on others. Just as important, I wanted my students to understand, how language arts/communication skills could be used to project one's own ideas and to assess more critically the ideas of others. Such instruction must be dynamic, as opposed to static or scripted, even by the best-intentioned curriculum materials. It must continually change in response to a number of stimuli. To do that, our teaching must be informed by a very deliberate analysis produced cooperatively by the trained professional teacher of English in continuous critical dialogue with him- or herself, and everwidening circles of students, parents, and colleagues.

I developed the term, *culturally engaged instruction* to describe how teaching and learning occur in my classroom. The students and I are engaged (committed to an interactive, mutually satisfying relationship over an extended period of time) in an exchange of cultural information. I have learned over time how dependent upon and integrated into the cultural context language arts instruction truly is. The students and parents must develop a level of trust with the teachers in order to compensate for the historically derived mistrust that language arts instruction has engendered within large segments of the African American community. This goes beyond just a superficial "I like my teacher" (although that may be the way the students articulate it). It is rooted in respect and communication.

Like that of so many of my colleagues, however, my classroom work has been affected by the current frenzy of reactions to the No Child Left Behind Act. I have spent years developing and analyzing my preassessments, only to have my school district insist I use a prepackaged pretest for all students. Similarly, the administration has attempted to move all the major assessments of students out of teacher control by requiring only district office-generated end-of-grading-period tests. This stripping of professional responsibilities from teachers cannot bode well for the development of quality teaching in our classrooms.

Nevertheless, I continue to implement three key lessons from my work. I continue to encourage my students to explore the truth behind "standard" English. I continue to use my own preassessments to learn about my students and their families and help create a truly individualized learning experience (to the extent possible given our class loads). Grammar instruction reflects my position that my students already have language and that language does not need to be "fixed" or "corrected." They need to learn a new way to communicate with a very different, sometimes hostile audience.

NOTE

I teach English and journalism at Broad Street High School in Shelby, Mississippi. Broad Street serves 370 students in Grades 8–12. There are 27 teachers on the faculty, one guidance counselor, a librarian, and a principal. Of our students, 99% are African American; 100% get free or reduced-price lunch. For more about my work, visit my website, *Culturally Engaged Instruction (CEI): Putting Theory into Practice*, at http://www.goingpublicwithteaching.org/rmoore/

REFERENCES

Delpit, L. (1986). Skills and other dilemmas of a progressive black educator. *Harvard Educational Review, 56,* 379–385.

———. (1988). The silenced dialogue: Power and pedagogy in educating other people's children. *Harvard Educational Review, 58,* 280–298.

———. (1991). A conversation with Lisa Delpit. *Language Arts, 68,* 541–547.

———. (1995). *Other people's children: Cultural conflict in the classroom.* New York: New Press.

Foster, M. (1992a). The politics of race: Through the eyes of African American teachers. In K. Weiler & C. Mitchell (Eds.), *What school can do: Critical pedagogy and practice* (pp. 177–202). Albany: State University of New York.

———. (1992b). Sociolinguistics and the African American Community: Implications for literacy. *Theory Into Practice, 31,* 303–311.

———. (1993). Urban African American teachers' views of organizational change: Speculations on the experiences of exemplary teachers. *Equity and Excellence in Education, 26,* 16–24.

Gilyard, K. (1991). *Voices of the self: A study of language competence.* Detroit: Wayne State University.

Hilliard, A. G. (1983). Psychological factors associated with language in the education of the African American child. *Journal of Negro Education, 52.1,* 24–34.

Ladson-Billings, G. (1997). *The DreamKeepers: Successful teachers of African American students.* San Francisco: Jossey-Bass.

Siddle-Walker, E. V. (1989). *Minority student perspectives on the use of intervention strategies in writing classrooms*. Boston: Annual Boston University Conference on Language Development. (ERIC Document Reproduction Service No. ED316860)

———. (1992). Falling asleep and failure among African American students: Rethinking assumptions about process teaching. *Theory Into Practice, 31.4,* 321–327.

Smitherman, G. (1983). Language and liberation. *Journal of Negro Education, 52.1,* 15–23.

PART II

The Content of the Curriculum: Expanding Classroom Understanding

This section of the book presents approaches that connect students' questions and concerns to key issues in a wide range of disciplines. Two different chapters delve into the teaching of mathematics. Ball takes on the difficult challenge of responding to the dilemmas of authenticity, community, and understanding in her elementary classroom. Copes mesmerizes high school and college students in an inquiry-based demonstration lesson that uses NCTM (National Council of Teachers of Mathematics) standards embedded in an engaging tale of a monk. Two teacher-authors use drama to deeply involve their students. Pincus, working in a magnet high school for academically talented students in Philadelphia, engages her students in a production of *The Laramie Project*, demonstrating how to scaffold learning that is both intellectual and emotional. Wolk's elementary students do participatory-action research in their town of Pio Pico, California, and learn that community action can sometimes make real change—as documented on her website. Levy captures the interest of his fourth-grade students by developing a question that is relevant to both the American Revolution and his students' lives. Hutchinson develops strategies and approaches to teaching in an urban secondary school that involve her students of African American and Latino cultures in the development of their literacy skills. Video, student work, teaching strategies, and student impact can be found on both Wolk's and Hutchinson's websites.

CHAPTER 7

With an Eye on the Mathematical Horizon: Dilemmas of Teaching Elementary School Mathematics

Deborah Loewenberg Ball

Over the past few years, school mathematics has been the target of a wave of reform recommendations (California State Department of Education, 1985; National Council of Teachers of Mathematics [NCTM], 1989, 1991; National Research Council, 1989, 1990).[1] Rather than acquiring basic operations and terminology, students should be "doing mathematics" (NCTM, 1989, p. 7). Students should learn to look for patterns and frame problems (National Research Council, 1990); to "explore, conjecture, and reason logically" (NCTM, 1989, p. 5); and to engage in mathematical argument within a community in which standards of mathematical evidence form the basis for judging correctness (NCTM, 1991).

These ideas about reforming school mathematics are part of a broader set of contemporary ideas about improving education. Across school subjects, current proposals for educational improvement are replete with notions of "understanding," "authenticity," and "community"—about building bridges between the experiences of the child and the knowledge of the expert. Teaching and learning would be improved, so the argument goes, if classrooms were organized to engage students in authentic tasks, guided by teachers with deep disciplinary understandings. Students would conjecture, experiment, and make arguments; they would frame and solve problems; and they would read, write, and create things that mattered to them. Teachers would guide and extend students' intellectual and practical forays, helping them to extend their ways of thinking and what they know as they develop disciplined ways of thinking and encounter others' texts and ideas.

These ideas are not new. Our contemporary hopes are rooted in the visions of our educational forebears—among them thinkers such as Bruner, Dewey, and Schwab. The notion that school curriculum could be much more substantial underlies Schwab's (1961/1974) claim that the disciplines themselves hold images of what learning entails. Examining what writers do, what it means to "know" something in history, how ideas develop in scientific communities—each of these, according to Schwab, should inform what students do in school. Dewey (1902) argued that we should think much more fluidly about the links between the lives and minds of children and the notion of "knowledge." We should, he claimed,

> abandon the notion of subject-matter as something fixed and ready-made in itself, outside the child's experience; cease thinking of the child's experience as also something hard and fast; see it as something fluent, embryonic, vital; and we realize that the child and the curriculum are simply two limits that define a single process. Just as two points define a straight line, so the present standpoint of the child and the facts and truths of studies define instruction. It is continuous reconstruction, moving from the child's present experience out into that represented by the organized bodies of truth that we call studies. (Dewey, 1902, p. 11)

Both Schwab and Dewey press me to think hard about my conception of curriculum and of the ways in which children might encounter content. Bruner's (1960) notion of "intellectual honesty," however, has most captured my imagination. Writing on the topic of readiness for learning, he argued: "We begin with the hypothesis that any subject can be taught effectively *in some intellectually honest form* to any child at any stage of development. It is a bold hypothesis and an essential one in thinking about the nature of a curriculum. No evidence exists to contradict it; considerable evidence is being amassed that supports it" (Bruner, 1960, p. 33; emphasis added).

Any subject? To *any* child? At *any* time? My undergraduate students sometimes squirm a bit and make weak, nervous jokes. "Calculus? Can a first grader learn calculus?" But I, more experienced with young children, am quite convinced. The things that children wonder about, think, and invent are deep and tough. Learning to hear them is, I think, at the heart of being a teacher. David Hawkins's (1972) wonderful essays provide multiple illustrations of the insights of young children and of the special dispositions entailed in the capacity to recognize such insights.

Bruner has with this passage inspired me to rethink what would be worthwhile activity for my third graders. The idea of intellectual honesty makes sense. Somehow what I do with children should be honest, both to who they are and to what I am responsible to help them learn. Intellectual honesty implies twin imperatives of responsiveness and responsibility. But I wonder: *How* do I create experiences for my students that connect with what they now know and care about but that also transcend their present? *How* do I value their interests and also connect them to ideas and traditions growing out of centuries of mathematical exploration and invention?

This chapter is about my investigation of these issues. Using myself as the object and tool of my inquiry, I teach mathematics daily to a heterogeneous class of third graders at a local public elementary school. Over half of the students are from other countries and speak limited English; the American students are diverse ethnically, racially, and socioeconomically and come from many parts of the United States. Sylvia Rundquist, the teacher in whose classroom I work, teaches all the other subjects besides mathematics. She and I meet regularly to discuss individual students, the group, what each of us is trying to do, and the connections and contrasts between our practices. We also spend considerable time discussing mathematical ideas, analyzing representations generated by the students or introduced by me, assessing the roles played by me and by the students in the class discussions, and examining the children's learning. My goal in this work is not to make claims about what other teachers should or should not do. Rather, my aim is to investigate some of the issues that arise in trying to teach mathematics in the spirit of the current reforms. It is a kind of research *into* teaching complementary to other research on teaching. By doing this teaching myself, I can offer a perspective that is different from not better than—what can be learned from other vantage points or methods.

This chapter draws on data from my teaching during 1989–1990. In this particular class, in which we had 22 students, 10 were from the United States, and 12 were from other countries—Indonesia, Taiwan, Korea, Nepal, Nigeria, Kenya, Egypt, Ethiopia, Nicaragua, and Canada. Four of the 10 U.S. students were African American. Although no standardized or district testing is done in this school until the end of third grade, informal assessment showed that these students' entering levels of mathematics achievement varied widely in both mathematical skills and concepts.

The mathematics period in my class is approximately 1 hour long. During this time, we often work on just one or two problems. My intention is to select problems that will be generative, rich with mathematical possibility and opportunity. Usually the problems are built from the previous day's work, with an eye to where we need to head. The class often begins with students exploring the problem of the day individually. As part of the class, students keep mathematics notebooks in which they record all their work and in which they also write about that work. Although I ask students to start by spending some time thinking about and working on the problem alone, I also encourage them to confer with others sitting nearby. After 10 minutes or so (depending on the problem), students move into small groups and work further together. We spend about half the class period in a whole-class discussion, during which individuals and groups present their solutions and discuss the ideas embedded in the problems. The character of some of these discussions is illustrated in this article.

Every class period is audiotaped, and most are videotaped as well. I keep a daily journal about my thinking and work. I also give quizzes and homework. The notebooks, quizzes, and homework are all photocopied and saved. To complement what can be learned from their written work, students are interviewed regularly, sometimes informally, sometimes more formally, sometimes in small groups and sometimes alone. Semistructured interviews at the beginning and end of the year explore the students' ideas and feelings about school, their developing epistemological orientations and beliefs, as well as their understanding of a sample of mathematical topics (e.g., place value and regrouping, fractions, integers, polygons, and probability). Informal interviews across the year probe students' reactions to classroom events and their developing ideas about particular content. I have also been developing ways to conduct whole-class interviews on a regular basis.

Among my aims is that of developing a practice that respects the integrity both of mathematics as a discipline *and* of children as mathematical thinkers. Three components of mathematical practice frame my work: the content, the discourse, and the community in which content and discourse are intertwined. Students must learn mathematical language and ideas that are currently accepted. They must develop a sense for mathematical questions and activity. They must also learn how to reason mathematically, including gaining an understanding of the role of stipulation and definition, of representation, and of the difference between illustration and proof (Kitcher, 1984; Putnam, Lampert, & Peterson, 1990). Schoenfeld (1989, p. 9) argues: "Learning to think mathematically means (a) developing a mathematical point of view—valuing the processes of mathematization and abstraction and having the predilection to apply them, and (b) developing competence with the tools of the trade, and using those tools in the service of the goal of understanding structure—mathematical sense-making."

Because mathematical knowledge is socially constructed and validated, sense making is both individual and consensual. Drawing mathematically reasonable conclusions involves the capacity to make mathematically sound arguments to convince oneself and others of the plausibility of a conjecture or solution (Lampert, 1992). It also entails the capacity to appraise and react to others' reasoning and to be willing to change one's mind for good reasons. Thus, community is a crucial part of making connections between mathematical and pedagogical practice.

I take a stance of inquiry toward my practice, working on the basis of conjectures about students and understandings of the mathematics; in my so doing, both my practice and my understandings develop. In the service of helping 8- and 9-year-old children learn, I seek to draw on the discipline of mathematics at its best. In so doing, I necessarily make choices about where and how to build which links and on what aspects of mathematics to rest my practice as a teacher. With my ears to the ground, as I listen to my students, my eyes are focused on the mathematical horizon. In this chapter, I explore the tensions I experience as I face this challenge.

A RESTATEMENT OF
THE PEDAGOGICAL CHALLENGE

Bruner (1960) argues that children should encounter "rudimentary versions" of the subject matter that can be refined as they move through school. This position, he acknowledges, is predicated on the assumption that "there is a continuity between what a scholar does on the forefront of his discipline and what a child does in approaching it for the first time" (pp. 27–28). Schwab (1961/1974), similarly, outlines a vision of the school curriculum "in which there is, from the start, a representation of the discipline" (p. 269) in which students have progressively more intensive encounters with the inquiry and ideas of the discipline. But what constitutes a defensible and effective "rudimentary version"? And what distinguishes intellectually honest "fragments of the narrative of enquiry" (Schwab, 1961/1974) from the distortions of the subject matter?

Wineburg (1989) argues that school subjects have strayed too far from their disciplinary referents. I agree. Still, trying to relate them to the disciplines is neither straightforward nor without serious conceptual and philosophical problems (Palincsar, 1989). Before considering the dilemmas that emerge in my own efforts to teach third-grade mathematics, I note three problems inherent in attempting to model classrooms on ideas about authentic mathematical practice, problems that persuade me to avoid the term "authentic" in this context.

First, constructing a classroom pedagogy on the discipline of mathematics would be in some ways inappropriate, even irresponsible. Mathematicians focus on a small range of problems, working out their ideas largely alone. Teachers, in contrast, are charged with helping *all* students learn mathematics, in the same room at the same time. The required curriculum must be covered and skills developed. With 180 days to spend and a lot of content to visit, teachers cannot afford to allow students to spend months developing one idea or learning to solve a certain class of problems. And the best and seemingly most talented must not be alone in developing mathematical understanding and insight. Moreover, certain aspects of the discipline would be unattractive to replicate in mathematics classrooms. For instance, the competitiveness among research mathematicians—competitiveness for individual recognition, for resources, and for prestige—is hardly a desirable model for an elementary classroom. Neither is the aggressive, often disrespectful, style of argument on which much intradisciplinary controversy rests (Boring, 1929). Finally, in any case, modeling classroom practice on *the* discipline of mathematics is, of course, impossible. As Schwab (1964/1971) points out, disciplines have multiple structures; these structures are also not easily uncovered. No one "knows" the structures of mathematics; there is no single view of "what mathematics is." My work, therefore, aims to create and explore practice that tries to be intellectually honest to both mathematics and the child. In this chapter I present and analyze three dilemmas I encounter in trying to create a practice of mathematics teaching that is defensibly—but not solely—grounded in mathematics.

The three dilemmas arise out of the contradictions inherent in weaving together respect for mathematics with respect for students in the context of the multiple purposes of schooling and the teacher's role. Teachers are responsible for helping each student learn particular ideas and procedures, accepted tools of mathematical thought and practice. However, a view of mathematics that centers on learning to think mathematically suggests that the teacher should not necessarily show and tell students how to "do it" but that they should instead learn to grapple with difficult ideas and problems. Yet creating such learning experiences may result in frustration and surrender rather than confidence and competence. Fostering a classroom mathematical community in the image of disciplinary practice may lead students to become confused—or to invent their own, nonstandard mathematics. The teacher thus faces contradictory goals. As Lampert (1985, p. 181) writes, "The juxtaposition of responsibilities that make up the teacher's job leads to conceptual paradoxes" with which the teacher must grapple, and for which there are not single "right" choices. This is because the teacher "brings many contradictory aims to each instance of her work, and the resolution of their dissonance cannot be neat or simple" (Lampert, 1985, p. 181). In trying to teach mathematics in ways that are intellectually honest—to the content and to students—I find myself frequently facing thorny dilemmas of practice. I explore three such dilemmas here. Rooted in the three components of mathematical practice that frame my work, one dilemma centers on representing the content, another on respecting children as mathematical thinkers, and the third on creating and using community. In each case, I begin by framing the dilemma. I have selected one example from my classroom to illustrate each dilemma, and I use a common structure across these examples. First, because the dilemmas arise directly from my explicit goals, I give some rationale for what the students and I were doing in the example. Why were we spending time on negative numbers in third grade? Why do I think it valuable for students to experiment with and invent mathematical ideas? What do I mean by "community," and why is it important to create and use such a community in helping third graders learn mathematics? Next, I describe and explain what I faced in each case and why it presented a dilemma for me. To elaborate on the presentation of the illustrative cases, I provide evidence of students' thinking and change. I conclude each case with a discussion of the dilemmas entailed.

DILEMMA NO. 1: REPRESENTING THE CONTENT: THE CASE OF TEACHING NEGATIVE NUMBERS

What concerns [the teacher] is the ways in which the subject may become part of experience; what there is in the child's present that is usable in reference to it; [to] determine the medium in which the child should be placed in order that growth might be properly directed. (Dewey, 1902, p. 23)

How can 9-year-olds be engaged in exploring measurement, addition and subtraction, fractions, and probability? What are the hooks that connect the child's world with particular mathematical ideas and ways of thinking? Shulman and his colleagues (e.g., Shulman, 1986, 1987; Wilson, Shulman, & Richert, 1987) have charted brave new territory with the concept of *pedagogical content knowledge*, "the most powerful analogies, illustrations, examples, explanations, and demonstrations—in a word, the ways of formulating and representing the subject that make it comprehensible to others" (Shulman, 1986, p. 9). Shulman (1986) argues that a teacher must have "a veritable armamentarium of alternative forms of representation" (p. 9); moreover, the teacher must be able to "transform" his or her personal understandings of the content. In Dewey's terms, "to see it is to psychologize it." Figuring out powerful and effective ways to represent particular ideas implies, in balanced measure, serious attention to both the mathematics and the children. This is more easily said than done. I will illustrate this with an account of my struggles to find a way of helping my third graders extend their domain from the natural numbers to the integers.

Rationale for Teaching Integers

When there is so much content to cover, why is teaching third graders about negative numbers worthwhile or appropriate? The justifications, I contend, are both experiential and mathematical. Children who live in Michigan know that there are a few days every winter when the temperature is below zero—and that means that it is too cold to go outside for recess. Many have also had experience with owing someone something or being "in the hole" in scoring a game—conceptually, experiences with negative numbers that have not been symbolically quantified. Still, they assert with characteristic 8-year-old certainty that "you can't take 9 away from 0." That third graders—indeed, many older children—think the "lowest number" is zero seems problematic. Teaching them about negative numbers is an attempt to bridge their everyday quantitative understandings with formal mathematical ones.

Analyzing the Content and Thinking about Learners

I began my pedagogical deliberations by reviewing the various models for negative numbers that I knew. The school district's curriculum (*Comprehensive School Mathematics Program* [CEMREL, 1979]) uses a story about an elephant named Eli who has both regular and magic peanuts. (The Comprehensive School Mathematics Program [CSMP] is an innovative mathematics curriculum developed in the 1970s for elementary classrooms [see Remillard, 1990, for a comparison of CSMP with other elementary mathematics programs].) Whenever a magic peanut and a regular peanut are in Eli's pocket at the same time, they both disappear (i.e., $-1 + 1 = 0$). This representation did not appeal to me, although I was sure that it would be fun and engage the children. I was concerned about the messages entailed in fostering "magical" notions about mathematics—peanuts just disappearing, for example—because of the widespread tendency to view mathematics as mysterious and beyond sense or reason. After considering other models such as money (and debt), a frog on a number line, and game scoring, I decided to use a building with many floors both above and below ground (see Figure 7.1). As is the case in many other countries, the ground floor is called the "0th" floor. This was a considerable adaptation of a model called the "Empire State Building" that appears briefly for one lesson in CSMP.

Figure 7.1. The "Building": A model for adding and subtracting

Why did I settle on this admittedly fantastic model? Analyzing negative numbers and operations with them, I saw that there were at least two important dimensions:

- Negative numbers can be used to represent an *amount of the opposite of something* (e.g., –5 can represent a $5 debt, the opposite of money).
- Negative numbers can be used to represent a *location relative to zero* (e.g., –5 can represent a position that is five units away from zero).

Any number has two components: *magnitude* and *direction*; from a pedagogical point of view, this seems to become particularly significant when the students' domain is stretched to include negative numbers. A focus on the magnitude component leads to a focus on *absolute value*. This component emerges prominently in many everyday uses of negative numbers (e.g., debt, temperature). Thus, comparing magnitudes becomes complicated. There is a sense in which –5 is more than –1 and equal to 5, even though, conventionally, the "right" answer is that –5 is less than both –1 and 5. This interpretation arises from perceiving –5 and 5 as both five units away from zero and –5 as more units away from zero than –1. Simultaneously understanding that –5 is, in one sense, more than –1 and, in another sense, less than –1 is at the heart of understanding negative numbers.

Just before beginning to work with negative numbers, I wrote in my journal:

I'm going to try the elevator model because its advantages seem to outweigh its disadvantages. It's like the number line in that it, too, is a positional model. The "up" and "down" seem to make sense with addition and subtraction: Artificial rules don't have to be made. And I think I might be able to use it to model adding and subtracting negative numbers as well as positives: When a person wants to add more underground floors, that would be *adding* negatives. If someone wants to demolish some of the underground floors, that would be *subtracting negatives*. But could something like 4 – (–3) be represented with this model? I'm not sure. I guess it would be like *moving away from the underground floors*, but . . . I don't like the money or game models right now because they both seem to fail to challenge kids' tendency to believe that negatives are the same as zero (owing someone five dollars—i.e., –5—seems the same as having no money). (Teaching journal, September 25, 1989, p. 28)

In this journal entry, I was settling on the building representation after weighing concerns for the essence of the content, coupled with what I knew to expect of 8-year-olds' thinking—for instance, that they tend to conceive negative numbers as just equivalent to zero. I hoped that this clearly positional model would help to deflect that tendency. I was aware from the start that the model had mathematical limits—for example, its capacity to model the subtraction of negative numbers.

We began to work with the building by labeling its floors. I was pleased to see that the students readily labeled the underground floors correctly. I used the language implied by the building: We had floors below the ground, sometimes referred to as "below zero." The circumflex (^) above the numerals on the building pictured in Figure 7.1 replaced the traditional negative sign (–). This is a convention from CSMP. The rationale for substituting the circumflex for the minus sign is to focus children on the idea of a negative number as a *number*, not as an *operation* (i.e., subtraction) on a positive number. Although I have found the symbol useful pedagogically, I do not use it in this chapter because it would be unfamiliar to most readers. We had floors above the ground, sometimes referred to as "regular floors." The unconventional system—with zero as the ground floor—did not seem to confuse the students who were, as a group, relatively unfamiliar with multistory buildings of any kind. I introduced little paper people who rode the elevator in the building: "Take your person and put her on any floor. Have her take the elevator to another floor and then write a number sentence to record the trip she took." Thus, if a person started on the fourth floor and came down six floors, we would record $4 - 6 = -2$. If a person got on at the second floor below ground and rode up five floors, this would be written as $-2 + 5 = 3$. I introduced these conventions of recording because I wanted to convey that mathematical symbols are a powerful way of communicating ideas, a consistent theme in my goals.

We worked on increasingly complicated problems with the building, for example, "How many ways are there for a person to get to the second floor?" This problem generated an intense discussion. Some children negotiated long, "many-stop" trips for their little paper people, for example, $-5 + 10 - 6 - 4 + 3 + 6 - 2 = 2$. Others stuck with "one-stop" trips, for example, $-3 + 5 = 2$. The students debated: Were there infinite solutions? Or exactly 25 solutions? This argument afforded us the opportunity to talk about the role of assumptions in framing and solving problems. Those who assumed one-stop trips were right when they argued that there were exactly 25 solutions to this problem. Our arguments about this evolved quickly from one child's proposition that there were 24 solutions—she argued that there were

12 floors above and 12 floors below zero—to another child's observation that the ground floor offered one more solution: $0 + 2 = 2$. However, those who assumed that trips could be as long as you like were also right when they argued that the problem might have "afinidy" or maybe 8,000,000,000, 000,000,000,000 solutions. As usual, the third graders reached out to touch the notion of the infinite with great fascination—and "afinidy" and 8,000,000, 000,000,000,000,000 are virtually equivalent when you are 8 or 9.

The work with the building generated other wonderful explorations. Nathan noticed that "any number below zero plus that same number above zero equals zero," and the children worked to prove that his conjecture would be true for all numbers.[2] Ofala produced "any number take away double that number would equal that same number, only below zero" (e.g., $5 - 10 = -5$).

Despite much good mathematical activity, such as our discussions of the number of solutions and the conjectures of Nathan and Ofala, I worried about what the students were learning about negative numbers and about operations with them. Writing the number sentences seemed somewhat perfunctory. I was not convinced that recording the paper people's trips on the elevator was necessarily connecting with the children's understandings of what it means to add or subtract with integers. I also saw that only partial meanings for addition and subtraction were possible with this model. For addition, we were only able to work with a change model (i.e., you start on the third floor and you go up two floors—your position has *changed* by two floors). For subtraction, we could model its comparison sense, but not the sense in which subtraction is about "taking away." I also thought that the building was not helping students develop a sense that -5 was less than -2. Although being on the fifth floor below ground was lower than the second floor below ground, it was not necessarily less. I wondered, not for the first or last time, about what may be gained by using and "milking" one representation thoroughly versus what may be gained by introducing multiple representations.

Finally, we hit a crisis—over what to do with $6 + (-6)$ (October 12, 1989). There was no sensible way to deal with this on the building. "If a person began at the sixth floor above the ground, what would it mean to go up "6 below-zero floors"? The children struggled with trying to make sense:

> *Betsy*: Here's how I do it. (She put a person on the sixth floor and on the sixth floor below ground and moved them toward each other.) 1 . . . 2 . . . 3 . . . 4 . . . 5 . . . 6. And so I move them both at the same time. And I got 0.
>
> *Sean*: But it says *plus*, not minus!
>
> *Betsy*: But you're minusing!

Riba: (To Betsy) Where'd you get the minus?

Sean: You should just leave it alone. You can't *add* six below zero, so you just leave it. Just say "good-bye" and leave it alone and it is still just six.

Mei: But this six below zero would just disappear into thin air!

Sean: I know. It would just disappear because it wouldn't be able to *do* anything. It just stays the same, it stays on the same number. Nothing is happening.

Trying Money

After some deliberation, I decided to try money as a second representational context for exploring negative numbers. Money had some advantages that the building lacked: It was not positional and it seemed as though it would work better for modeling relative quantities—that –5 was less than –2, despite the fact that 5 was more than 2. Moreover, all meanings for addition and subtraction were possible. The expression 6 + –6 could have meaning: having 6 dollars and also owing 6 dollars. Still, I saw potential problems on the horizon. As I wrote in my journal, "One keeps bumping into the absolute value aspect of negative numbers—for example, –$5 ($5 of debt is *more* debt than –$2. You have to talk about how much *money* (or `net worth') in order to make it focus on negative numbers being *less*" (Teaching journal, October 12, 1989, p. 63).

I struggled with the language "props" that would structure the fruitful use of money as a representation for negative numbers. I decided that I needed an 8-year-old's version of "net worth" so as to focus the children on the inverse relationship between debt and money, on financial *state* rather than on *actions* of spending or getting money. Our first money problem—about their teacher, Mrs. Rundquist—was very structured as I tried to create the representational context (see Ball, in press). Instead of our usual pattern of some small-group or independent work followed by a whole-class discussion, we discussed this problem together:

Ms. Suzuka has 4¢ (represented two ways: "4¢" and with 4 magnetic checkers).

She wants to buy a pencil that costs 10¢. (*She needed _____?*)

She borrowed 6¢ from Mrs. Rundquist. Mrs. Rundquist gave her an IOU for 6¢ (*written as "–6¢" and also represented with six "negative" checkers*).

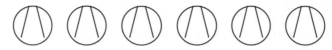

Later, she was lucky and got an envelope with 15¢ in it.

She had to pay back Mrs. Rundquist. What did she have for herself then?

To resolve the debt, I had the students pay off 1¢ of what was owed at a time, matching one negative checker (representing 1¢ of debt) with one regular checker (representing 1¢). We arrived at the answer of 9¢ without much difficulty. When I wrote the 6¢ debt as –6, I asked, "Why do you think I wrote 6 below zero?" It seemed that the students found it sensible.

But when I asked them to write a number sentence to represent the story, they wrote $15 - 6 = 9$, not using any negative numbers at all. And that made sense when I thought about it: Their number sentences represented the *action* of paying off the debt (i.e., you take 6¢ from your 15¢ and give it to the person you owe). I realized that I would need to structure the use of this representation to focus on *how much money there was*, rather than on *actions*. I decided to do another problem in which the key question would be how much money Ms. Suzuka had *for herself* at any given point. So when she owes Mrs. Rundquist $10 and also has $13 in her pocket, one can ask, "What does Ms. Suzuka have *for herself* right now?" and that would support the use of negative numbers—that is, $-10 + 13 = ?$ I conceived the idea of "for herself" as a representation of net worth; I hoped it would focus the students on balancing debt with money in ways that would illuminate positive and negative numbers. I felt that, if I could get it to work, money would be a good complement to our work with the building.

I realized as we continued, though, that the students did not necessarily reconcile debt with actual money, that they were inclined to remember both but to keep them separate. For example, if I talked about Jeannie having $4 in her pocket and owing $6 to her mother, they were not at all disposed to represent her financial state (how much money she had for herself) as –$2. Instead, they would report that "Jeannie has $4 and she *also* owes her mother $6." With money, they seemed to avoid using negative numbers—maybe precisely because the representation entails quantity, not position. As Jeannie argued, quite rightly, "There is no such thing as below-zero dollars!"

Negative numbers seemed sensible on the building to denote different positions relative to the ground. But on the building, we used negative numbers only in the first or answer positions of the number sentences, ____ + 2 = ____, because we never figured out what it would mean to move a negative amount on the building. With money, many children never used negative numbers to represent debt: They were inclined to report that someone had "$6" and "also owes so-and-so eight dollars" rather than using –$8 to represent the debt. They were also inclined to leave positive values (money) and negative ones (debt) unresolved.

Students' Learning

Uncertain about where we were and where we could reach, I gave a quiz. I found that, after exploring this new domain via the representations of the building and money, all the students were able to compare integers correctly, for example,

$$-35 < 6$$
$$6 > -6$$

and explain why (e.g., "–35 is below zero and 6 is above zero so –35 is less than 6"). They were also all newly aware that there *is* no "smallest number." However, about half of them, when asked for a number that was less than –4, produced one that was more (e.g., –2). Note that producing a number less than –4 requires still more solid understanding of negative numbers than comparing a negative with a positive number. It is easier to see that –35 is less than 6 than to see that it is less than –6. Children will typically explain that –35 is less than 6 simply because it is below zero and 6 is not. But when they examine –35 and –6, they are often inclined to think that –35 is greater than –6, on the basis of the magnitude of the numbers. When students focused only on the magnitude of the number, –2 seemed less than –4. As I thought about how wary some of them still were of "these numbers" below zero, I reminded myself that it took over a thousand years for negative numbers to be accepted in the mathematical community—due principally to their fundamental "lack of intuitive support" (Kline, 1970, p. 267). Why should I expected my third graders to be quicker to accept a difficult idea?

Dilemmas of Content and Representation

Clearly, the representation of negative numbers is fraught with dilemmas. I had to think hard about numbers below zero. And as I did so, I realized how rare such content analyses are for any of the topics typically taught. Moreover, the children's understandings and confusions provided me with more information with which to adapt my choices, yet the mathematics helped me to listen to what they were saying. Thus, it was in the ongoing weaving of children and mathematics that I constructed and adapted my instruction.

My analysis made me aware of how powerful the absolute-value aspect of integers is—that is, that –5 is in many ways more than 2: It is farther from zero than 2 is. Moreover, –5 is also equal to 5 in some senses: They are equidistant from zero. So, given this insight, I faced the dilemma of what I should try to get my students to learn: Could they learn to manage simultaneously the sense in which –5 is more than 3 and the sense in which it is less than 3? In school, they will be required to say that –5 is less than 3. Am I confusing them when I allow them to explore multiple dimensions of negative numbers and what these numbers represent?

I also had to think about what 8-year-olds could stretch to understand. Although there is research on student thinking, it has not investigated many topics that teachers teach: What are 8-year-olds' conceptions of proof and of what makes something true—in different domains? Our knowledge about primary-grade children's solving of arithmetic word problems or of place value, for instance, does not necessarily help us to predict how they understand the notion of numbers below zero, or the relationship between positive and negative integers.

Constructing good instructional representations and figuring out how to use them well are not the same thing. Even after I developed these two models for negative numbers and had analyzed them with respect to the mathematics and to each representation's accessibility for students, I still had to figure out how to use them—what kinds of problems to work on while using each tool, what should be the supporting language that would structure and focus the representation's key features for illuminating the content. For example, I discovered that I needed some kind of notion of "net worth" in order to steer the children's use of the money model away from attention to *actions*—buying (subtraction) or earning (adding)—to attention to *balances* and states. If I wanted the students to have a need to use negative numbers to represent quantities, then how money was engaged as a representational context was crucial (Ball, in press).

No representations capture all aspects of an idea; nor are all equally useful for particular students. No formulas exist for generating fruitful representations. Good teachers must have the capacity or be provided with the support to probe and analyze the content so that they can select and use representations that illuminate critical dimensions of that content for their students. Threaded throughout must be thoughtful consideration of students' current ideas and interests. A teacher must also figure out how to support and use the representational contexts that students construct. And teachers need alternative models to compensate for the imperfections and distortions in any given representation (Ball, 1988). When Bruner (1960) argues that constructing intellectually honest representations "requires a combination of deep understanding and patient honesty to present physical or other phenomena in a way that is simultaneously exciting, correct, and rewardingly comprehensible" (p. 22), this is no simple observation. As I try to do this, I struggle with dilemmas and unanswered questions. And, if all the uncertainties were not enough, I face persistent uncertainties about what sense my students are making, about what they are learning.

DILEMMA NO. 2:
RESPECTING CHILDREN AS MATHEMATICAL THINKERS: THE CASE OF "SEAN NUMBERS"

Good teachers respect children's thinking. They view students as capable of thinking about big and complicated ideas, although what that actually means in mathematics is, at times, not clear. Mathematics is, after all, a domain in which there *are* "right answers." Respecting children as authors or artists seems somehow different. Mathematics teachers must respect students' thinking even as they help students to acquire particular tools, concepts, and understandings. Mathematics teachers must respect students' thinking even as they strive to enculturate students into the discourse of mathematics. Hawkins (1972, p. 113) captures some of this tension when he writes that the teacher must be able to "sense when a child's interests and proposals—what I have called his trajectory—are taking him near to mathematically sacred ground. . . . A teacher-diagnostician must map a child's question as much as his answer, neither alone will define the trajectory; and he must be prepared to anticipate something of what the child may encounter farther along the path."

Rationale for Teaching Invention

When my students excitedly noticed that only some numbers could be formed into squares out of the ceramic tiles we were using to explore multiplication and division, and that many of the odd numbers yielded only two different rectangles, they were reaching out to square and prime numbers. They were also reaching out to a kind of mathematical thinking: seeing patterns and conjecturing about their generalizability. Riba suggested that there would be more odd numbers that could be made into squares than even numbers; Betsy countered, pointing out the even-odd pattern in the squares they had found thus far (1, 4, 9, 16, 25, 36, 49, 64).

When Jeannie and Sheena announced that "you can't *prove* that an even number plus an odd number would always be an odd number—because numbers go on forever and so you can't check every one," the class was shocked:

> *Mei*: (Pointing at the "theorems" posted above the chalkboard) Why did you say *those* were true?
> *Sheena*: She just *thought* of it today.
> *Ofala*: I think that an even plus an odd will always equal an odd because I tried . . . (counting in her notebook) . . . 18 of them and they always came out odd.
> *Jeannie*: But how do you know it will *always* be odd? (January 26, 1990)

Third graders tread frequently on "mathematically sacred ground" (Hawkins, 1972). They also tread on mathematically uncharted ground. Surely "respecting children's thinking" in mathematics does not mean ignoring nonstandard insights or unconventional ideas; neither must it mean correcting them. But *hearing* those ideas is challenging. For one thing, teachers are responsible for helping children acquire standard tools and concepts—ideas of mathematical heritage. However, the unusual and novel may consequently be out of earshot. For another, making sense of children's ideas is not so easy. Children use their own words and their own frames of reference in many ways that are not necessarily congruent with the teacher's ways of thinking. Both Dewey (1902) and Hawkins (1972) suggest that a teacher's capacity to hear children is supported by a certain kind of subject-matter knowledge. Hawkins describes it:

> A teacher's grasp of subject matter must extend beyond the conventional image of mathematics. . . . What is at stake is not the . . . end-product that is usually called mathematics, but . . . the whole domain in which mathematical ideas and procedures germinate, sprout, and take root, and in the end produce visible upper branching, leafing, and flowering. (1972, p. 114)

So, even when the teacher *hears* the child, what is she supposed to do? What does it mean to respect children's thinking while working in a specialized domain that has accepted ways of reasoning and working and accepted knowledge (Kitcher, 1984)? Here I explore this problem in the context of one child's unconventional idea, an idea I chose to extend and develop in class.

Appreciating the Mathematics in the Child

We had been working with patterns with odd and even numbers. One day, as we began class, Sean announced that he had been thinking that 6 could be both odd *and* even because it was made of "three twos." Challenged by often-quiet Temba to "prove it to us," Sean drew on the board,

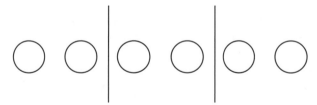

and explained that since three was an odd number, and there were three *groups*, this showed that six could be both even and odd. At this point, the only explicit definition of even numbers that we had developed held that a number was even "if you can split it in half without having to use halves."

Six is even because you can split it in half without having to use halves.

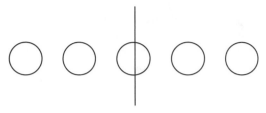

Five is not even because you have to split one in half. Five is odd.

Sean had broken from this convention by dividing six into *groups of two* rather than into *two groups*. Although the other children were dubious, they seemed interested.

> *Mei*: I think I know what he is saying . . . is that it's, see. I think what
> he's saying is that you have three groups of two. And there is an
> odd number so six can be an odd number *and* an even number.
> *T*: Is that what you are saying, Sean?
> *Sean*: Yeah.

Mei said she disagreed. "It's not according to, like . . . can I show it on the board?"

Pausing for a moment to decide what number to use for her argument, she drew 10 circles and divided them into five groups of two:

> *Mei*: Then why don't you call *other* numbers an odd number and an
> even number? What about ten? Why don't you call ten an even
> and an odd number?
> *Sean*: (Paused, studying her drawing calmly and carefully) I didn't
> think of it that way. Thank you for bringing it up, and I agree. I
> say ten *can* be odd or even.
> *Mei*: (with some agitation) What about *other* numbers? Like, if you
> keep on going *on* like that and you say that *other* numbers are odd
> and even, maybe we'll end up with *all* numbers are odd and even!
> Then it won't make sense that all numbers should be odd and

even, because if all numbers were odd and even, we wouldn't be even *having* this discussion!

Ofala, jumping into the fray, was the first to address directly the issue of divisibility by two as including dividing into groups of two. She said she disagreed with Sean because "if you wanted an odd number, usually, like (and she drew some hash marks on the board), . . . even numbers are something like this. Even numbers have two in them (she circled the hash marks in groups of two) and also *odd* numbers have two in them—except they have *one left*":

I called attention to what I referred to as "Ofala's definition for odd numbers," which she restated as "an odd number is something that has one left over." Her formulation was, I realized, in essence, the formal mathematical definition of an odd number: $2k + 1$. The children tried some experiments with it, with numbers that they expected to work because they already knew them to be odd. Temba tried 3, Betsy tried 21, and Cassandra tried 17. Each time, when they represented the numbers with hash marks and circled groups of two, they found that they had one left over.

Later, Riba was still thinking about what Sean had proposed about some numbers being both even and odd. She said that "it doesn't matter how much circles there are—how much times you circle two, it doesn't prove that six is an odd number." Ofala agreed.

But Sean persisted with this idea that some numbers could be both even and odd. On the one hand, Sean was wrong. Even and odd are defined to be nonoverlapping sets—even numbers being multiples of two and odd numbers being multiples of two plus one. He was, as Riba pointed out, paying attention to something that was irrelevant to the conventional definitions for even and odd numbers—that is, how *many* groups of two an even number has. On the other hand, looking at the fact that six has *three* groups of two and ten has *five* groups of two, Sean noticed that some even numbers have an *odd* number of groups of two. Hence, they were, to him, special. I thought about how I could treat this as a mathematical invention—and whether I should. I wrote in my journal:

I'm wondering if I should introduce to the class the idea that Sean has identified (discovered) a new category of numbers—those that have the property he has noted. We could name them after him. Or maybe this is silly—will just confuse them since it's nonstandard knowledge—i.e., not part of the wider mathematical community's shared knowledge. I have to think about this. It has the potential to enhance what kids are thinking about "definition" and its role, nature, and purpose in mathematical activity and discourse, which, after all has been a major point this week. What should a definition do? Why is it needed? (Teaching journal, January 19, 1990, pp. 184–185)

I thought about how I want the children to be learning about how mathematical knowledge evolves. I also want them to have experience with what a mathematical community might do when novel ideas are presented. In the end, I decided not to label his claim wrong and, instead, to legitimize Sean's idea of numbers that can be "both even and odd." I pointed out that Sean had invented another kind of number that we had not known before and suggested that we call them "Sean numbers." He was clearly pleased, the others quite interested. I pressed him for the definition of Sean numbers and we got the following: "Sean numbers have an odd number of groups of two." And, over the course of the next few days, some children explored patterns with Sean numbers, just as others were investigating patterns with even and odd numbers. Sean numbers occur every four numbers—why? If you add two Sean numbers, do you get another Sean number?[3] If a large number ends with a Sean number in the ones place, is the number a Sean number?

Students' Learning

Often I must grapple with whether or not to validate nonstandard ideas. Choosing to legitimize nonstandard *content*—"Sean numbers"—was more difficult than valuing unconventional *methods*. I worried: Would children be confused? Would "Sean numbers" interfere with the required "conventional" understandings of even and odd numbers? Or would the experience of inventing a category of number, a category that overlaps with others, prepare the children for their subsequent encounters with primes, multiples, and squares? How would their ideas about the role of definition be affected? I was quite uncertain about these questions, but it seemed defensible to give the class firsthand experience in seeing themselves capable of plausible mathematical creations.

When I gave a quiz on odd and even numbers, a quiz that entailed some of the kinds of mathematical reasoning we had been using, the results were reassuring. Everyone was able to give a sound definition of odd numbers and to identify and justify even and odd numbers correctly. And, interestingly, in a problem that involved placing some numbers into a string picture (Venn diagram), no one placed 90 (a Sean number) into the intersection between even and odd numbers. If they were confused about these classifications of number, the quizzes did not reveal it.

Dilemmas of Respecting Children as Thinkers

As a mathematics teacher, I am responsible for certain content. My students are supposed to be able to identify even and odd numbers, add and subtract, measure, understand fractions, and much more. Often my problem is to figure out where they are in their thinking and understanding. Then I must help to build bridges between what they already know and what there is to learn. Sometimes my problem is that it is very difficult to figure out what some students know or believe—either because they cannot put into words what they are thinking or because *I* cannot track what they are saying. And sometimes, as in this example, students present ideas that are very different from standard mathematics. The ability to *hear* what children are saying transcends disposition, aural acuity, and knowledge, although it also depends on all of these. And even when you think you have heard, deciding what to do is often a trek over uncharted and uncertain ground. Although Sean was, in a conventional sense, wrong—that is, six is *not* both even and odd—his claim was magnificently at the heart of "doing" mathematics.

DILEMMA NO. 3: CREATING AND USING COMMUNITY

Classrooms as learning communities (Schwab, 1976) are not a new idea. In my teaching, I am trying to model my classroom as a community of mathematical discourse, in which the validity for ideas rests on reason and mathematical argument, rather than on the authority of the teacher or the answer key (cf. Ball, 1988; Lampert, 1986a). In so doing, I aim to develop each individual child's mathematical power *through the use* of the group. I aim to develop the children's appreciation for and engagement with others different from themselves. In Schwab's (1976) terms, we strive to be a learning *community* and also to be *learning* community.

In working our way through alternative ways of approaching and solving problems, we confront issues of shared definition and assumptions, crucial in using mathematics sensibly. I am searching for ways to construct classroom discourse such that the students learn to rely on themselves and on mathematical argument for making mathematical sense. My role in this is tricky: Surely I am the one centrally responsible for their learning the content of the third-grade curriculum. I am also responsible for fostering their capacity and disposition to learn more mathematics and to use it in a variety of life situations. In my work, I often encounter traces of what students learn from their math classes in school and how authority for knowing figures into that learning. For example, one of my students, explaining why she put a little 1 above the tens column when she was adding, said, puzzled, "That's what our teacher in second grade *told* us to do whenever you carry." Never mind that in this case she should have carried a 2 instead of a 1—the underlying principle for the strategy was not the reason, but teacherly authority. Of course, teacherly authority plays a role in my classroom, as it does in any classroom. I aim, however, to use my authority to encourage a set of intellectual and social norms to support a kind of work unusual in students' prior experience in school. Rather than establishing myself as the final arbiter of truth, I strive to develop and distribute in the group a set of shared notions about what makes something true or reasonable. The dilemmas inherent in trying to use the group to advance the individual and vice versa, all while keeping one's pedagogical eye on the mathematical horizon, are not trivial.

In this section, I use a segment from a lesson on integers, on one of the days we were struggling with the building model (introduced previously under dilemma no. 1) and trying to make sense as a community of mathematical thinkers. The vignette spotlights the dilemmas of my role, of authority for knowledge, and of the clarifying-confusing tensions inherent in group discussions—all critical aspects of creating and maintaining a community.

Community Learning

The students were stuck on a problem involving negative numbers. What could it mean to try to do $6 + (-6)$? What could be the answer? All of them were convinced that $-6 + 6 = 0$. This was established by use of Nathan's conjecture (which was actually a theorem, but had not been yet labeled as such): "Any number below zero plus that same number above zero equals zero." It was a little surprising to me that no one put this together with the commutativity of addition to argue that, if $-6 + 6 = 0$, then

6 + (–6) would have to equal zero as well. That not one child made this connection was striking and reminded me of the shifts we assume in conventional mathematics teaching. When children are introduced to rational numbers, for instance, they are simply supposed to carry their notions about operations with them into this new domain.

Perhaps I might have chosen at this point to pose a challenge: "What if someone in the other third-grade class came over and said, 'Nathan's conjecture says that any number below zero, plus that same number above zero equals zero and I think you could turn it around because 3 + 6 is the same as 6 + 3, so you can turn Nathan's conjecture around too, and so I think that the answer to 6 + (–6) is 0?' What would you say?" This is one strategy I use when the group has entrenched itself in an inadequate or incorrect conclusion or assumption. I did not do this in this case, however. It seemed to me that the students were right not to assume that what they knew for positive numbers would automatically hold for negatives. Still, you ask, why not press them a bit? It seemed to me a big step to figure out and reason about the arithmetic of integers, and I wanted to let it simmer for a while. I thought, too, I could construct an alternative representation with which they could figure out what made sense.

Recall the children's struggles over this problem of 6 + (–6). Sean had argued that 6 + (–6) should just be six "because it wouldn't be able to *do* anything. It just stays the same, it stays on the same number. Nothing is happening." And Betsy had, intuitively, put two little paper people on the drawing of the building and moved them toward each other until they met—at zero. In both cases, I remained silent, not presenting the children with questions to challenge their solutions. I might have asked Sean, as Riba did, "It says plus six below zero. You're supposed to do *something*. You can't just leave it alone." Or, I might have pressed Betsy, whose conclusion was right but whose reasoning incomplete, "What would you do if it said 6 + (–2)? Or, "Why don't you put two people on the building and move them toward each other when you add two numbers *above* zero— like 6 + 6?" Instead, however, the other children pressed them:

Betsy: Instead of Sean's, I got zero.
Teacher (T): You'd like to put zero here for 6 + (–6)?
Betsy: Do you want to see how I do it?
T: Okay.
Other students: Yeah!
Betsy: Here. You're here, but you can't go up to twelve, because that's six plus *six*. So, I say it's just the opposite. It's just six minus six.

Sean: But it says plus, not minus!!!

Betsy: But, you're minusing.

Riba: Where'd you get the minus?

Sean: You should just leave it alone. You can't *add* six below zero, so you just leave it. Just say "good-bye" and leave it alone and it is still just six.

Mei: But this six below zero would just disappear into thin air!

Sean: I know. It would just disappear because it wouldn't be able to *do* anything. It just stays the same, it stays on the same number. Nothing is happening.

Betsy: But, Sean, what would you do with this six below zero then?

Sean: You just say "good-bye" and leave it alone.

Riba: You can't *do* that. It's a *number*.

Sean: I know, but it's not going down. It's going up because it says plus.

Mei: I think I disagree with Betsy and Sean because I came up with the answer nine.

T: Okay, why don't you come and show us how you did that. (At this point I did not have a clue what Mei was thinking.)

Mei: (Reaches up and places one of the little paper people on the building) I start here (at 6 above zero) and then I add three to that, because when you go three and three—it's six. Yeah, and then I got nine, so I think the answer is nine.

T: Lucy?

Lucy: Where did the other three go then?

Mei: Well, see 'cause it's three below zero. . . .

Sheena: I know what you're saying.

Mei: So when we put two in each group in order to make one because it's below zero.

(I still had no idea what she was doing, but I assumed that if she explained it further, it would make sense in some way.)

T: I don't understand this part—put two in each group in order to make 1.

Mei: If we take six and add six to it, we get twelve above zero, but it's below zero, so—and three plus three is six, so we add three more to the six above zero.

Riba: Mei, is this what you're saying? Three and three makes six. And then you're saying six below, and since it's *below*, you have to go up to the three?

Mei: I'm making, this is one of the numbers, these are two of the numbers below zero (she made two hash marks to represent two of the numbers), and two of these equals 1 (she wrote 1), and if I have about, like—

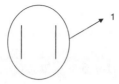

Betsy: What numbers are these? Can you put the numbers in yet?
Mei: (She paused, wrinkling her face and pondering this request, and then drew the following on the board):

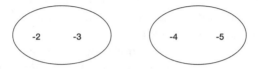

Okay, let's see. Two below zero and three below zero, and this could be four below zero and five below zero, equals 1.

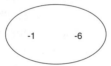

And then I have two already, and that means you will go up to eight. (She moved the paper person from the 6 to the 8 on the building.) And then I make one more. One below zero and six below zero, so there's one more then to go up, and now I end up on nine. (She moved the person one more floor up.)

When she put in numbers at Betsy's request, I realized that Mei had not been thinking of particular numbers. She had meant any two numbers below zero would equal 1 (see the first drawing) and that you could make three pairs of "below zero" numbers because the problem said "–6." I think Mei was working off a memorized "fact" that "a negative plus a negative equals a positive," something she may have been told by some helpful person. So, taking six below zero and pairing the six into three groups of negative numbers (again, look at her drawing with the hash marks), you would get three positive and would add that three to the six above zero—hence, the answer 9.

Sean: I don't understand what you're trying to say. I thought that you were starting from the six, plus six below, not like 1 plus 1 below zero plus six or any other. You're doing all different numbers.

The discussion continued for about 10 more minutes. Ofala said she didn't agree with either Betsy or Mei "because it says plus, and you are supposed to be going *up*." Mei replied that if you go up, you end up on the twelfth floor, and that is the answer for 6 + 6, not 6 + (–6). This made sense to Ofala, who then revised her answer. (We use the term "revise" to denote "changing one's mind," in place of more traditional notions of correcting or fixing or being wrong.) Other children spoke up, either agreeing with one of the presented solutions or questioning one, for example, "If you're going to start with 6, then you have to go up because it's plus?" Sheena objected, "So you're saying that six plus six equals 12 and six plus six below also equals 12? I don't get it."

Jeannie, who had been quiet all this time, raised her hand. "Jeannie?" I asked. "I'm *confused*," she began slowly. "Betsy said that it is zero, and Mei says that it is nine, and Ofala says that it is twelve, and Sean says that it is six, and I don't know who to believe." I asked her what she had thought when she worked on it before we started the discussion. She said she thought it was zero (the correct answer), "but now I'm not sure."

At this, Cassandra raised her hand. She had changed her mind, listening to the discussion. "I get my person and I started at six and I went down six more and I ended up at zero." Although this was the end of class and came on the heels of Jeannie's confusion, I still refrained from sealing the issue with my approval. I asked Cassandra why she thought she should go down. "Because it says below zero." Cassandra was now getting the right answer, but her reason was problematic. For instance, when she tries to subtract a negative number someday, "going down" will be wrong. This is a problem that arises regularly: Children say things that are true in their current frame of reference, in relation to what they currently know, but that will be wrong in other contexts later on. (An example may help here. When a first grader announces that 3 is the next number after 2, he is right—in his domain, which is the counting numbers. But, for a sixth grader considering rational numbers, there *is* no next number after 2, for the rational numbers are "infinitely dense," which means that between any two rational numbers, there is another rational number. Between 2 and 2.1 are 2.01, 2.02, and so on. Between 2 and 2.01 are 2.001, 2.002, and so on. Consequently, there is no "next number" unless you specify a context—e.g., the next hundredth.) I chose *not* to correct Cassandra's statement, believing that my qualification of what she said would just pass the children by anyway. But, as I always do when this happens, when I leave a problematic assertion or answer alone, I felt a sense of unease and dishonesty.

I knew that some others probably felt as confused as Jeannie did at that moment. She seemed matter-of-fact about her confusion, rather than distressed. Still, she was confused. And here we were, at the end of the class period. I glanced at the clock and saw that we had 15 minutes, and I made a decision. Moving up by the board, I announced,

> I want everybody to stop talking for 1 minute now, just think for a minute. I'd like you to find in your notebook where there's an empty space right now. I want you to write down two things. Listen very carefully because you'll have 5 minutes to do this and I want you to do it carefully. The first thing I want you to write down is what the argument was about that we've been having today, what are we trying to figure out? And then I want you to write down who you agree with most, or if you don't agree with anybody who's up on the board right now, write what you think about this argument. You might not be sure, but write down what you think right now as of October 12, on Thursday at 1:50 P.M. The first thing is, what do you think we've been arguing about, and the second thing is, what do you think about the argument? What do you think the answer should be? And why you think that. There's the first question, what have we been arguing about? The second one is, what do you think and why? (October 12, 1989)

The room was silent as the children wrote intently in their notebooks. Ten out of the 17 children who were in class that day agreed with Betsy, who had argued that $6 + (-6) = 0$ (the correct answer). Riba said that "Betsy's ikspachan [explanation]" caused her to change her mind. Two agreed with Sean that the answer should be six. Sheena wrote that she disagreed with Betsy: "betsy is using a minece instead of a plus and its says plus not minece." Three students were not sure. Jeannie said she wasn't "srue hoo to balve [sure whom to believe]," although she soon thereafter became convinced that the answer was zero.

Students' Learning

We continued to struggle for the next few days with making sense of adding and subtracting negative numbers. I tried to think of better representations for exploring this. When we moved on from negative numbers a week or so later almost every student was able to add and subtract integers accurately if the negative number was in the first position, for example, $-5 + 4$, or $-3 - 8$. And many who relied on commutativity or money were able to operate readily with addition and subtraction sentences in any form. This was not a bad achievement.

In addition to learning specifically about operations with integers, what might the students have been learning about community or about the roles of different people—their peers, the teacher, themselves—in their learning? Evidence on this is harder to obtain, but a few snatches from other points, later in the year, help to illuminate some possible learnings. One day, after we had had a particularly long and confusing session on even and odd numbers, I asked the students for comments on the discussion (January 19, 1990). Sheena commented that "it helps" to hear other people's ideas because "it helps you to understand a little bit more." She gave an example: "I didn't think zero was even *or* odd until yesterday and then someone said it could be even because one below zero and one above zero are both odd, and that made sense."

Mei made a comment that was reminiscent of Jeannie's confusion over the $6 + (-6)$ discussion: "I thought zero was an even number, but from the meeting [the discussion] I got sort of mixed up because I heard other ideas I agree with and now I don't know which one I should agree with." Once again, I saw that children were becoming confused *from* the discussions. But then I asked Mei what she was going to do about this. What she said was significant for what it revealed about what she may have been coming to understand about herself and about learning mathematics: "I'm going to listen more to the discussion and find out." Both Sheena and Mei, like many of their peers, seemed by midyear to have the sense that they could figure things out together, in group discussions, as well as alone.

I asked the class how they felt when, during a discussion, they were arguing a position with which many other people disagreed. Jeannie said that it did not bother her: "I don't really care how *many* people think [something]. If they changed my mind—if they convince me, then I would change my mind" (January 19, 1990). I asked how they felt when they took a position that no one else in the class was taking. Sean said he "felt fine" about that and that he, too, changed his mind when he was convinced: "I have just changed my mind about 1—that it *is* an odd number." Some children, however, have complained that some of their classmates argue *too* much and that the discussions go on for a long time and "we never find answers" (January 19, 1990).

In general, though, the students seemed to be developing a sense for what they could learn from one another. Riba commented that discussions are helpful because one person may have a good idea when it is taking a long time to figure it out all by yourself. Mei added that, in discussions, "we get ideas from other people." And Sheena said that "it helps us to learn what other people's thoughts are about math because they might teach something new that you never knew before." Or give us a good example, added Ofala. Even, said Riba, maybe the whole class would agree that something was right and only one person in the class would be able to prove that it was wrong.

Dilemmas of Creating and Using Community

Despite evidence that the third graders learn to learn on their own as well as from one another, there are many days on which I ask myself whether this is time well spent. Take the discussion of 6 + (–6), for example. We spent over half an hour discussing what would be a sensible answer for that one problem. The correct answer was given, but with a problematic explanation. Moreover, two other answers were presented and given equal discussion time. I did not tell or lead the students to conclude that 6 + (–6) equals zero—by pointing them at the commutativity of addition or at the need for the system of operations on integers to be sensibly consistent. At the end of class, only slightly over half the students knew the right answer. And some misconceptions were floating around—that any negative number plus another negative number equals one positive, for example. Still, the very fact that Mei had carried this misconception into class—probably based on something someone had explained to her about subtracting a negative number—is the kind of thing that keeps me thinking that time spent unpacking ideas is time valuably spent. I have too often been confronted with evidence of what students fail to understand and fail to learn from teaching that strives to fill them efficiently with rules and tools. It is not clear to me that *telling* them that 6 + (–6) = 0 will result in more enduring or resilient understanding, or in better outcomes in terms of what the children *believe* they are capable of learning.

Two issues lie at the heart of creating and using community in a third-grade mathematics classroom: one centered on my role and authority for knowing and learning mathematics, and another on balancing confusion and complacency in learning. These two issues are intertwined all of the time: How much should I let the students flounder? Just because it took hundreds of years for mathematicians to accept negative numbers does not necessarily imply that third graders must also struggle endlessly with incorporating them into their mathematical domain. How much "stuckness" is productive to motivate the problems that are being pursued? Deciding when to provide an explanation, when to model, when to ask rather pointed questions that can shape the direction of the discourse—is delicate and uncertain. Certainly mathematical conventions are not matters for discovery or reinvention—for instance, how we record numbers or what a square is. But that 6 + (–6) must equal zero, or that an even number plus an odd number will always be odd, or that the probability of rolling a seven with two standard dice is 6/36 are things that children *can*—through conjecture, exploration, and discussion—create. Children can also create—as Sean did—new mathematics, new beyond its novelty only for third graders. When is this important?

As the teacher, I know more mathematics than my third graders. There is a lot of mathematics for them to learn. If I understand that 6 + (–6) equals zero and can explain it clearly, it may make sense for me to show them how you add a negative number, and get on with more important things. Yet orchestrating a classroom community in which participants work together to make sense, developing strategies and ideas for solving mathematical and real-world problems, implies a set of goals that do not exclude, but are not limited to, the children's developing understandings of operations on integers.

The classroom community is often, as the children themselves note, a source of mathematical insights and knowledge. The students hear one another's ideas and have opportunities to articulate and refine or revise their own. Their confidence in themselves as mathematical knowers is often enhanced through this discourse. Still, as the story about 6 + (–6) shows, the community can also be a stimulus for confusion. Students with right answers become unsettled in listening to the discussion and sometimes end class uncertain and confused. Are their apparently fragile understandings best strengthened by exposing them to alternative arguments? I worry and I wonder about providing more closure: I as often open or conclude class discussions with a summary of what our open problems, conjectures, and puzzlements are as I do with a summary of what we have learned. Are the students learning from this slow progress to tentative conclusions that anything goes, that there are no right answers? Or are they learning, as I would like them to, that understanding and sensible conclusions often do not come without work and some frustration and pain—but that they can do it, and that it can be immensely satisfying?

DILEMMAS OF TRYING TO BE "INTELLECTUALLY HONEST" IN TEACHING MATHEMATICS

In what sense is my practice with third graders "intellectually honest" (Bruner, 1960)? It is honest in its frame—in my concern for students' opportunities to learn about mathematical content, discourse, and community. I try to focus on significant mathematical content and I seek to fashion fruitful representational contexts for students to explore. To do this productively, I must understand the specific mathematical content and its uses, bases, and history, as well as be actively ready to learn more about it through the eyes and experiences of my students. My practice is also honest in its respect for third graders as mathematical thinkers. In order to generate or adapt representations, I must understand a lot about 9-year-olds: What will make sense to them? What will be interesting? How will they take hold of and transform different situations or models? I must consider the mathematics in relation to the children and the children in relation to the mathematics. My ears and eyes must search the world around us, the discipline of mathematics, and the world of the child with both mathematical and child filters. And from all of these aims and principles come the dilemmas that lie at the core of creating a defensible practice: If children believe that zero is not a number, and they are all convinced and agree, what is my role? If all the fraction models I can think of still mislead and distort in some ways, what should I do? When students construct a viable idea that is, from a standard mathematical perspective, reasonable but incorrect, how should I respond?

Dilemmas such as these are not solely the product of the current educational reform rhetoric; many are endemic to teaching (Lampert, 1985). Practice is, after all, inherently uncertain (Jackson, 1986; Lortie, 1975). Still, aiming to create a practice that is, at once, honest to mathematics and honoring of children clearly heightens the uncertainties. The conception of content is more uncertain than a traditional view of mathematics as skills and rules, the view of children as thinkers more unpredictable. Lampert (1985) argues, however, that embracing—rather than trying to resolve—pedagogical dilemmas gives teachers a power to shape the course and outcomes of their work with students. My understandings and assumptions about 9-year-olds equipped me to make decisions about mathematical representation and activity that served their opportunities to learn. Similarly, my notions about mathematics allowed me to hear in the students' ideas the overtures to important understandings and insights.

Because no rules can specify how to manage and balance among competing concerns, teachers must be able to consider multiple perspectives and arguments and to make specific and justifiable decisions about what to do (Lampert, 1986b). Teachers need "the resources to cope with equally weighted alternatives when it is not appropriate to express a preference between them"; they need to be comfortable with "a self that is complicated and sometimes inconsistent" (Lampert, 1985, p. 193). We need to learn more about what are the crucial resources for managing the dilemmas of mathematical pedagogy.

Like many others, I have assumed that teachers who understand subject matter deeply are better equipped to help students learn with understanding a mathematics that has both personal and disciplinary integrity and worth. And, as a teacher educator, I have worried about the problem of helping teachers transcend their own school experiences with mathematics in order to create new practices of mathematical pedagogy. That mathematical knowledge is helpful is obvious; the kind and quality of such knowledge are less clear. The same is true for knowledge about students and about learning. Although learning mathematics has often, at least in the United States, been considered an exclusively psychological matter, other perspectives—linguistic, cultural, sociological, historical—are equally helpful in learning to listen to and interact with children as learners. And I am increasingly aware that there are many resources beyond knowledge that contribute to wise practice: patience, respect, flexibility, humor, imagination, and courage, for instance.

In a society in which mathematical success is valued and valuable, reforms that herald a richer understanding and power for students are attractive. But the pedagogical courses are uncertain and complex. How teachers learn to frame and manage the dilemmas of "intellectually honest" practice in ways that do indeed benefit all students is crucial to the promise of such work. (See, e.g., Lampert, 1992; Lensmire, 1991; Wilson, 1990, all of whom write about the special dilemmas they have found in their efforts to construct alternative pedagogies in mathematics [Lampert], writing [Lensmire], and social studies [Wilson].)

In the face of these kinds of challenges, attention to and debates about what teachers need to know—while important—seem insufficient. Another resource worthy of development is the professional community of teachers and the discourse about practice in which teachers might engage. Typically teachers face the problems and dilemmas of their work alone. Isolated from one another, rarely do they have satisfying or helpful opportunities to talk about practice. To begin with, the structure of teachers' work mitigates against these kinds of opportunities. Furthermore, the incentives for honest and constructive conversation are lacking. On the one hand, acknowledging pedagogical difficulty is too often tantamount to admitting professional incompetence. On the other hand, the tone of some articles and workshops seems to convey that there is "a right way" to motivate children, to teach place value, or to respond to certain kinds of questions from students. Between these two opposing approaches to problems of practice lies little territory for thoughtful teachers to discuss with others the uncertain challenges of their work.

Representing content, respecting students, creating and using community—these are not aims simply resolved. However, that these aims present tough challenges does not mean that all efforts are equal. That all representations have limitations does not mean that any representation is as good as any other. Not every claim to respect students stands up to critical scrutiny. And not all applications of the concept of community are equally defensible. Developing shared standards for evaluating pedagogical interpretations and actions is a necessary step toward restructuring the social and intellectual parameters of teachers' work. Recently I experimented with using videotape from my classroom to engage others in thinking about my dilemma with Sean's numbers. I am still unsure about the choices I made across those few days in my class, and it felt risky to open up my practice to the scrutiny of strangers. I thought people might scoff at my labeling this a dilemma. I thought others might just tell what I should have done— which, while possibly helpful, would underestimate the complexity of my dilemma. The videotape did prove to be a fruitful context for discussion: I watched and listened to alternative interpretations and ideas about that lesson, about what Sean was thinking, about what the other students were doing. My own thinking about how I responded was expanded, as was the thinking of the other participants in the conversations. I saw the promise of a kind of professional discourse that does not expect single answers to complicated problems of practice, but which, instead, proffers tools for interpretation and choice. Such tools, gleaned in forums for professional exchange, could become a important resource for improving teaching and learning in ways that are both responsive to students and responsible to content. Dilemmas endemic to this kind of teaching could be identified and explored. The important terrain between "it's all a matter of individual style," on the one hand, and five-step models of instruction, on the other, could be developed. What makes the building model a useful representation—and for what purposes? What makes it a troubling one? What are the arguments for and against following Sean's assertion that six is both even and odd? This requires developing a kind of principled discussion that has been all too rare in either research or practice.

Although such discussion would require changes in the structure of teachers' work, structural change is not all that is needed. These kinds of exchanges would require substantial revisions in the norms of professional discourse—in what educators (teachers and others) talk with one another about and in what ways. This would require rethinking assumptions about what counts as evidence for believing or doing something in teaching. And such exchanges would require teachers letting one another and others behind the proverbial classroom door, to explore one another's practices, to raise hard questions, and to help one another grow.

NOTES

1. An earlier version of this article was presented at the annual meeting of the American Educational Research Association, Boston, April 1990. This work was supported in part by a grant from the National Science Foundation (grant TPE-8954724). The opinions herein are the author's and do not reflect the position, policy, or endorsement of the foundation. I gratefully acknowledge colleagues Magdalene Lampert, Margret Buchmann, David Cohen, Helen Featherstone, Jessie J. Fry, S. G. Grant, Nancy Jennings, Mary Kennedy, Margery Osborne, James Reineke, Sylvia Rundquist, Deborah Schifter, Kara Suzuka, and Suzanne Wilson for their comments on and contributions to this work.

2. All names used are pseudonyms and are drawn appropriately, to the extent possible, from the individual children's actual linguistic and ethnic backgrounds. They also accurately reflect the students' gender.

3. Because a Sean number has an odd number of groups of two, the sum of two Sean numbers will have an *even* number of groups of two (because odd + odd = even) and so will *never* equal a Sean number.

REFERENCES

Ball, D. L. (1988). *Knowledge and reasoning in mathematical pedagogy: Examining what prospective teachers bring to teacher education.* Unpublished doctoral dissertation, Michigan State University, East Lansing.

Ball, D. L. (in press). Halves, pieces, and twoths: Constructing and using representational contexts in teaching fractions. In T. Carpenter, E. Fennema, & T. Romberg (Eds.), *Rational numbers: An integration of research.* Hillsdale, NJ: Erlbaum.

Boring, E. G. (1929). The psychology of controversy. In R. Watson & D. Campbell (Eds.), *History, psychology, and science* (pp. 67–86). New York: John Wiley & Sons.

Bruner, J. (1960). *The process of education*. Cambridge, MA: Harvard University Press.

California State Department of Education. (1985). *Mathematics framework for California public schools, kindergarten through grade twelve*. Sacramento: Author.

CEMREL. (1979). *Comprehensive school mathematics program*. St. Louis: Author.

Dewey, J. (1902). *The child and the curriculum*. Chicago: University of Chicago Press.

Hawkins, D. (1972). Nature, man, and mathematics. In D. Hawkins (Ed.), *The informed vision* (pp. 109–131). New York: Agathon.

Jackson, P. (1986). *The practice of teaching*. New York: Teachers College Press.

Kitcher, P. (1984). *The nature of mathematical knowledge*. New York: Oxford University Press.

Kline, M. (1970). Logic versus pedagogy. *American Mathematical Monthly*, 77, 264–282.

Lampert, M. (1985). How do teachers manage to teach? Perspectives on problems in practice. *Harvard Educational Review*, 55, 178–194.

Lampert, M. (1986a). Knowing, doing, and teaching multiplication. *Cognition and Instruction*, 3, 305–342.

Lampert, M. (1986b). Teachers' strategies for understanding and managing classroom dilemmas. In M. Ben-Peretz, R. Bromme, & R. Halkes (Eds.), *Advances in research on teacher thinking* (pp. 70–83). Lisse, the Netherlands: Swets & Zeitlinger.

Lampert, M. (1992). The practice and problems of teaching and learning authentic mathematics in school. In F. Oser, A. Dick, & J. Patry (Eds.), *Effective and responsible teaching: The new synthesis*. San Francisco: Jossey-Bass.

Lensmire, T. (1991). *Intention, risk, and writing in a third grade writing workshop*. Unpublished doctoral dissertation, Michigan State University, East Lansing.

Lortie, D. (1975). *Schoolteacher: A sociological study*. Chicago: University of Chicago Press.

National Council of Teachers of Mathematics. (1989). *Curriculum and evaluation standards for school mathematics*. Reston, VA: Author.

National Council of Teachers of Mathematics. (1991). *Professional standards for teaching mathematics*. Reston, VA: Author.

National Research Council. (1989). *Everybody counts: A report to the nation on the future of mathematics education*. Washington, DC: National Academy Press.

National Research Council. (1990). *Reshaping school mathematics: A framework for curriculum*. Washington, DC: National Academy Press.

Palincsar, A. (1989). Less charted waters. *Educational Researcher*, 18(4), 5–7.

Putnam, R., Lampert, M., & Peterson, P. (1990). Alternative perspectives on knowing mathematics in elementary schools. *Review of Research in Education*, 16, 57–150.

Remillard, J. (1990). *Is there an alternative? An analysis of commonly-used and distinctive elementary mathematics curricula* (Elementary Subjects Center

Series No. 31). East Lansing: Michigan State University, Institute for Research on Teaching, Center for the Learning and Teaching of Elementary Subjects.

Schoenfeld, A. (1989, December). *Reflections on doing and teaching mathematics*. Paper presented at a conference, "Mathematical thinking and problem solving," Berkeley, CA.

Schwab, J. J. (1961/1974). Education and the structure of the disciplines. In I. Westbury & N. Wilkof (Eds.), *Science, curriculum, and liberal education* (pp. 229–272). Chicago: University of Chicago Press.

Schwab, J. J. (1976). Education and the state: Learning community. In *Great ideas today* (pp. 234–271). Chicago: Encyclopaedia Britannica.

Shulman, L. S. (1986). Those who understand: Knowledge growth in teaching. *Educational Researcher*, 15(2), 4–14.

Shulman, L. S. (1987). Knowledge and teaching: Foundations of the new reform. *Harvard Educational Review*, 57, 1–22.

Wilson, S. (1990). *Mastodons, Maps, and Michigan: Exploring the uncharted territory of elementary school social studies* (Elementary Subjects Center Series No. 24). Michigan State University, East Lansing, MI: The Center for the Learning and Teaching of Elementary Subjects. ERIC Document No. ED 326470.

Wilson, S., Shulman, L., & Richert, A. (1987). "150 different ways of knowing": Representations of knowledge in teaching. In J. Calderhead (Ed.), *Exploring teachers' thinking* (pp. 104–124). Eastbourne, England: Cassell.

Wineburg, S. (1989). Remembrance of theories past. *Educational Researcher* 18(4), 7–10.

CHAPTER 8

Messy Monk Mathematics: An NCTM-Standards–Inspired Class

Larry Copes

Host teacher is introducing me. Glad they all have name tags. The class looks lethargic. Hope I can wake them up. I'm on. Stand and smile.

I'm really delighted to be here, although you might prefer to be taking an afternoon nap.

Good. Some laughter. Not much, but a little is better than none. Pause. Set the mood. Stare into space. Try to get them wondering what I'm up to.

Once upon a time there was a monk. He lived at the bottom of a not-so-high mountain in . . .

Short pause. Mary is looking a little startled. Bruce appears to be skeptical. Shrug my shoulders.

. . . Tibet? He has this strange habit. So to speak.

Good. Another titter. Who was that? Jane?

Precisely at sunrise on the last day of every month, he leaves his hut at the bottom of the mountain. He walks up a path to the top of the mountain, timing it so that he arrives at the top precisely at sunset. Got that?

A few nods. Bruce is still skeptical. Sara there on the front row is nodding hard. Wonder if she's heard the problem before. Hope not.

I need you to nod or shake your head, if only to stay awake. Got it?

Yeah. Everyone's nodding except Jon.

Jon? Maybe I was looking elsewhere. Are you OK? Good. The monk meditates all night, or whatever monks do. The next morning, the first day of the new month, he leaves the top of the mountain precisely at sunrise. He walks down exactly the same path to the bottom of the mountain, arriving back at his hut precisely at sunset. OK? Nod or shake.

They're all nodding, except Sara. She is sitting back, looking smug. What do I do if she can already solve the problem? Even though she's not nodding, I don't dare ask her if she understands. Pause for the dramatic moment.

The question is, "Is there necessarily a point on the path at which the monk arrives at the same time of day on both days, both on his trip up the last day of one month and on his trip down the first day of the second month?" We'll concentrate only on one round trip, forgetting other months.

Don't know if I should make that last stipulation, but when I don't it leads to all kinds of confusion. Confusion is not necessarily bad, but in this case it seems to distract from the investigation. Considering more than one roundtrip can always be used as an extension. Oh, no! Sara's hand is up. If I call on her and she announces her result now, it could cause real difficulties. When people hear an answer, especially from someone who's probably always correct, they stop thinking about the problem, even if they don't understand the ideas very well. I'll try to ignore her for a minute and get some others involved.

Now, at first, I just want your gut reaction, your intuition. Mary?

Mary: I don't know.

Good. If you knew, I'd be intimidated by your brilliance. At this point I just want intuition. Intuition is important in mathematics, though it has to be checked against logic eventually. What's your intuition?

Mary: No.

Most people who understand the problem would agree. Mary must not be assuming a constant pace. Hope I find someone who does right away, or they'll reconsider their response and that possibility won't be raised. But first, I need to give Mary some reinforcement. And repeat the statement to emphasize the quantifiers.

You're saying that no, there's not a point on the path at which the monk arrives at the same time on each leg of his trip?

Sara's hand is still up. She's pretty eager. I shouldn't really ignore her much longer.

Mary: Yes. I mean, yes, that's what I'm saying.

Thanks, Mary.

Maybe one more before Sara. Jennifer is looking as if she might tune out.

Jennifer, what's your gut feeling? No defense is needed at this point.

Jennifer: No.

Good. Carl is shaking his head. He may bring up the midpoint. But I've got to let Sara go next. Her hand is really waving.

Thank you, Jennifer. Sara?

Sara: Yes, there has to be a point. Imagine two monks, one going up and the other coming down. They have to cross, and it will be at the same place on the path at the same time of day.

Very clearly put. What now? The teacher's eyebrows are raised. Thinks the investigation is over. Maybe it is. But if I just stop when someone says an answer I'm happy with, I'm violating the spirit of inquiry. Let's find out what the others think of her idea.

Who agrees with Sara?

Oh. They're looking puzzled. No hands up. Aha! Filters! Maybe they're filtering out what they're not ready to understand.

Does anyone understand what Sara just said?

Still no hands. A lot of blank looks. Maybe this won't be such a short session after all! But Sara could feel she needs to explain more, and that could stop others' thinking. I don't want her to say more yet, but she needs some encouragement.

Thank you, Sara. Hold that thought. You've probably planted a seed. Carl, what's your intuition?

Carl: The answer is yes. The point will be the midpoint.

I want to get more people involved before we begin justifying. But that seed is planted, too.

Thank you, Carl. Lesley?

Lesley: Oh. I was going to say no, but now I'm not sure.

Is it Carl's magnetic personality or something he said that cast doubt in your mind?

Lesley: I hadn't thought about the midpoint.

But your gut feeling was no?

Lesley: Yes.

Thanks, Lesley. Tom?

Tom: I think the midpoint is the point.

OK. Jon?

Jon: My gut feeling is no.

Good. Cathi?

Cathi: Did you say that the monk walks at a constant pace?

Should I answer that question or repeat the problem? I think I should re-peat it. They need to know it well, especially the quantifiers in the question. And that gives us another chance to focus on just two days.

Did I? Let me repeat what I said. The monk leaves his hut at the bottom of the mountain precisely at sunrise the last day of the month. He walks up the path, timing his journey to arrive at the top precisely at sunset. The next day, he leaves the top precisely at sunrise, and walks down the path, arriving back at the hut precisely at sunset. Is there necessarily a point on the path at which he arrives at the same time of day on each of those two days? What's your intuition now, Cathi?

Cathi: No.

She settles back comfortably. Maybe she has some justification in mind.

OK. Thanks. You back there, the woman with the red T-shirt. Sorry, I can't read your name tag. Sue? Thanks. What's your gut feeling about the monk, Sue?

Sue: I don't like him.

Good. Everyone's laughing. She is funny. Look chagrined.

Thanks for sharing that, Sue. Would you like to talk about it?

They're more relaxed now.

Sue: Not really.

Does she replace thinking with humor? Another chance to restate the problem.

Feel free any time. To rephrase my question, what's your intuition about whether or not there's a point on the path at which the monk arrives at the same time of day on each of the two days?

Sue: There's no such point. Sunrise and sunset change.

Aha! She thinks! Cathi's nodding vigorously. I'd better acknowledge that she had the same idea.

Thanks, Sue. Was that your idea too, Cathi?

Cathi: Yeah. The days aren't the same length.

José: And . . .

That was José. Good. Wish he hadn't stopped to wait for my permission, but I can't expect otherwise this early in our first session together.

José?

Maybe if I sit on the edge of the table they'll feel that they should converse with each other.

José: Also, the times of sunrise and sunset are different at the top of the mountain and at the bottom.

Good thinking. That point doesn't always come up. On the other hand, everyone seems stunned. Oh, there goes Sara's hand again. They're probably mostly convinced that there's no point, so it wouldn't hurt to have her come in again. We're moving into justification, even though not everyone has expressed a gut feeling. Jon's hand is up, too, but I want to get to everyone before too much repetition. Otherwise a small bunch will take over.

Ooh! Good thinking, José. Despite the fact that I was looking for gut feelings, several people have given some justification for their intuition, looking for a proof.

There. I slid in the idea that proof is justification. Now maybe I can use the word "argument" synonymously. Some folks think of argument as conflict, to be avoided. Sara's hand is down.

One argument that there is a point is that it's the midpoint. Who agrees?

Few hands. Time for quantifiers. Who hasn't said much?

Do you disagree, uh, Bruce? Why?

Bruce: I don't know.

Jane?

Jane:. I'm not sure, but the question was, "Is there *necessarily* a point?" *If* he walks at a constant pace, there *might* be a point—the midpoint. But if he doesn't, I don't think there's *necessarily* a point.

Was that clear? Some nodding. Sara's hand is back up. Maybe I should rephrase it, but I don't want it to sound like a pronouncement from me, which could indicate that we're finished.

Are you saying that to prove there's necessarily a point, we have to consider all cases?

Jane: Well, yeah.

So that would make the constant-pace situation a special case?

Jane: Yeah.

Lots of nods. Sara's hand is down.

Often in working on a problem it helps to consider special cases. So what about this special case in which the monk's pace is constant? Do we have a solution then? What do you think, Amin?

Amin: Sure.

Do you agree, Tina?

Tina: Uh-huh.

Not sure either is really thinking. She at least is probably taking the easy way out. Who was it who first raised the sunrise and sunset times?

Sue?

Sue: Yes.

She's supposed to object!

Yes what?

Sue: Yes, if the monk's pace is constant then the midpoint is the point.

Who else?

José?

José: I don't think so. Sunrise and sunset will still make a difference, even if the pace is constant.

Thank you, José.

Sue: But don't sunrise and sunset change symmetrically?

That was Sue. That's why she agreed with the claim about the special case. I'm glad they're not relying on me as a mediator. But I wonder if I can push her to show us a graph or something.

What do you mean, Sue?

Yes. She looks as if she wants to draw something. I bet she's enough of a ham not to resist leading the way.

If you'd like to use the board, feel free.

Of course she's hesitating. Get a marker and hand it to her.

The board is our collective scratch paper.

Yes, she's eager. Oh, she's going to write some formulas.

Sue: Distance is rate times time, right? So the first day let's say you go a distance of 6 miles. And you take 12 hours. So your speed is 1/2 miles per hour.

Tina: That's average speed.

Thank you, Tina, for waking up.

Sue: Oh, yeah. But speed is constant in the special case. So at the midpoint you've gone 3 miles in 6 hours. And the second day you go faster, right, because you're going downhill. Like, 6 miles in 10 hours, or 6/10 miles per hour. And you're halfway down, 3 miles, in 5 hours. Like, at the midpoint.

Terry: But that assumes you're going at a constant speed.

Well, yeah, Terry. But it also misses another point. . . .

Troy: You can't take less time the second day. You still have to travel from sunrise to sunset.

Thanks, Troy. They seem to be conversing well without me. I'll just sit back on the edge of the desk.

Melissa: I don't think sunrise and sunset are symmetric. I heard that sometimes sunset comes earlier even though the days are getting longer, so sunrise is much earlier.

I've heard that too, Melissa. Wonder if anyone will agree.

Sara: It doesn't matter. Look, if you have two monks, then they'll meet no matter when they leave the ends of the path.

Yeah, Sara now feels free to participate without being called on. Time for a little more control. Stand up. I'm glad she's on the front row so I can reinforce her without others' noticing so much. They're beginning to talk among themselves anyway.

Thanks, Sara. I like your thinking.

Someone: There's definitely not a point.

Keep talking to Sara.

But apparently you haven't convinced everyone yet. Keep trying, and listen to see if someone else has a better idea.

Now to take advantage of that "definitely not" that came out of the class somewhere. Need to get to the objective of the exercise, concerning proofs and justification.

There's definitely not a point? That's pretty strong. I asked if there was necessarily a point. I have heard arguments that there is *necessarily* a point if the monk's pace is constant; in fact, that point is the midpoint. I've heard the claim that he can walk at a varying pace and avoid having such a point. I haven't heard an example of such a walk yet. And now I heard someone claim that there was definitely no point. To support that argument you'd have to show what was wrong with the case of the constant pace and midpoint.

Jane: I meant that there wasn't *necessarily* a point.

Thanks, Jane. Does anyone believe that there is definitely no point at which the monk arrives at the same time of day on each of the two days?

Silence. I think they'd all feel comfortable saying so if they believed it, but perhaps I'm wrong.

Well, let's take a vote between definitely yes and not necessarily. All who think there's definitely such a special point, raise your hands.

Sara now has company in Maurice. Wonder what his idea is. He looked pretty eager in voting; I imagine he isn't assuming the constant pace.

All who think there's not necessarily a point?

Not everyone else. Guess we need a third option after all.

All who don't think?

Again some laughter. Controversy engages them. But need to get them more open to Sara's opinion.

Great! I love controversy! But since so many of you agree, you must be right. Right? OK. If it's so obvious, maybe you can prove it. What's involved in a proof that there's not necessarily a point? Terry?

Terry: I have no idea.

OK. Chris?

Chris: Just show how to walk up and down the mountain.

How could you show it?

Chris: Maybe make a chart. Or draw a picture.

A picture? How? Would you come up and draw one?

Good. No hesitation. Chris draws the diagram shown in Figure 8.1.

Maybe you can label under the line the times for the monk going up, and above the line the times for the monk going down.

Chris draws, hesitatingly, the diagram shown in Figure 8.2.

Great idea, Chris. I want everyone who thinks there's not necessarily a special point to draw such a picture. Please get together with your neighbor and come up with a picture that supports your claim. Sara and Maurice, can you conspire to produce an argument that will support your position? Lori, why don't you join Troy and Amin, since we have an odd number?

Lots of noise. Good. Wander around. Everyone's involved. Some groups challenging their own pictures. Josh and Derek arguing. Troy and Amin seem to be ignoring Lori. Terry and Chris look very puzzled. Andi and

---

Figure 8.1. Chris's first diagram

Figure 8.2. Chris's second diagram

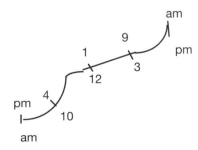

Mary are working individually. Hope they get around to looking at each other's pictures. Kerry and Toni look satisfied. Have them put their work on board. Others will challenge it. Sara and Maurice are discussing a graph as well as two-monk model. The teacher is missing some interesting ideas by remaining seated. We have only 20 minutes left. Difficulty in getting them back together means they're involved.

We have a picture on the board. Is everyone happy with it?

Good silence. Nobody's taking a nap. Feel the wheels turning. Lots of hands. They're not speaking out spontaneously any more. Amin hasn't said much, but Lori needs some attention.

Lori?

Lori: What about between 12 and 1? I think if you break that down, you'll find a point where he passes at the same time of day each day.

Good. Using the same phrase. Say so.

I'm flattered that you used my words. Thank you, Lori. Amin?

Amin: I agree.

Thanks, Amin. Kerry and Toni, can you help Lori see why there's no point?

Good that they both are walking up to the board. But they don't understand.

Kerry and Toni: What?

Can you give details about what happens between 12 and 1, so others will be convinced by your picture?

They could draw enlarged picture, but they're trying to squeeze in the numbers on the original picture. Oops, they switched the order. Time is going backward on the top. Should I correct? It's better if one of the students catches it.

Toni: Oops, we switched the numbers.

Thank you, Toni. Saved being corrected by someone else. Can they see it now? Apparently. They're looking puzzled, especially Kerry.

Did anyone else get a picture you're happy with?

No hands. Now Maurice is tentatively raising his. Should he and Sara go? Maybe with the graph.

You folks had a graph, didn't you Maurice? Would you please draw it for us?

Maurice: OK.

He's shy, but he's doing it. Sara doesn't look offended. Maybe she's sure she'll get her chance. Maurice draws the graph shown in Figure 8.3.

Maurice: You can't get from here to there without crossing the other line.

Silence. Let it sit for a minute.

Carl: No. That's the same point on the path, but it's not the same time.

Thanks, Carl. If nobody had said that, I'd have to play devil's advocate, since I'm sure some people are wondering.

Lesley: And the mountain just goes one way.

Oh, yeah. Lesley. Also confused about the axes. It's tricky. Can Maurice explain? He's taking his time to consider.

Maurice: You have to think of what's on each axis. The *x*-axis represents time of day, not just time. And the *y*-axis represent height on the mountain. Neither graph is a picture of the path. They're graphs of height compared with time of day.

Good explanation, though there's no x or y in the picture. Who gets it? Carl is nodding. Derek looks very confused. Can't tell about Lesley.

Derek?

Derek: I don't get it. What do you mean by height on the mountain?

It flowed right out. Not wondering why I asked. We're communicating. Should I explain? Or suggest to Maurice. . . .

Maurice, do you mean that the vertical axis represents distance along path from the bottom?

Figure 8.3. Maurice's graph

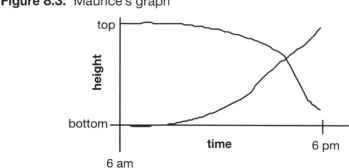

Maurice: Sure.

Should I have said that? Is it too leading? Telling is rarely teaching. It doesn't do much good to answer questions that the students haven't asked. On the other hand, filters will probably work. Oh, there's Josh. He was pretty adamant before that there was no point.

Josh: I don't know how to draw a picture, but I like Sara's idea about two monks.

Really? He understood it? Is the pendulum swinging toward thinking there's a special point?

Josh: Can I do a demonstration?

Sure.

Sara doesn't look offended. It was kind of Josh to give her credit.

Josh: Bruce, can you get at that end of the room, and Mary, at this end? Now, Bruce is the monk going up the mountain, and Mary is the monk going down the mountain the next day. So start walking toward each other. See? When they meet, it's not the same time, because they're on two different days.

Oh. He's pretty confused. But what a wonderful intermediate step! Will there be controversy? Andi's eager.

Andi: Of course they meet at the same time. When else would they meet?

Kind of chaos now. Jane, Lesley, and José seem most eager to point out Josh's error. Wonder if they realize that they're convincing themselves of the weakness of their earlier position. Don't want Josh to be turned off. He's looking a little dazed. Not much time left, though. Perhaps they're ready to hear Sara.

Thank you, Josh. Maybe Sara can answer the challenges. Sara?

She looks confused. Of course, she's agreeing with the challenges. Keep her thinking, though. I suspect she can handle the confusion.

Sara: As Josh said, imagine that you have two monks, one at the top and one at the bottom. Like Bruce and Mary. Bruce follows the original monk's every movement on the first day, going up the mountain. Mary follows the original monk's movement on the second day, coming down the same path. Even with changes in sunrise and sunset, or even stopping for lunch, the two monks have to meet. They'll meet at a point where the original monk arrived at the same time of day on both days.

Lots of nods this time. But it's not unanimous. Heather still isn't convinced. Filters haven't stopped working. Given time, I'd survey individuals to see what they think. and question Heather more. But I'll have to skip a step, because it's not my own class.

Nice, Sara. Who thinks Sara's two-monk model is equivalent to the original problem? Melissa?

Melissa: No.

How many think that one monk on two days is equivalent to two monks on one day?

We're having to go too fast. Only about half. Sara is looking astounded. Perhaps she's thinking that her peers are pretty dumb. But they're thinking well; they just aren't ready to see her approach. Anyway, some of those who don't believe the two-monk model may have been convinced by the graph.

Either because of the two-monk model or the graph, who now thinks that there's necessarily a point on the path at which the monk arrives at the same time of day each of the two days?

Aha! Almost unanimous. Who doesn't agree? It doesn't matter now. I have to stop. Only about a minute left.

Great. Still some disagreement. Keep messing with it. I'll mention briefly that you may want to relate this to a theorem called the intermediate value theorem.

Glad I took a few seconds to write that on the board. Some people actually are copying it down.

But there's one more step. We've been deepening understanding on the forefront of our own mathematical knowledge. It's been pretty messy as our intuition has clashed with our logic. The same kind of mess happens when mathematicians do research, building understanding on the frontiers of knowledge of the mathematical community. So you have experienced some of the frustration and exhilaration and perhaps even beauty of doing mathematical research.

When doing research, unlike when studying mathematics traditionally, we don't stop when we solve a problem. Every solution leads to more questions, making more research in the future. What questions can we ask about the monk problem? One question might be, "How do we prove that those two lines in the graph have to cross?"

Will they come up with questions? It's difficult to ask open-ended questions you can't answer. Wish we had more time to do it. Maybe just one tool . . . What can they do if I take an extra minute or two? At least nobody seems eager to leave.

Often good research questions begin with "What if . . . ?" Asking *what if* can impress the heck out of all your teachers.

Good. More laughter. But will they have any ideas?

Sue: What if the monk walked backward?

The clown with a brain can still make people laugh.

Good. Not exactly a *deep* question . . .

Be sure to grin broadly. Lots of laughter now.

. . . but a researcher might ask lots of questions before getting one that leads somewhere. Troy?

Troy: How do sunrise and sunset really differ?

Pretty. Kerry?

Kerry: Are the endpoints actually points on the path? If not, then do the monks really need to meet on the path?

Oooh. Nice question. Tom?

Tom: What if we consider more than one month, more than two days?

Lots of heads shaking. They're still engaged. Should I wrap it up? Nah. Someone once said that closure marks the end of thinking. If you feel you have to summarize, do it the next day.

Excellent. Now you have lots to think about for a while. Let me know what your thoughts are.

My students never applaud like this at the end of a class session! But the clapping is somewhat distracted; some of the students are still more interested in the problem than in me. Guess they woke up.

NOTE

This piece is dedicated to Stephen I. Brown, an inspiration for inquiry-based teaching and learning, on the occasion of his retirement.

CHAPTER 9

Learning From Laramie: Urban High School Students Read, Research, and Reenact *The Laramie Project*

Marsha R. Pincus

How Pa. heartland went for gay rights.
The hate-crimes law extends even to the transgendered.
Observers are stunned.

A remarkable thing has happened in Pennsylvania. The state legislature passed an amendment to the hate-crimes law that made Pennsylvania only the fifth state in the union to protect not only gays, lesbians, and bisexuals, but also those who are transgendered. (Harris & Worden, 2002)

This story appeared on the front page of *The Philadelphia Inquirer* on Sunday December 15, 2002. The article chronicled the road to the passage of this legislation in a state that is commonly thought to be very conservative, not particularly sympathetic to gay issues, and maybe even a little hostile. It included stories of gay activists and parents of gay children working tirelessly to convince legislators of the need for this bill. In the article the writers cited the beating death of Matthew Shepard in 1998 as an important milestone in awakening people's concern for gay rights. As I reprinted the article for my senior drama students at Masterman High School, I thought that the journey taken by the activists and legislators toward passage of the bill was similar to the one I had hoped my 43 senior drama students would take after reading, researching, and reenacting Moises Kaufman's play about the Matthew Shepard murder, *The Laramie Project*.

BACKGROUND AND CONTEXT

I have been teaching English at Masterman High School since 1998. Masterman is a small, highly selective magnet school located on the fringes of Center City that draws academically talented students from all neighborhoods of the city. Prior to teaching at Masterman, I taught at Simon Gratz High School, a comprehensive neighborhood high school located in North Philadelphia, in the heart of the African American community. During my 20 years at Gratz, I was involved with Philadelphia Young Playwrights, an arts-in-education organization that pairs classroom teachers with professional playwrights for the purpose of teaching students to write and produce original plays. I was able to integrate this program into my English program at Gratz, and my students there were extremely successful. (Every year at least one of my students won the local playwriting competition and three of my students won the national competition and had their plays produced off-Broadway.)

I spent nearly 10 years as a teacher-researcher studying the meaning and significance of what I learned from my students at Gratz. One of the most important lessons I learned came from the insights of my student Terrance Jenkins about authorial intent. The author of the award-winning play *Taking Control*, Terrance said of his work, "I had a message I wanted to get across. I had a story to tell. I wanted people to see these things and I wanted then to begin to make a change" (Patterson & Strosser, 1993).

Terrance's words reminded me of Iser's (1978) ideas about the pragmatic nature of literature as expressed in *The Act of Reading*. "What is important to readers, critics, and authors alike is what literature *does*, not what it *means*," (p. 53) Iser writes. Literature has a pragmatic meaning and an intersubjective goal: "the imaginary correction of deficient realities" (p. 85). To imagine is to take the first step toward taking action in the world. The process of writing original plays involved a kind of reflective thinking about the world, and it offered the student playwrights the opportunity to (in Terrance's words) "take control" of the trajectory of their lives. I saw my students' outlooks on life and education change as their reading and writing powers developed. I also saw many of them go on to college. It is still my greatest source of pride that so many of my former Gratz High School students became social workers and educators.

When I arrived at Masterman, I initially tried to include the playwriting program in my English classes. I soon discovered that it was not a good fit;

the academic requirements and the pressure for students to perform well on standardized tests did not allow for this kind of curricular "deviation." I became dismayed by the implications of this kind of teaching and I began to feel used and exploited by the system. What I was being asked to do was not consistent with my own sense of mission and purpose. Simply stated, I teach to "tikkun olam," or heal the world. I do not teach to earn a profit for some nameless investors (despite the incursion of for-profit companies into the public school arena); I do not teach to get the most privileged kids into the best schools (despite the assumptions and demands made by some of the parents); I do not teach to pass on unexamined traditions of literature or history; I do not teach to perpetuate racism, sexism, classism, ethnocentricism, heterosexism, or any of the other damaging *isms* that threaten to diminish the lives of some and aggrandize the lives of others. I do not teach to maintain the status quo.

For me teaching is a hopeful act, one of possibility and transformation. And it has been a struggle. The struggle became more difficult for me in a school of relative privilege. It wasn't just that the playwriting program didn't fit; my own philosophies and values appeared to be in conflict with the dominant values of the school at large.

With the support of the Carnegie Academy for the Scholarship of Teaching and Learning (CASTL), I began to explore alternative approaches to what I was doing in my English classes at Masterman. With the assistance of CASTL, I was able to develop an interactive website titled *Playing with the Possible: Teaching, Learning, and Drama on the Second Stage*. On this website, and for my Carnegie project, I was able to (a) outline my process and history as a teacher researcher, (b) present my thinking behind the development of a new elective class called Drama and Inquiry, and (c) explain my burgeoning theory of "second stage" school reform, which I thought might be possible at a school like Masterman.

Many theaters have two performance areas: a main stage upon which works are performed with a wide audience appeal and a second stage (sometimes called a black box) where new plays and experimental works can be developed. The second stage often serves as an incubator for main-stage productions. In rethinking my approach to teaching at Masterman, I developed an elective class called Drama and Inquiry that grew out of my decade-long association with Philadelphia Young Playwrights and was consistent with my critical pedagogy approach to teaching and learning. While my English classes remained "main stage" productions, my elective became the alternative, experimental space—my second stage on which I could enact a different kind of pedagogy, which might eventually have an impact on the pedagogy of the main stage. In Figure 9.1, I have identified some of the characteristics of teaching and learning on these different stages.

For 3 years of their high school experience, Masterman students have little choice in their course selection. In their senior year, they are able to select from among a small number of electives that take the place of some of the more selective AP (advanced placement) courses. The purpose of the Drama and Inquiry course, as I stated to the students in the syllabus, was to "explore questions about multiple perspectives, shifting identities, and our coexistence in a diverse, complex, and ever-changing world." It was my hope that we could "become a true intellectual community filled with members who raise heartfelt and complex questions and explore answers together in an engaged ethical dialogue." In this course, we read plays by contemporary American playwrights that dealt with issues of race, class, gender, ethnicity, and identity. Students wrote their own monologues and dialogues and eventually wrote and acted in their own one-act plays. They participated in alternative types of classroom discourse, including Socratic seminars, collaborative inquiry, reflective conversations, and journal groups. At the end of the year, the students of this class produced a theater performance titled *Split Open. Split Open* contained original scenes and was written, acted, and directed by the students and performed for a small audience in an intimate space we created on the stage of the auditorium.

The study I conducted of *The Laramie Project* occurred in the 3rd year of this class. Over the years, the course has continued to create a second-stage space. In this space, alternative discourses and values have been developing in relation to the discourses and values of the main stage that are

Figure 9.1. Characteristics of the main-stage and second-stage teaching and learning

Main Stage	Second Stage
Emphasis on answers	Emphasis on questions
Lecture and debate	Dialogue
Competitive	Collaborative
Knowledge transmission	Knowledge construction
Canonical texts	Non-canonical texts
Individual rewards	Group accomplishments
Individual acheivement	Social justice

embodied in the courses, assessments, structures, and rituals of the school. It is helpful for me to think about the ways in which what happens in this class can affect what is happening in classes on the main stage. The course has grown in popularity among the students. The first year it was taught, 16 students were enrolled; the second year found 28 students in the class. This year, I am teaching two sections of the class with a total of 43 students.

THE LARAMIE PROJECT

While I had previously studied the impact that writing original plays had on my high school students, I had not looked closely at the impact that reading and performing the plays of others could have on them. I had been planning to teach *The Laramie Project* to my drama classes. I was familiar with reader-response theory, particularly Rosenblatt's (1995) ideas about the relationship between efferent and aesthetic responses to literature. These ideas intrigued me and raised questions about the ways in which my students would respond to this play. Because the play was about homosexuality, homophobia, murder, and religion, I knew that they would have deep emotional responses to the text. I was less certain how they would relate to the text intellectually and what my role as the teacher in this process should be. In addition, I had planned to have my students perform parts of this play for an audience. I was not certain how that process would affect their responses to the text.

I devised a study in which I asked the students to write a two- to three-page written response to *The Laramie Project* at three junctures in the process:

1. After reading the play independently with very little background explanation.
2. After reading about Moises Kaufman and the Tectonic Theater Group, about their philosophy and process, researching accounts of the actual events that happened in Laramie and surrounding stories, events, websites, and so on.
3. After performing key moments from the play that groups of students blocked, staged, and directed themselves.

I was particularly interested in the level of engagement students experienced at each of these points in the process. I hypothesized that they would become increasingly more engaged as the project intensified. For this study, I collected 129 responses from all 43 students at the three different moments. An additional piece of the study that I did not systematically record and transcribe is the discussions that took place in class in response to the play and the journals. In addition, there were several group e-mails that I sent to the class Listserv and student responses that make up the data for this study.

MY INTELLECTUAL JOURNEY
AS TEACHER-RESEARCHER ON THIS PROJECT

As a teacher-researcher, I am constantly engaged in what Lytle and Cochran-Smith (1993) have called "systematic and intentional" inquiry into my classroom practice. This process of inquiry allows me to raise questions; search for answers both inside and outside of my classroom; make sense of what is happening there; and develop new ideas, strategies, and curricula. In short, I can have an active intellectual life that is linked to my teaching, each feeding the other. Teacher-researchers, unlike outside educational researchers, have a unique responsibility to the students they are teaching *while* conducting their research. Their theory and practice are inextricably linked as they must simultaneously question, observe, read, analyze, make sense, and teach. Thus these teachers' intellectual journeys are as much a part of the story as are their students.

My original goal in selecting *The Laramie Project* was to teach a play that would challenge my students to think differently about the world and show them the transformative power of drama. Before teaching *The Laramie Project,* I researched the actual events upon which the play was based, the process used by the Tectonic Theater Project in creating the play, and the underlying ideas about theater held by the director of the group, Moises Kauffman. Shortly after the murder of Matthew Shepard, a gay University of Wyoming student, Kauffman (2000a) posed these questions to the members of his theater company: "What can we as theater artists do as a response to this incident? And more concretely: Is theater a medium that can contribute to the national dialogue on current events?" In response to his own questions, Kaufman and his theater company traveled to Laramie, Wyoming, and over the course of 15 months conducted more than 200 interviews with more than 50 people. From the transcripts of those interviews and other public documents relating to the murder and subsequent trials, Kaufman and his company created a play in which the actors played themselves and the dozens of characters they had interviewed. The play was constructed as juxtaposed and related moments and performed with minimal scenery, props, and costume changes. By presenting these multiple perspectives and contrasting moments, Kaufman was inviting the audience to synthesize the material for themselves, an approach that was pioneered by Bertolt Brecht in his Epic Theatre.

My desire to understand more about Kauffman's theories about theater lead me to the work of Augusto Boal (1985), who in his seminal work, *Theater of the Oppressed,* contrasts Classical Aristotelian Theatre and Epic Theatre. He explains that Aristotelian drama appeals to the spectator's emotion, while epic drama appeals to the spectator's thought. Aristotelian drama creates empathy and provides an emotional catharsis that cleanses the spectator, while epic drama appeals to the spectator's reason and, through knowledge, arouses his or her capacity for action. Boal says that for Brecht, a play is meant to provoke the audience into reforming society not only by thinking about the play, but also by challenging common ideologies. Because there is no denouement or resolution to the conflicts enacted in the play, the spectator can see the fundamental contradictions in society and be moved to make decisions for action.

I found this distinction between feeling and thought as described in these two types of theater very provocative in thinking about students' efferent and aesthetic responses to *The Laramie Project.* I felt assured that given Kaufman's stated objectives in creating this play, it would be appropriate for my students to enter into a complex dialogue about the issues and events the play evoked.

I also read the work of Brian Edmiston (2000), one of the leading researchers in drama education. I was intrigued by his ideas about drama as a form of ethical education that could provide students with multiple and sometimes conflicting views of events. He writes, "To judge myself ethically, I must be answerable to others' evaluations of my actions at the same time I expect them to be answerable to me and to others" (p. 66). Reflection on action is essential to acting ethically and one must get outside of one's own intentions to view one's actions from the perspective of those affected. He goes on to argue that drama enables young people to imagine life from other people's positions. Such positioning offers them the opportunity to imagine "how the world could be different and what our lives could be like if we acted in different ways" (p. 67).

Thus, I concluded, reading a play such as *The Laramie Project* and providing students with the opportunity to reflect upon and engage in real dialogue about the issues and events it presents can translate into action. This is of no little consequence. Our students are future participants in our democracy and will one day be called upon to make decisions relating to gay rights and hate crime legislation. There are real-life consequences for real people of Bill Clinton's "don't ask, don't tell" policy or George Bush's failure to include gay people in Texas's hate crime legislation.

My students' responses to this play and the way that I shape their classroom experiences are also of grave consequence. This is a frightening and daunting realization for any teacher to have. However I was encouraged and reassured by these words of John Dewey (as quoted in Rosenblatt, 1995):

> More "passions" not fewer is the answer. To check the influence of hate, there must be sympathy, while to rationalize sympathy there are needed emotions of curiosity, caution, respect for the freedom of others—dispositions which evoke objects which balance those called up by sympathy and prevent the degeneration into maudlin sentiment and meddling interference. Rationality once more is not a force to invoke against impulse and habit. It is the attainment of a working harmony among diverse desires. (p. 217)

Literature, Rosenblatt contends, can foster that kind of rationality. "The literary experience may provide emotional tension and conflicting attitudes out of which spring the kind of thinking that can later be assimilated into actual behavior" (p. 217). This process of reflection can lead the student to seek additional information concerning the work, the author, and their social setting as a basis for understanding him- or herself and the literature. "Through the process of self scrutiny, he [the student] may come to understand himself as well as the outside world better. A certain inner readjustment may have started that will modify his response to the next person or next situation encountered" (p. 214).

Throughout all my preliminary research, I couldn't help but think about Aaron McKinney and Russell Henderson, the two young men who beat and killed Matthew Shepard. If only they had been educated to think rationally about their emotional responses. If only they had been engaged in an empathetic and ethical dialogue about difference. If only they had learned to make a habit of reflection and self-scrutiny. They were not that long ago students in a Laramie High School English classroom. What were they then thinking about their lives and their futures? What might their teachers have done to interrupt the flawed and circular logic that enabled them to justify their brutal beating of a young man because they said he had made a pass at them?

PRELIMINARY FINDINGS

This question leads me back into my own classroom and the 129 journal responses I collected from my students during this project. I have read and reread these journals many times, marking them and trying to begin an analysis. For this chapter, I will share some of my initial impressions and make some preliminary connections to theory.

One of my expectations in designing this project was that students' level of engagement would increase and deepen as they moved through the different processes. I thought that their stepping back from the work itself and researching the event as well as Moises Kaufman's theories of theater would offer a kind of efferent detachment and intellectual inquiry. I had also hypothesized that they would return to a more aesthetic or emotional stance when they performed the play, thereby creating an even more intensive "lived through" experience than the one they had had when they initially read the text alone. While this was true for many of the students, it was not universally the case.

Some students had their most intense responses to their initial reading. I was surprised by the number of students who wrote in their first journals about how this play made them feel. Several students used the term "emotional roller coaster" to describe their experience reading the book. Many wrote about having a physical reaction to the text. Some had to stop reading and take a break from the intensity. Here is a sampling of some of their responses:

- "Halfway through act II, I actually started to cry."
- "The content was not easy to swallow. At one point, I put the book down and just took a breath because the book really affected me."
- "*The Laramie Project* is one of the few books I actually had to take a break from not because I was bored but because I was deeply moved by Matthew Shepard's story."
- "I actually found myself becoming physically upset as I read some of the moments."

Some were able to pinpoint the exact moment and where they had their most intense aesthetic response. Steve explains his in this excerpt from his first journal:

At the end, Dennis Shepard's statement may have single-handedly made me like this play. It was so heartfelt and sincere and as he was

talking, I could picture all the things he was talking about like the way
he used to watch the stars with his son. . . . When he said not only
his son but his hero he lost on that dreadful day, I felt so bad for him.
It was just an amazing speech that was so powerful and so heartfelt
that I had to stop and just read it again. I don't like a large majority
of the books I have read in my years at this school and I don't think
anything I have read had made me feel as bad as this speech but it is
probably the only thing I ever stopped to read over and over again. A
book has never really touched me as much as this one. (Journal 1)

One of the areas of response that has intrigued me is how the work we
did after reading the play aroused students' thinking about social action.
Adam addresses this question in this excerpt from his final journal:

I have been inclined to believe that little good has come from
Matthew's death, but another thought has come to mind. While
sudden newsworthy stories of any cause may dominate our thoughts
as a public in an ever changing barrage of new victims and new
villains, it is the slow progress fueled by activists and regular people
that produces change. A story and the martyrs and heroes it produces
serve as a symbol for the fight. However, the fight is not won by the
symbols, but by the fighters. Civil Rights for minorities were not won
by the deaths of Martin Luther King and Malcolm X but by the years
of steady and unspectacular pushing for equality in policy and public
opinion. (Journal 3)

He goes on to say that that the play keeps us "at a safe distance, where
our intellects are at work as much as our emotions." This echoes Rosenblatt's and Dewey's ideas about the relationship of rational reflection upon
emotion and the kind of ethical action it can engender.

This change is evident in what Derek writes in his final journal:

I know it made me more conscious of what of what I say and do.
I have to admit that I have called things "gay" before. It was not
meant to belittle gay people. It just seemed like a word to describe
something you didn't like. When we started talking about *The
Laramie Project* and gay people, I realized how wrong I was to say
these things. I have never felt any form of hate towards gay people
but I can see how I was using a form of discrimination and I felt bad
about it. Whenever I hear someone say, "that's gay" or something like

that I think about what we learned in class and most of the time I'll say something to that person. (Journal 3)

Derek is able to step outside his own benign intentions and see the ways in which his act could be hurtful to others. This is what Edmiston means when he discusses drama as ethical education. Bakhtinian answerability is at work in Derek's reassessment of his past behavior. His decision to "say something to that person" is a difficult one for many high school students.

One of the reasons for this difficulty is the very popular notion among high school students that "everyone is entitled to his or her opinion." I call this "raging relativism" and I have found it to be very hard to combat in the classroom when controversial issues are being addressed. This idea has as its corollary among some that "all opinions are equal." This makes it difficult for teachers to engage those students who articulate hateful, racist, or other harmful opinions in class discussions. I have often been accused by some students of being close-minded and too didactic when I have challenged those students. Seeing the hateful rhetoric on the website of Reverend Phelps (www.godhatesfags.com) changed the way many thought about people's "rights" to their opinions.

Ariel struggled with this throughout the process. In her second journal, written after several days of online research and heated class discussions, she notes:

> At Masterman the majority likes to think that we're so open-minded. But we're close-minded to people who we think are close-minded. . . . I am judgmental to the judgmental. And I'm not sure that isn't okay either, because I think that if the people who insist on controlling other people's lives go undisputed, then they might succeed. (Journal 2)

It's as if she needs to convince herself that it is OK to judge the ideas of others. She sees the prevailing ethos of Masterman as one of "open-mindedness." However, she is beginning to question the usefulness, even the rightness, of that approach. She seems to reach a decision about this in her final journal as she contemplates the consequences of the "haters'" views:

> This reminds me of what Angus said about being close-minded to the close-minded. And I'm still not sure if that's okay. I mean, I'm that way, but that's kind of bringing myself down to the haters' level,

right? But also, they deserve it. I mean why should they expect good treatment if they dish out the opposite? But I learned a lot from thinking about this. People have opinions that you can't change. But you should try to change them anyway. If people had spoken out in Laramie when they heard homophobic slurs, maybe McKinney and Henderson wouldn't have become what they are. Zubaida was right. Laramie had to own this. And I realized that at Masterman there are a whole lot more anti–gay people than I thought. . . . All in all I am grateful for this play. I found a new courage in myself to do the right thing. I lost a bit of innocence. Seeing this kind of tragedy jades you (and I know about the Holocaust so that is saying a lot). Matthew did make a difference. I wish that he was still alive, but he did make a difference. (Journal 3)

In his final journal, Angus addresses the impact the process has had on him. While he acknowledges that the project has come to an end, the thoughts, feelings, and discussions live on:

This whole process has been one long emotional journey. I thought that after a while I might become numb to the subject matter and every period wouldn't evoke some sort of emotional distress within me. This was definitely not the case. I'm relieved that this inquiry into *The Laramie Project* has come to a close. However I know that this is by no means the end to the inquiry itself, especially as it exists outside the classroom. This is an issue that will have relevance and importance to my generation probably for the rest of our lives.

He goes on to explain why this learning experience has been different from others he has experienced in school:

Our inquiry into *The Laramie Project* will go down in my memory as the most powerful educational experience of my life. Usually, classroom discussions and subject matter tend to avoid the really controversial issues, especially those that have relevance in people's lives. Too often in education, it seems that educators and students alike avoid topics that make people uncomfortable and really change their thought processes. Usually, when we discuss upsetting events, it's in a subject like history and you can easily write it off as "oh, that's history, that's in the past." The reality of *The Laramie Project* is that you absolutely cannot do that. It's real, it's present and it's scary.

Perhaps that is why I had such a strong personal reaction. I read it and I have to realize, "This is how we are." I can't just say, "This is how we were." And write it off as a mistake of the past that we have since learned from. Obviously, we have yet to learn. (Journal 3)

This lack of closure is appropriate and one of Epic Theatre's desired results. Moises Kaufman intended for audience members to find their own meanings in this play, search their own conscience, and be moved to take their own action. In his initial reading of the play, Ahmed wrote:

I would be interested in reading similar plays about Columbine and such tragedies. It's not so much I want to relive the horror but I want closure. Is it fair for an outsider to want closure on a tragedy that didn't directly affect him? Is it fair to the insider who probably will never find such closure? (Journal 1)

Later, after conducting the research and preparing for the performance, he comes to understand that the closure he sought will not be provided for him.

I have learned that major events do not have the ability to have defined beginnings and endings. The story began before the actual murder and continues even as I type. It has been carried on through discussions, hate crime legislation, straight-gay relations nationwide among other things. It is impossible to ever have the complete story and I have learned that in research that the goal is not always to have the complete story. I can only hope to find better understanding for myself. (Journal 3)

Bianca's journal entries present a dramatic example of the process by which one finds a better understanding for oneself. A passionate and outspoken African American young woman, Bianca wrote in her first journal that she thought that "it is the best play that I have ever read, (yes even better than *Fences*). I have never read anything like it and it allowed me to reflect on my views not only on homosexuals but on people whom [*sic*] are different from me."
She goes on to write:

I personally think homosexuality is wrong, but that doesn't mean that I would ever hurt or think about hurting someone whom [*sic*] is gay. People need to learn that "to each his own." It is not our place to judge anyone, because we all have skeletons in our closets. I would never treat anyone differently because they are gay, my views are simply my views and I have no right to impose them on others. (Journal 1)

Bianca expresses her initial reaction to hearing of the Matthew Shepard murder in 1998 in self-centered terms.

When I first heard about the tragedy, I was shocked, but I really didn't dwell on it. I was like, oh that's a shame what happened to that boy," and I just sort of forgot about it. Maybe if it had been a black boy or girl beaten and bound to a fence and left to die, I might have reacted differently. . . . I'm not gay, so I didn't have to worry about being tied to a fence in the middle of nowhere and left to die. (Journal 1)

In her second journal, she writes about an article she has come across during her research into *The Laramie Project*. The article frightens her.

The article was about a white supremacist who had killed a homosexual couple. It scared me to death because the killer felt that he was completely justified in his actions, claiming that he carried out the will of God. He even went as far as to criticize others for not taking similar actions against homosexuals and Jews. The killer was very alert and sure of himself, which was the scariest part. He felt that his murder was not a crime because it was the will of God that these two men burn in hell. (Journal 2)

Here she is beginning to make the connections between thought and deed. While she doesn't make the direct connection to her first journal in which she has written that she personally thinks homosexuality is wrong, she is appalled that other people have used Christianity to justify their heinous acts.

The idea that people are murdering innocent people in the name of God is just sad. Why would God want someone to die because they are gay? Not my God. The world is a scary place and crazy things happen all of the time. I can't control someone dragging me on the back of a pick-up truck for miles because they feel that all African Americans should die. (Journal 2)

In the performance, Bianca played Reggie Fluty, the police officer who was the first official to arrive on the scene of the crime. Bianca writes:

> Playing Reggie Fluty, who was the first police officer to report to the scene of the crime, I learned exactly how he was murdered. He was beaten, tied to a fence with a rope and left there overnight to die. This is a crime that would make me cringe if it was done to an animal, nevertheless a real person. Reading it for the first time, I could not believe that people could have such hatred in their hearts towards gays. . . . Sometimes my world is so black and white. I just do not consider homosexuals like me and when I think of discrimination or hatred, I think of it as being done against people who look like me. Honestly, before I started reading the play, I was like, why is this guy so special? He is no different than any black man that got killed in the struggle. For instance, the case in Texas where the black man was dragged only a couple of years ago; where's his play? Doing this project helped me move a little past that however. Once I began looking at *The Laramie Project* as a true story, not just a play, I began to care and feel like I had a duty to change things. (Journal 3)

This change becomes evident in her closing comments and final epiphany.

> In all of our discussions, Giana always says that she does think that homosexuality is wrong but she would never publicly judge someone gay or disrespect their space. That is sort of my feelings about homosexuality. [See comments in Journal 1.] But I was thinking today. Our feelings are hurtful too. As long as we think that homosexuality is wrong, as long as the majority sees it as an abnormality, hate crimes such as this will be sort of okay. The way that whites justified racism against blacks is by training themselves to believe that we were animals [reference to Toni Morrison's *Beloved* and the character known as schoolteacher]. They forced themselves to believe that we were not normal, and therefore inferior, making slavery acceptable. In *The Laramie Project,* Rob's character has the line that always sticks in my head: "I would sit them down and I would tell them, this is what gay people do, okay? This is what animals do." If we all believe that homosexuality is abnormal and animalistic, then the crime becomes almost justified. This scares me because no crime like this should be accepted. But

then I know deep down, I do think that the man who was dragged from the truck in Texas suffered more than Matthew did, even after reading the play. I relate that to me, because shit like that has been happening to us for years. Like I said, sometimes I see things in black and white, I think a lot of us do. We're so busy with our own prejudices we're dealing with, it's sort of hard to think about gays. (Journal 3)

While Bianca still sees things in "black and white," through her involvement in the reenactment of the play, she has reached a deeper understanding about the process of dehumanization and the ways in which it can lead to violence against people who are different and vulnerable. And she has come to question her own complicity in that process.

NEXT STEPS AND
IMPLICATIONS FOR PRACTICE

I have been surprised and overwhelmed by the depth and variety of my students' responses to *The Laramie Project*. I have been intrigued by some of the connections I have been able to make between their responses and reader-response theory. I believe that my preliminary findings indicate that there is a powerful and important role that drama education can play in the ethical development of young people.

Some of the issues and questions I would like to pursue include

1. *The ways in which students connected this text to their own lives.* During the 3 weeks in which we read this play, two students were severely beaten at a party. Another lost her father after he was felled by a sudden heart infection. These events affected their responses and the responses of the other members of the class.
2. *The ways in which students' ethnic, racial, sexual, and religious identities played into their responses to the play.* Many students wrote about their own experiences as minorities. Others struggled with their religious beliefs as they related to homosexuality. It is also interesting that at this particular time at Masterman, in the entire high school, there are no students who are "out." This has not been the case in the other years I have taught there and I have questions about the implications of that.

3. *The ways in which students connected to individual characters in the play.* Because the interviews were done over a period of 15 months, the Tectonic Theatre Company was able to chronicle the change in attitude of several characters, particularly Jedidiah Shultz, a young Morman acting student who changed his thinking about homosexuality, and Romaine Patterson, a lesbian and friend of Matthew Shepard's who became a human rights activist. Several students cited these characters or described emotional and intellectual journeys similar to theirs.

4. *The nature of the intertextual connections made by the students.* As was illustrated by Bianca's story, students turned to other texts as well as historical and current events such as Columbine, September 11, and the brutal dragging death of the Black man in Jasper, Texas (James Byrd).

5. *The way students responded as actors.* Some students' responses addressed their concern with acting in this play. One student, who had been in the annual school play for 3 years, addressed all his journal responses to the daunting and very unpleasant task of having to play a hateful character such as Reverend Phelps or one of the murderers.

6. *The ways in which individual students moved along a continuum of engagement and detachment.* I would like to look closely at the responses of several individual students and chart their responses in terms of their own expressed engagement and detachment looking at the activities, issues, or moments in the text that triggered their involvement or detachment.

7. *The ways in which individual students expressed their emotional and intellectual responses.* While I understand Rosenblatt's theory of a continuum of response, some of my students seemed to express simultaneous emotional and rational responses. I would like to look at this more closely.

8. *The ways in which students responded to one another's responses.* Many times in their journals, students cited the ideas, comments, or performances of other students. In addition, students engaged in some group e-mails on the class Listserv in response to class discussions. I would like to take a closer look at these intersections and interactions in light of Edmiston's ideas about dialogism and answerability in the drama classroom.

9. *Students' responses to the structure, goals, and impact of Epic Theatre.* The students read *The Laramie Project* with little

introduction from me. Most of them responded to the unexpected
structure of the play and their own feelings about it. I would like
to look more closely at the ways in which their thoughts and
feelings changed as they learned more about Kaufman's intentions
and the tradition from which he was working. I am also interested
in knowing whether acting in and seeing the play performed
affected the students' responses to the work.

These are just some of the ideas that I would like to pursue, and they
all have at their root questions about implications for practice. While my
work in analyzing and making sense of this project has only just begun, the
daily responsibilities to my two drama (and three English) classes march
on. The insights and ideas that I have gained while writing this chapter will
no doubt continue to inform my teaching.

CODA

Meanwhile, the impact of this project continues to ripple out from my classroom. The director of the school play, a social studies teacher (and a friend)
came to my Drama and Inquiry classes' performances of *The Laramie Project* after deciding that he would like to do it as the school play. When the
call came for auditions, nearly 50 students tried out. (There are only 400
students in the entire high school.) And this number does not include the 20
students who will work on the stage crew designing sets and props for the
performance. On the day before opening night, the cast members performed
their dress rehearsal for the entire eighth grade. Student leadership groups
planned and led workshops relating to homophobia for the middle school
students following the performance. The work of the "second stage" had
literally become a main-stage production and the students' thoughts, feelings, and reflections were translated into actions that brought about positive
change in the school and the community. Such a result is what we hope for
from our citizens and what we sometimes get from our legislators.

NOTE

To learn more about Marsha Pincus's teaching, see Playing with the Possible:
Teaching, Learning, and Drama on the Second Stage, at her website, http://www.
goingpublicwithteaching.org/mpincus/

REFERENCES

Boal, A. (1985). *Theatre of the oppressed.* New York: Theatre Communications Group.

Doyle, C. (1993). *Raising curtains on education: Drama as a site for critical pedagogy.* Westport, CT: Bergin & Garvey.

Edmiston, B. (2000). Drama as ethical education. *Research in Drama Education, 5*(1), 63–84.

Harris, L. K., & Worden, A. (2002, December 15). How Pa. heartland went for gay rights. *The Philadelphia Inquirer,* p. 1.

Iser, W. (1978). *The act of reading.* Baltimore: Johns Hopkins University Press.

Kaufman, M. (2000a). Into the West: An exploration in form. *American Theater, 17*(5), 20–23.

Kaufman, M. (2000b). *The Laramie Project.* New York: Dramatist Play Service.

Lytle, S. L., & Cochran-Smith, M. (1993). *Inside/outside: Teacher research and knowledge.* New York: Teachers College Press.

Patterson, N., & Strosser, M. (1993). *I used to teach English.* Philadelphia: Scribe Video.

Pincus, M., Pointer, D., Hatch. T., & Iiyoshi, T. (2001). *Playing with the possible: Teaching learning and drama on the second stage.* Retrieved April 1, 2004, from http://www.goingpublicwithteaching.org/mpincus/

Rosenblatt, L. (1995). *Literature as exploration.* (5th ed.). New York: The Modern Language Association.

Wilhelm, J., & Edmiston, B. (1998). *Imagining to learn: Inquiry ethics and integration through drama.* Portsmouth, NH: Heinemann.

CHAPTER 10

Pio Pico Student Researchers Participatory Action Research: From Classroom to Community, Transforming Teaching and Learning

Emily Wolk

My ultimate goal—as a teacher, and as an individual who cares about children—is to have students internalize a feeling of powerfulness, a feeling that we can persuade a community to take action. Not just to think about "what I'm going to do in my community" or just to complain about "what I can do in my community," but to actually go out and make a difference in the community. Through that action, they become invigorated, they become powerful, they say to themselves, "You know what, I persuaded the city to put in a four-way stop"—not a lot of people can say that they've done that. As they grow and meet challenges in the face of which they feel frustrated, they can pull on that experience and say, "I've done this before in my past; I can do it right now."

The excerpt in the next section, "Getting the Green Light," is part of the work on my website, *From Classroom to Community, Transforming Teaching and Learning*.[1] The website (see Figure 10.1) documents my work with the Pio Pico Student Researchers, a group of students ages 8 through 11 who work together to take action in our school neighborhood and in the larger community. Through a participatory action research (PAR) approach, I work with my students to identify important issues in our community and work together with them to effect change.

Figure 10.1. Home page of Wolk's website

For example, in the years since the inception of the Pio Pico Researchers group, the students identified a major local problem of traffic safety and pedestrian fatalities worked with local law enforcement and city planners and used urban-planning data to craft a persuasive argument that more needed to be done in our neighborhood to protect students and their families from speeding traffic. Our first success was that the students were able to get a four-way stop put in place near the school. As a result of subsequent presentations by the students, the four-way stop was replaced by a signal light, and pedestrian injuries have plummeted. The Pio Pico researchers and I have presented our findings to an international conference for transportation engineers, at which the U.S. national director of transportation safety praised the students for taking part in transforming traffic safety in their community.

The website describes the journey of the Pio Pico Student Researchers, the ways they have had an impact on local concerns, and my evolving ideas about what makes the group effective. The site includes two videos of local newscasts about the students' research, a project time line, and a variety of writings about my work, including narratives that document key moments in the group's development and a full version of "Getting the Green Light."

EXCERPT FROM "GETTING THE GREEN LIGHT"

Edwin: Hey, Mrs. Wolk! I've got an idea. What about a parade?
Mrs. Wolk: A parade? Do you think . . . ? (pause)

Brenda: Yeah, we should have a parade and we'll invite everyone. We'll invite all the families. We'll ask the classes to make something. Yeah, the teachers will help us out if we ask. Maybe they could have the kids make like those things people carry in parades.

Mrs. Wolk: Do you mean banners? Those things that people carry in front of a marching band?

Edwin: Yeah.

Mrs. Wolk: Hey, maybe we could get some balloons.

Esme: How about green or red or yellow ones like the light we want.

Cristina: And we'll have a band or something. Let's get Britney Spears.

Mrs. Wolk: I don't know if we could get Britney Spears.

Edwin: Yeah, yeah, Britney Spears.

Cristina: She's so cool! (E. Wolk, personal communication, April 3, 2001)

REFLECTION

Edwin's idea was the beginning of one of our most successful events to engage our urban elementary school and our surrounding neighborhood in addressing a serious problem in our community: pedestrian safety. On the day of the event, nearly 700 students—kindergarteners with stop-sign hats, third graders with banners and whistles, fifth graders with carefully designed posters with the logo "Cuidado cuando cruces" (Be careful when you cross) marched and chanted to the rhythm of the Santa Ana High School Marching Band, "Walk safe, be safe!" The chanting and the drumbeats echoed off the large tenement buildings that make up a large percentage of the housing in one of our nation's most densely populated several square miles.

Onlookers watched curiously from windows and balconies, wondering why, at 2 o'clock on a warm California afternoon, the streets were flooded with a pedestrian parade: moms with strollers, police officers on motorcycles, business leaders, city officials, and 1,400 little feet. Reporters from our neighborhood Spanish language newspaper, *Rumores*, and the local television station came to cover the parade. This was quite an event. This had been quite a research project.

Starting this group of students called the Pio Pico Researchers seemed a natural corollary of my years as a classroom teacher. But it also filled a tremendous need to reestablish myself as a teacher, after my having just left the classroom to support our large numbers of young, inexperienced staff grappling with their first year in our "underperforming school."

For years, as a classroom teacher, I worked collaboratively with my students and their families on what we called "action-based projects" to make positive changes aimed at social justice in our school and community. My desire to implement this kind of alternative curriculum was fostered, in part, by our school's commitment to preparing students to become problem solvers and critical thinkers. Yet I also noticed that when my students and I worked within our community on this type of curriculum, engaging in such efforts as beautifying our streets through projects like Operación Limpieza (Lubetkin, 1996), my students and I became invigorated and both teaching and learning somehow changed. It was this spark that carried me through the challenges of being a teacher in a school in a large urban district: the stacks of mandatory accountability pieces, such as the endless checklists of what was taught and mastered; the pressures to improve student performance on standardized tests; and the mandated curriculum and assessment schedules.

Now, faced with little classroom contact and even more endless paperwork as a school-based project coordinator, I felt I was losing my connection to my own identity as a teacher and, perhaps, my own integrity, which allowed me to address other teachers about teaching. Moreover, I was unable to realize my personal commitment as an educator to teach my students—all Latino, mostly first generation—the skills necessary to look at their world critically and to address the injustices that I knew they faced in their own lives. Therefore, I decided that I had to find a way to stay connected to students.

In late 1997, I initiated a club with a small group of interested students that we later came to call the Pio Pico Researchers. The idea came from my classroom practice, in which my students and I became coresearchers. I was deeply influenced by my university advisor, Dr. Suzanne SooHoo (1991, 1993, 1995), who used various techniques and strategies to "capture" the essence of a problem. In her study (SooHoo, 1991), students received notebooks to record their observations, and cameras to photograph "meaningful learning experiences." Students met twice weekly to discuss and analyze observations, clarify misconceptions, or volunteer any other data. Like my advisor, I wanted to deepen my understanding and check my own perceptions of teaching and learning with my students in my classroom. These initial steps in my classroom became my foundation as a teacher-researcher, coresearcher with my students, and a member of what later would become a participatory-action research project.

NOTE

1. Wolk, E., Pointer Mace, D., Hatch. T., & Iiyoshi, T. (2002). *Pio Pico Student Researchers Participatory Action Research: From Classroom to Community, Transforming Teaching and Learning.* Retrieved April 1, 2004 from http://www. goingpublicwithteaching.org/ewolk/

REFERENCES

Lubetkin, M. T. (1996, April). How teamwork transformed a neighborhood. *Educational Leadership, 53*(7), 10–12.

SooHoo, S. (1991). *Lessons from middle school students about learners and learning.* Unpublished doctoral dissertation, Claremont Graduate University.

SooHoo, S. (1993). Students as partners in research and restructuring schools. *The Educational Forum, 57*(4), 386–393.

SooHoo, S. (1995). Emerging student and teacher voices: A syncopated rhythm in public education. In B. Kanpol & P. McLaren (Eds.), *Critical multiculturalism: Uncommon voices in a common struggle* (pp. 217–234). Westport, CT: Bergin & Garvey.

CHAPTER 11

Was the American Revolution Completed Before the War Began?

Steven Levy

I am required by the Lexington Public Schools to teach the American Revolution as part of my fourth-grade social studies curriculum. There are textbooks that predictably recount the acts and tariffs imposed by the British, the reactions of the colonists, the succession of battles, and the eventual winning our independence. There is some value in learning these facts. They become part of the national lore that we share as Americans. But if we stop with the "tit for tat" events that culminated in a war, our students will gain only the most superficial understanding of what the American Revolution was about. I wanted to inspire my students to find out what the revolution meant, the part it played in the evolution of our civilization, and its relevance to their own lives. I needed a question that would open the door to understanding on a deeper level. My first step was to read about the American Revolution myself.

FINDING THE GRAND QUESTION

In my reading, a jewel of a question gleamed in a letter by John Adams. It promised to open the many facets of exploration and discovery that would lead us to the deeper aspects of what the revolution was about. Adams wrote in 1818, "The Revolution was completed before the war ever commenced. The real American Revolution was in the minds and hearts of the people. Their changing opinions, values and sentiments, that was the real American Revolution." What did he mean by this perplexing paradox: the

Revolution completed before the war ever began?! This incongruity is the kind of puzzle that can be reconciled only from deep levels of understanding. What was changing in the minds and hearts of the people? is the kind of grand question that launches a complex investigation. Grand questions like this have no single right or wrong answer. They compel viewing the topic from multiple perspectives. They lead us back to original documents in our research. They provide opportunities for the students to develop skills and master content in the course of the investigation.

When I asked my students what they thought of when they heard the words *American Revolution*, I heard nothing but images of "soldiers," "Redcoats," "muskets," "Paul Revere," "'the rockets' red glare, the bombs bursting in air.'" So when I put this quotation from John Adams before them, they were quite puzzled. They had only a vague idea what Adams was talking about. The vocabulary was new for most of them, and the concepts quite sophisticated. I gave them words like *revolution, sentiments, affections, opinions*, and *commenced* for their spelling words the first week. They learned the definitions and wrote the words in sentences.

Then I told them their challenge was to figure out what John Adams meant. I thought this approach would lead them to discover the genius of the American Revolution, which I saw emerging in the tension between authority and freedom, between dependence on the powers that be and the desire to decide for oneself. All the ways that we might see the American Revolution, all the lenses that highlight different aspects of it, share the development of a powerful sense of self. In the late 18th century, the importance and value of the individual was supplanting the prevailing loyalty to the established hierarchies of authority and power. A person's identity was beginning to be expressed as an individual rather than through the authorities to which he or she was subject.

LEARNING FROM THE PAST

What was changing in the minds and hearts of the people? To explore this change, we looked back to the preceding centuries to see what the relationships were like between the individual and the authorities. We took a brief look at medieval life, in which the common people were totally bound by the political, economic, and religious governance of the federal system. There was no room for individual expression. From there we went on to study the lives of leading personalities from the Renaissance. Of particular interest were persons whose lives reflected the genius of the times. Where could we find seeds of this new sense of self, of the value and dignity of the individual, that would flower in the ideals of the American Revolution? Galileo stood out in science, Martin Luther and Joan of Arc in religion, Oliver Cromwell in politics, and Leonardo da Vinci in the arts. Their biographies are vivid illustrations of individuals who stood up against the authorities, championed new frontiers, and paid a significant price. They demonstrated on a personal level the dramatic change in the minds and hearts of the people that would later be manifest in society, where individual dignity and independence became prizes worth dying for.

Galileo

First I told my class about Galileo, who was born in Pisa, Italy, in 1564. As a child, he loved to tinker, making little toys with levers and pulleys that fascinated his sisters. As a young man he wanted to be a monk. However, his father hoped Galileo would become rich and replenish the dwindling family fortune, so he sent him to medical school to become a doctor. The school was torture for Galileo. His impatience made it difficult for him to listen to his teachers, who taught by lecture and demonstration. He frequently questioned the facts they taught him. "Why is this so? What would happen if we treated the patient this way instead of that?" His teachers would tell him, "This is always the way it has been done. We do not ask why." Galileo was expelled for his constant questioning.

Galileo left the school and went into a nearby church. I let the children imagine his thoughts at this time. He must have been terribly worried about how his father would react. He may have returned to his boyhood dreams of becoming a monk. But while he was in the church, he watched the priests come by and swing the great incense lamps that hung on long chains from the ceiling. He noticed that no matter how far the incense lamps were swung, it took the exact same time for them to make one complete arc. Aristotle had said that the longer arc would take a longer time. "Aha!" he shouted. "Aristotle was wrong! And now I can prove it!" Here I asked the children how they thought Galileo might have measured the swinging lamp.

"With a clock," someone said.

"That would have been very handy, but alas, they had no clocks in Galileo's time."

"He counted," someone else surmised. I had them close their eyes and count up to 30. We noted how much time it took. Then we did it again and found it took a different amount of time.

"Counting is good. It gives us a good approximation of the time. But it might not be precise enough for Galileo to use to prove Aristotle was wrong."

"Maybe he had a sand-dial type watch."

"Well, that would give an accurate measure of a longer period of time, but would he be able to use it to measure the few seconds of the lamp's arc?"

"Maybe there was music in the church and he used the beat of the music." I love the ideas the children come up with.

"Ingenious, but alas, there was no music in the church that day."

Eventually, with a hint or two, they got it. Medical student that he was, Galileo timed the arc with his pulse. This led into a fascinating discussion of time and how it can be measured. Why can I use the sun but not the wind? Why isn't counting accurate? What is it about time, anyway? Why can I use my pulse but not my breathing? One child disputed using the pulse. She said Galileo's heartbeat would change because of his excitement at proving Aristotle wrong!

I challenged the children to design an experiment that would prove whether Galileo or Aristotle was correct, first teaching them the proper procedure for writing up a scientific experiment. They conducted their experiments, and we compared results (one group's documentation of their experiment is shown in Figure 11.1).

The students were very accurate in their measurements, using a stopwatch that showed results in hundredths of a second. One group listed their results: the long arc took 2.52 seconds; the small arc took 2.47 seconds. I was pleased—the results confirmed that the two arcs took the same amount of time—so I was shocked to hear their conclusion: Aristotle was correct. It did take longer for the long arc. While I naturally attributed the slight variance of .05 seconds to the imprecision of fourth-grade technique and measurement, the children took the results literally (or do we say, in this instance, mathematically?). They were being much more scientific than I. We all have a tendency to see results in terms of the outcomes we expect. On many occasions I have seen students ignore the actual results and record instead what they think the answer should be. I stood condemned by this same inclination. This led us into an important discussion about the variables that we could not precisely control, and how all measurement is approximate to the degree our instrument can measure. We learned the concept of "margin of error." We also learned why it was important to repeat an experiment multiple times and determine averages in order to get more accurate results. In this way I was able to teach the methods and

Figure 11.1. Experiment to determine whether Galileo or Aristotle was correct

Aristotle verses Galileo

Purpose: To see if Aristotle or Galileo is right.

Procedure: We are going to put the string on the ball of beeswax and swing the string. Then we will time the big arc and the little arc.

Materials: 1 yard of string, 2 inch ball of beeswax, and a watch.

Results: When we did our experiment we found it takes 3 seconds to make a big arc and 3 seconds to make a small arc.

Conclusion: We found that it takes the same amount of time to make a big arc as it does to make a small arc and therefore Galileo was right.

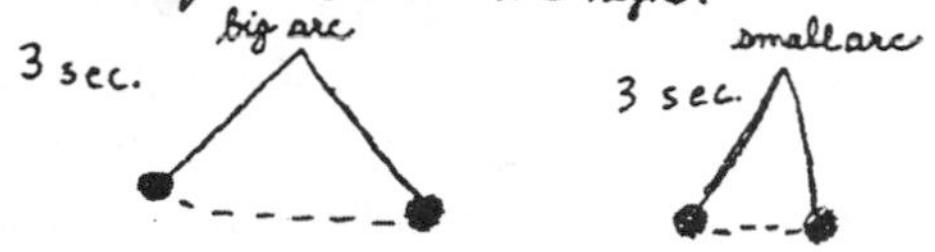

3 sec.   big arc   small arc   3 sec.

skills of scientific procedure in an authentic context, one that arose from our own activity and experience.

After his epiphany, Galileo rushed out of the cathedral and set up a laboratory in which to prove Aristotle was wrong. He conducted many experiments; this was remarkable because the whole idea of doing experiments to find out what was true was heretofore unknown. Galileo is regarded as the father of modern experimental science. Before Galileo, if you wanted to find out what was true you looked in the books of Aristotle, the unquestioned authority. But this did not satisfy Galileo. He would not base his understanding on what the authorities said. He had to find out for himself! He represents in the scientific world this spirit of the individual that we would trace to our ancestors in the founding of our country. Just as Galileo insisted on finding the truth for himself, the English colonists insisted on being part of the process that would formulate the laws of our land.

I went on to recap the rest of Galileo's life. (I tell the story rather than have the children read about it. If knowledge is dependent on reading, then the children will have unequal access to it. I have books available for those who want to go into more detail, but I don't want to hinder the less able readers from taking part in the discussions and activities.) If Aristotle was wrong about the pendulum, what else might he be wrong about? Galileo staged a public demonstration from the (not yet leaning) tower of Pisa. He dropped a heavy ball and a light ball from the tower as all the professors, religious authorities, and curious townspeople watched. Sure as the eye can see, both balls hit the ground at the same time.

Nevertheless, the authorities still did not believe him, even though they had seen it with their own eyes! Aristotle had said that a heavier weight would fall faster than a lighter weight. What Aristotle said was their truth! Their conceptions were so inflexible there was no room to adjust them in the light of new data.

The children were quick to reprove the authorities for their stubborn rigidity. "I mean, they saw it, how could they not believe it?" But we always have to be careful in judging others, especially across the centuries. Is there anything we have today that we can see with our own eyes but still refuse to believe? How about magic? We cannot believe the tricks some magicians are able to perform, even though we see them with our own eyes. So it was not so unusual for the authorities to dismiss Galileo's experiment on the grounds of magic: It was an understandable hypothesis given the context in which they lived and thought. Just as we know a magician doesn't really saw a woman in half, they knew that the ideas of Aristotle and the church could not really be wrong.

The children were outraged to learn that Galileo was called to trial for his ideas and that his books were burned. They were disappointed that he recanted at the trial and admitted that all his books were false. They were thrilled that students came to visit him while he was under house arrest and smuggled his manuscripts out to other countries to be published. The truth can never die! (The story ends in 1992, when the church formally admitted it made an error in condemning Galileo and issued an official apology and pardon.)

Martin Luther

After Galileo, we turned our attention to Martin Luther. I told the story of his life in the same way I had with Galileo's. Luther insisted that there need be no higher authority to mediate the relationship between humanity and God, that every individual needed to develop his or her own relationship with the Creator. He translated the Bible into German so the people could read it and interpret it for themselves. Luther wrote 95 theses detailing the errors and hypocrisies he saw in the church, and he, like Galileo, was brought to trial for his beliefs. The children were especially heartened to hear that Luther retained his conviction at his trial. Their longing to champion the courage of humanity, dampened by Galileo's retraction, was restored by Luther's refusal to recant. I had them memorize his response to the court, the heart of which is, "I cannot and will not retract anything. It is neither safe nor right to go against one's conscience. Here I stand. I cannot do otherwise. God help me. Amen." This is the same rock the American patriots stood on almost 300 years later.

Oliver Cromwell

In politics, we studied Oliver Cromwell and the Glorious Revolution. The "Roundheads," as Cromwell's followers were called, were not willing to accept laws, believe laws to be righteous, just because they came from the hand of the king. They wanted to have a say in the making of those laws. We experienced their struggle in deciding whether or not to revolt against King Charles. He clearly refused to share his power with anyone, but what about the precedent set if the people seized power? What authority would ever again be safe?

The night before the king's execution Charles and his enemies prepared themselves for the final struggle. For Charles, the only victory left was in dying bravely. His enemies hoped to weaken his courage. Each side was fighting for the minds and hearts of the people. If Charles winced even a little, if by his behavior on the scaffold he showed himself unworthy of the thousands who had died defending him, the throne would be tarnished forever.

The king wore two shirts on the day of his execution to avoid the appearance of being fearful if he shivered in the cold January morning. Cromwell had moved the crowd far enough away from the scaffold so they would not be able to hear anything the king said. Nevertheless, Charles spoke, ending his remarks with a summary of his political philosophy. "For the people, and truly I desire their liberty and freedom as much as anybody, but I must tell you that their liberty and freedom consists in having, of government, those laws by which their life and their goods may be most their own. It is not for having a share in the government, sirs; that is nothing pertaining to them." To the end, Charles stood by his own ideas of government. It was for the king to decide what was good for his people. The people had no business sharing in the government.

The ax fell, and parliament tried to rule. But in a few years the people demanded a king once again, and Charles II came back from France to rule.

Although certain individuals were ready for a new kind of government, the general public had not yet broken free from their dependence on the king.

Finally, in the arts we saw the rise of the individual reflected in paintings. Before this time, the subjects of art were primarily religious or royal. In the paintings of Brueghel and Leonardo the common peasant began to emerge as a worthwhile subject.

In addition to these in-class examples, I had the children read other biographies of the Renaissance in search of more examples of the changing minds and hearts of the people.

EVALUATING WHAT THEY LEARNED

I was able to evaluate the children in a variety of ways. I learned a lot about their understanding through their participation in class discussions. The children all wrote biographies of a Renaissance person that concluded with a paragraph on how this person relates to the spirit of the American Revolution.

At the end of our study, they all wrote about what they thought John Adams meant by his statement. Emily's response represents the understanding I hoped they'd come to:

The Real American Revolution

John Adams said that the American Revolution started in the minds of the people long before the war of independence.

Before King Charles I, people believed that the royal family was blessed by God. During King Charles I's time the people were beginning to question the idea of the king having special powers to rule. Did they really need a king to rule over them?

This was happening in religion also. A monk named Martin Luther helped people form the idea that Pope and priest were not the only ones who could have a relationship with God. They thought they should be able to read the Bible for themselves and decide what it meant for themselves.

A century before the American Revolution, old ideas in science were being questioned also. Aristotle had been the greatest scientist in the world for hundreds of years, until Galileo, a young scientist, proved some of Aristotle's works wrong. But finally he was forced into saying his ideas were wrong because the church said they would kill him if he didn't. All of Galileo's books were burned in Italy, but he sent his manuscripts to scientists in other countries. Galileo was the first scientist to base his work on experiments and to find out for himself how nature worked.

These are all examples of what the American Revolution was about. These are the things that started in the hearts and the minds of the people, that they should be able to choose their own government, that they should be able to worship God in their own way, and that they should not be put in jail for their ideas.

I also evaluated the children on the scientific aspects of the project: the design and execution of their experiment, how they recorded and reported on the data, and the conclusion they drew from their results. (I like the approach taken in Figure 11.2!)

I hold all my students to high standards, but I don't expect them all to achieve the same level of understanding. For example, some children were able to retell the lives of the Renaissance personalities in their own words and write coherently about them. They designed experiments to find out if Galileo or Aristotle was correct. However, when I challenged them to think about the relationship between Galileo, Luther, Cromwell, and Leonardo, they had a vague sense that they are related but weren't able to articulate it. And they had very little understanding that these lives had anything to do

Figure 11.2. Galileo–Aritstotle

with the American Revolution. A second group of students were able to see and articulate the relationship between the four biographies, that they all are individuals who stood up to the authority, the system, the conventions of the time. They also had a sense of the relationship between these persons and the American Revolution but had trouble articulating it. The final group enjoyed the stories, saw the connections between the four characters, and also understood how they were the seeds of the American Revolution.

I push all my students to think more deeply and stretch them to demonstrate their understanding, but because of very different levels of development and abilities, I do not expect them all to reach the third stage. What I like about a project like this is that children who do not reach the deepest levels of understanding will still be challenged and actively engaged. They, too, will feel success from the hard work they were able to accomplish. Each level of understanding has its own challenges and fills the children with a sense of accomplishment when they meet them.

CHAPTER 12

A Friend of Their Minds: Capitalizing on the Oral Tradition of My African American Students

Yvonne Divans Hutchinson

As a child, I thrived on reading and learning. In addition to fairy tales, novels, and poetry, I read the Bible, the newspaper, comic books by the hundreds, all 10 volumes of my Spiegel Catalogue edition encyclopedia, parts of the dictionary, the backs of Kellogg's Corn Flakes and Quaker Oatmeal cereal boxes, and anything in print that I could get my hands on. I read incessantly, in the bed under the covers at night with a flashlight, out on the porch or in the yard, in the car during family trips. To me the written word was sacred, inviolate.

Although I have since learned not to believe everything that I read, I still regard the act of reading with the awe I felt as a 6-year-old. I still love learning with the fervency sparked during my first year of school. This is the legacy handed down from my teachers, beginning with my mother and continuing through the fourth grade with the three African American women who guided my education through the land mines of segregation and discrimination in the South, helping me to realize that literacy is the road to freedom, and from all the great teachers since, of all hues, who sparked my intellect and touched my spirit, who have passed on the legacy: a love for humanity and lifelong learning. It is this legacy that I hope to share with my students.

As a teacher, I have focused for many years on developing strategies to engage all my students in substantive discussions of literary texts and the issues those texts raise for their own lives. In this approach, I build on the oral traditions of my students' African American and Latino cultures and seek to support the development of their literacy skills through high standards, explicit expectations, and rigorous literature experiences.

My initial instruction centers on guiding students to respect themselves, to recognize, appreciate, and tolerate differences. Our school, King/Drew, has a majority black population (72%), including many students from Africa and the Caribbean Islands, and a smaller group of Latinos (22%) and others (6%). In establishing a learning community in my classroom, I seek to establish a sense of harmony. Since race has the potential to be problematic, I find it futile to attempt to teach subject matter without first making sure that my students appreciate one other as human beings. In this case, understanding the content of their classmates' character, as Martin Luther King Jr. would say, matters more than understanding the content of the course.

Fortunately, the study of literature and language lends itself to the exploration of social justice issues such as race, but even before we examine literary texts as a mirror of society, I invite students to reflect on the importance of respecting others and tolerating diversity. It is imperative that they have this understanding and awareness if they are to become intellectual leaders in the classroom and to establish the global outlook that I believe is an important habit of mind of the lifelong learner.

MY WEBSITE

The piece that follows later in this chapter, "Thinking with Text," is part of the work on my website, *A Friend of Their Minds: Capitalizing on the Oral Tradition of My African American Students*[1]—a documentation and analysis of one instructional period that exemplifies my approach to teaching (see Figure 12.1).

The website juxtaposes video clips with commentary and samples of classroom documents. In the video clips, I reflect on my expectations for the day's class; a student orally presents the "class scribe" notes from the previous day (see Figure 12.2); the students engage in small-group and large-group discussions about a racially charged literary selection that had been assigned the night before (see Figure 12.3); and after the class, four students reflect with me on their experiences in my classroom and how our rigorous approach and emphasis on dialogue and diversity prepares them for other academic work.

The website also includes instructional materials, a video interview in which I share my beliefs about my teaching, a full-length video of the entire class period, and a time line that captures the beginning, middle, and end of the school year with various groups of students.

Figure 12.1. Home page of Hutchison's website

Figure 12.2. Image from video clip of "class scribe" presentation on Hutchinson's site

Figure 12.3. Image from video clip of class discussion on Hutchinson's site

THINKING WITH TEXT:
AN EXERPT FROM *A FRIEND OF THEIR MINDS*

"I don't get it," A. J. exclaimed. With his brow furrowed in bewilderment, he protested, "Where does it say that?"

A bright ninth grader who navigates the Internet handily and who is always reading a book, A. J. nevertheless was perplexed by the explanation of the metaphor in the poem "Fog" by Carl Sandburg. He couldn't "see where it says" that the fog appears with the same quiet stealth as a cat. Although he reads incessantly, he wasn't in the habit of analyzing what he read. For him and many of his classmates, reading and thinking were not simultaneous acts.

At the beginning of the year, I give an open-ended reading assessment, a remnant from the days of the California Learning Assessment System (CLAS), which almost invariably reveals that the majority of my students read at a literal or thoughtful level of comprehension. On the CLAS 6-point reading scoring guide, most of the class score at 3 and 4. And although a few avid readers demonstrate perceptive and insightful achievement, all of them are perplexed when I ask, "What do you do when you read?" Almost to a person, they stare at me blankly and shoot back, "What do you mean, what do I do? I just read." To introduce them to the idea that reading is more than the simple recognition of words, I give them my whimsical Informal Reading Assessment, asking them to "read" the word *cat* in isolation (decoding), then in a simple sentence and answer a question: *The cat has a black tail. What color is the cat's tail? Black (literal comprehension).* Then Sandburg's poem*: The fog comes in on little cat feet/It sits looking over the harbor and city/on silent haunches/and then moves on"* (1994). At this point, many students, like A. J., are stymied. They offer various interpretations of the poem, all of them literal: "The cat is walking around in the fog. The cat has fog on its feet." In A. J.'s ninth-grade honors English class, one student was able to explain the metaphor.

"Thinking with text" is an unaccustomed habit for the average teenager. Recounting his days as a middle school teacher, reading expert Richard T. Vacca (Kent State University) realized that he wasn't actually teaching reading, but rather teaching kids to "think with text" (Vacca & Vacca, 2002). "Thinking with text" is where I begin with my students: avid readers, indifferent readers, struggling readers, functionally illiterate readers. After almost all of them "fail" the informal group reading test, they realize that reading is more than just being able to pronounce words and pick out details. A. J. was bowled over by our discussion of the poem—clueless, but intrigued.

Next, we explore what it means to read. We reflect on the nature of reading, using the image of a tree as a metaphor. I ask the class to fold a paper from top to bottom, draw a dotted line on the fold and draw a tree, showing the part that grows above ground on top of the dotted line and the part that grows underground below it. When we look at our trees and compare it to reading a text they discover that reading is *understanding what the text says* as represented by the trunk, leaves, and branches, and *what it means,* as shown by the roots that are below the surface. They realize that it is the invisible "beneath the surface" reading that requires interpretation and analysis—that is, thinking.

They learn the active reading strategies: question, connect, predict, clarify, reread, evaluate. They learn to annotate, to mark up text, from two wonderful articles about close reading: high school AP teacher Victor Moeller's article "Creative Reading," and the article that inspired it, "How to Mark a Book" by Mortimer Adler (1940). As they learn more ways to "think with text"—levels of questions, question-answer relationship, metacognitive marking, reciprocal reading, literature circles—A. J. and his classmates continue to grow as readers, writers, and speakers, as demonstrated by their written response to core literature texts and in their recent book talks, enhanced by music, performance, art, research, interviews, and PowerPoint presentations.

But what I treasure most from this enthusiastic and delightful evidence of thinking *with* and *about* texts is the moment when A. J. reached epiphany, at one point looking up from his copy of *I Know Why the Caged Bird Sings* (Angelou, 1970) and chirping, "*Now* I get it, Ms. Hutch, this is getting interesting," as he articulated a "beneath the surface" idea about a passage in the book. When he finished reading a few days later, he looked up from the page and declared triumphantly, "This is the first time I've ever read a metaphorical book by myself."

"A. J.," I chuckled, " I'm proud of you. The *fog* has lifted!"

NOTE

Hutchinson, Y. D., Pointer Mace, D., Hatch. T., & Iiyoshi, T. (2003). *A Friend of Their Minds: Capitalizing on the Oral Tradition of My African American Students.* Retrieved April 1, 2004 from http://www.goingpublicwithteaching.org/yhutchinson/

REFERENCES

Adler, M. (1940, July). How to mark a book. *The Saturday Review of Literature,* pp. 200–204.

Angelou, M. (1970). *I know why the caged bird sings.* New York: Random House (Bantam Books).

Earnest, D. (1998). *The Plan Press reader: AP English.* Detroit Lakes, MN: Schoolhouse Books.

Sandburg, C. (1994). *Chicago poems.* Mineola, NY: Dover Thrift Editions.

Vacca, R. T., & Vacca, J. A. L. (2002). *Content area reading: Literacy and learning across the curriculum.* Boston: Allyn and Bacon.

PART III

Issues of Equity, Race, and Culture

Issues of equity, race, and culture are among the most difficult—and yet among the most important—aspects of teaching that teachers face. As the pieces in this section illustrate, addressing these issues can be risky and complicated and often require the authors to examine their own backgrounds and perspectives. While investigating the underachievement of African American males in her AP English class, Carter delves beyond the factors commonly cited for underperformance and seeks understanding from research literature while adding her own observations and knowledge. Cone explores the persistence of the institutional and individual factors that can undermine efforts to build a culture of high achievement for all students, even after the success of some detracking efforts. Diaz-Gemmati engages her eighth-grade students and herself in a quest to initiate and sustain conversations and understandings about questions of race and prejudice in literature and life. A piece about the growth of a shy Hmong fifth grader reflects Campano's efforts to develop teaching strategies that acknowledge and dignify the sometimes tumultuous experiences of children from migrant and refugee backgrounds that are often overlooked by traditional curricula. Struggling to understand her own beliefs and those of her 4-year-old Haitian students, Ballenger learns about the clash of cultures, particularly in terms of what motivates students.

CHAPTER 13

Helping African American Males Reach Their Academic Potential

Marlene Carter

At 8:00 A.M. the bell rings and my AP English literature class begins. Four young men, all African American, sit at the front, ready to lead the discussion of chapter 16 of Ralph Ellison's *Invisible Man* (1952). I sense something different in the room, an anticipation that was not here yesterday when the previous group led the chapter 15 discussion. This group of students is, by their choice, all male. I am hoping that their discussion will be as thorough and insightful as that led by the co-ed group the day before.

Kevin writes the chapter number and the names of the group members on the board. He sports an Afro and wears the fashion of the day, an oversized athletic jersey, sagging jeans, and name-brand tennis shoes. Next to him is Randy, a tall, lean, built-for-basketball type. His hair is freshly braided. He wears an oversized T-shirt and sagging shorts. To Randy's right is Joseph, who has been quite distracted recently by a combination of needing to make decisions about college and having fallen in love with an AP English student in another class. (They will get married at the end of their freshman year at UCLA.) The last student, Stanley, sits quietly, turning through the pages of his book. He smiles a lot, but seldom speaks. He is a modest young man; I later learn from his friends that he has earned a football scholarship to a major university.

I introduce the group, then settle down to become part of the class as the young men assume control of the classroom. As the conversation heats up, I hear . . .

> *Kevin*: So we agree this prize fighter is symbolic of Invisible Man. IM says he was "blinded by the light."
> *Elaine*: I disagree. When Invisible Man was in the ring he was able to see.
> *Jared*: IM is being blinded by the underlying meaning of the Brotherhood like the boxer is blinded by boxing. and IM is . . .
> *Kevin*: They talk a lot about light and darkness, blindness, and sight.
> *Eric*: When he approaches the stage he is blinded (refers to page 338)—
> *Kevin*: I have a question. If light represents truth, how is he blinded by light?
> (Three girls respond simultaneously. Finally, a male voice emerges.)
> *Jared*: I think this light goes back to the boxer in the ring. There is a lot of parallelism.

We have come a long way together to get to this day. I had struggled for years to get more African American males into my AP class. The young men had fought stereotypes and low expectations from some teachers, a rigid educational system that does not cater to the needs or learning styles of young men, and gatekeepers who would exclude them from opportunities to learn. I had worked hard over the past 3 years to prepare more African American males for AP classes and, more than that, to see that they were successful in those classes.

Four years earlier, my AP class of 23 included only 3 boys. I made a commitment to nurture the ninth-grade boys I had that year and encourage them to take AP. When the young men became seniors, I was pleased to have 11 boys in a class of 27, but most of them were content to do mediocre work, doing just enough to get by. This year my class of 23 AP students included 6 African American males. Five of them consistently demonstrated the ability to excel in the course.

As documented in this chapter, my concern about African American male achievement led me to conduct a 2-year teacher-research study as a K–12 scholar with the Carnegie Foundation for the Advancement of Teaching. I began my study with the following question: What curriculum, strategies, and attitudes best help African American males to be successful in advanced placement English and college? During the first year I focused on the factors that may have caused most of the young men in my senior AP English literature class to underperform. During the second year, I looked at factors that may have led the young men in my senior AP English class the following year to be so successful.

LIVING AND LEARNING IN LOS ANGELES

I teach in a neighborhood situated between the glitz of Hollywood and the harshness of what has come to be known as South Los Angeles. Located in southwest Los Angeles, this urban high school is surrounded by a stable neighborhood of working- and middle-class families, on one side; a prosperous upper-middle-class area, in the nearby hills; and several blocks of low-income apartment complexes, adjacent to the school. The families in the hills rarely send their children down to our high school. They have been scared away by the school's low test scores and the gang violence that plagues the surrounding community, sometimes spilling over onto the campus. At the time of the study there were slightly more than 2,000 students enrolled in the school, of whom about 65% were African American and 34% Latino.

I am a graduate of this school and have lived in the community continuously since sixth grade. My passion for finding answers to my questions about improving education for African American male students grew out of decades of watching young men, first my classmates, then my students, and later my own son, struggle in a school system that did not meet their needs. I have heard the regret in the voices of 40-year-old men who say they wish they had done better in school; they struggle to make a living on jobs barely above minimum wage. I hear the sadness when I talk each year with young men in their senior year who realize their options are limited because of their academic performance during the previous 3 years. They sometimes sign up for community college, but more often go straight to work in low-paying jobs. I agonize with my son, now a student at my alma mater, as he complains, frustrated, that he is bored with school. These complaints began in fourth grade and have intensified every year.

These issues took on even greater importance for me as I encountered other parents and teachers who shared my frustration. I talked about it with two friends who are also teachers and mothers of African American sons. We discussed the research we had read on how school systems do not meet the needs of African American males. We also shared stories of how most teachers seemed to misunderstand our sons, how disappointed we are in the system, and how we would like to see the system change. As we talked, I felt that I had to be part of that change. Since young men were not succeeding in my class, I needed to make some changes in my curriculum, strategies, and attitudes in order to be a more effective teacher. In addition, I knew that I was not the only one who had to do some changing. I wondered how I could help my students (and my own son) take more of an interest in their academic education and have a more positive attitude toward learning. I pressed forward by developing a study to look specifically at the factors that might be influencing the performance of my African American male students and others like them.

WHY SOME AFRICAN AMERICAN MALES
UNDERPERFORM IN SCHOOL

As I began my research, I listed possible reasons why the young men were not reaching their academic potential. I wondered if curriculum, teaching strategies, teacher attitudes, student attitudes, or a combination of these could be responsible for the achievement gap. If this were the case, I decided, I would make changes in my teaching style, offering the students more choice in reading material, essay topics, and class activities.

In November I had the opportunity to share my study as a work in progress at a session of the National Writing Project Urban Sites Network Conference. This session was valuable in helping me to expand my thinking and become open to other possible factors. A group of about 50 teachers, composed mainly of Writing Project fellows from urban cities across the United States, collaborated with me to compile a list of factors that may affect African American male achievement. I later grouped the responses into categories.

Home Environment
Lack of encouragement at home
Lack of spiritual foundation in home/school
Absence of male role models at home

Role Models
Too much emphasis on sports and entertainment figures
Lack of alternative role models
Lack of Black male teachers
Positive media portrayal of thugs

Teacher Attitudes
Lack of cultural sensitivity
Overstressed teachers who have no time for caring
Perception of Black males as hostile
Image of African American males as tough and rough

Student Attitudes

Not cool to be "geek"
Don't see benefits of academic success
Anger over powerlessness
Achieving is "acting White"
Acculturation—feeling like they have to give up something
Don't relate to female instructors
Influenced by peer groups
Image in school is that African American males are tough and rough
Lack of proper motivation

Curriculum

Literacy curriculum excludes texts males find interesting
Lack of awareness of literary heritage
What's offered doesn't support emerging identity of what is a man

Teaching Strategies

Teaching strategies and methodology don't support active learning

Miscellaneous

More hyperactive (K–1)
Break a cycle of gangs within family structure
Alienation and rejection from dominant culture

I reviewed the literature on African American learning and achievement. The College Board's *Reaching the Top: Report of the National Task Force on Minority High Achievement* (1999) identifies several factors that influence achievement:

1. *Economic circumstances*: "A high concentration of poor youngsters in schools is associated with lower achievement for poor and nonpoor students alike. . . . These schools do not have sufficient resources to meet student needs and these schools have high student mobility" (p. 14).
2. *Education of Parents*: "Students from low-income homes, or who have parents with little formal education, are much more likely to be low achievers and much less likely to be high achievers than students from high-income families or who have parents with bachelors or advanced degrees" (pp. 8–9).
3. *Racial and Ethnic Prejudice and Discrimination*: "A sufficient

number of whites still harbor doubts about the educational
potential of some minority groups for these views to continue
to take a toll on the academic performance of many minority
students" (p. 16).

Jawanza Kunjufu, an educational consultant, attributes the high African American male high school dropout rate to factors that include "our
children being bored, lack of finances, lack of rewarding experiences in
school, lack of positive adult reinforcement, and concern for gangs and
safety."

In *Young, Gifted, and Black: Promoting High Achievement among
African American Students* coauthor Theresa Perry states: "In order for
African-American children to achieve in school they have to be able to
negotiate three distinct social identities: their identity as members of a
castelike group, their identity as members of mainstream society, and their
identity as members of a cultural group in opposition to which whiteness
historically and contemporarily continues to be defined" (Perry, Steele, &
Hilliard, 2003)

Using this information, I began to explore factors that did or did not
affect my students. I used a combination of written surveys, classroom
observations, and student work to find out more about the skills, attitudes,
and lives of the 11 young men in my senior AP English class.

YEAR 1: JUST GETTING BY

Are you presently performing at your academic potential?
Nope. I'm lazy.
No, I actually slacked off a lot, but I was able to bring it back up.
No. I am slacking off because I am tired of school.
No, there is a lot of improvement needed.
No, because I haven't begun to fight.

The students who responded to the survey question above were African
American males who, by their own admission, were not doing as well academically as they could. Surprisingly, these seniors were not struggling in
remedial classes, happy to just get their high school diplomas. They were
students who had elected to take advanced-placement English. In June,
when the survey was given, all the young men had been accepted into
4-year universities and would start college in 3 months. The survey con-

firmed what I had determined from their essays, tests, and projects during Year 1 of my study—they were not doing their best academically.

As I shared my study with other teachers, I could see that some did not understand my concern. They congratulated me for having 11 young Black men in my AP class. They were aware that most high schools, urban or suburban, public or private, have surprisingly few African American males in the higher level classes. At one high-performing high school in Los Angeles, for example, an AP English teacher reported that there were no African American males in any of the AP English classes. But I had come to realize that getting the young men into the AP class was only half the battle. The young men, with one exception, lacked the motivation and drive of their female counterparts. The young men were less likely to complete the reading, to write multiple drafts of a paper, and to engage in deep conversations about the literature. Most of them did just enough to get by.

I began reviewing the data I had collected thus far: student surveys, student writing, and teacher observation. Using that data, I would try to rule out factors that did not appear to affect my students. I do not mean to suggest that such factors do not inhibit students in other classrooms from excelling. However, I determined that it was essential to focus only on factors that might be the cause of underperformance for *my* students.

Factor 1: African American Males Do Not Achieve Because Their Parents Are Not Involved in Their Education

This factor did not affect my students. Nine of the 10 African American males in my AP English class had a parent who attended at least one school meeting to conference with teachers. (The 10th student had an adult cousin who made several contacts with me.) Two students had parents who were very active in parent groups in the school. Whenever a student received a grade of less than C on a progress report, parents initiated contact with me about their child's progress. One pair of parents asked for weekly updates even though their son received satisfactory grades on all the school-generated progress reports.

Parental involvement went beyond policing grades. One student told me that when he was having a hard time reading *Hamlet* his father read through act III with him. At graduation a mother approached me to say that she was dissatisfied with the final project her son's group had submitted. (She had taken the time to read a 30-page magazine project.) I recalled that another young man had been in my ninth-grade English class. On a survey that I sent home to all parents, his mother noted that she felt her son was underchallenged in his classes. Her comment caused me to review his school records and recommend to his counselor that he be moved to honors classes. These parents are involved and for the most part aware of what is needed for their children to succeed in high school.

The cause of the underachievement, I believed, did not lie in the parents. I did not feel that these parents needed special "training," as is given in the classes being offered in many urban schools these days. The assumption in these classes is that parents are not educated and don't understand or are intimidated by the educational system. The parents of my students had no trouble communicating with (and in some cases making demands of) the school. My parents understood the educational system, but they were as puzzled as I was about why their sons were not achieving.

Factor 2: African American Males Do Not Succeed Because They Do Not Have Male Role Models in the Home

I met the fathers of 5 of these 10 students. All the fathers were employed. All showed through their conversation with me and with their sons that they valued education and expected their sons to achieve in school. All the sons showed respect for their fathers. The fathers of the other 5 did not attend any school events. The boys' mothers, however, were fine role models who showed that they valued education. One was a journalist; another was a businesswoman who had to travel for her job; another was a realtor. The students with fathers in the home did not do significantly better than students who did not live with their fathers.

Factor 3: Teachers Are Not Culturally Sensitive to African American Males

Some educators suggested that African American males were alienated by the dominant culture. But in the safe cocoon of our high school, where African Americans constitute the majority of the student population, the faculty, and the administrative staff, students did not report feeling such alienation. Instead, they were confident in their abilities. On the survey, they rated themselves as above-average students, despite the C grades they earned in my class. They saw that in comparison to all other students, they were above average. Their confidence also grew out of their affiliation with sports. As varsity players and college-bound students, they had status in the eyes of their peers and their teachers.

I believe that there are teachers who are not culturally sensitive to African American males. These teachers often lack experience with males from this culture and base their beliefs on images from books and the media. There are teachers who misinterpret the language or body language of Black boys, who misread their facial expressions. This was not a factor in my classroom. After leaving my Period 1 AP English class, students typically went to Trigonometry or AP Calculus, AP Government, and Physics or AP Chemistry. By coincidence, all these classes were taught by African American teachers who had a reputation for being both challenging and caring. As an African American woman, I am definitely in tune with the culture. I live in the community. I am the mother of three African American sons who attended schools nearby. At no time did students ever complain of cultural insensitivity. (They did complain about other things, mainly the amount of homework they were expected to do.)

Although I believe that cultural sensitivity is a factor that explains lack of achievement in some school situations, I did not feel it was a factor for my students.

Factor 4: African American Males Will Achieve
Better If They Have African American Male Teachers

I agree that Black boys need Black male teachers as role models. However, having African American male teachers did not solve the achievement problem for my students. My AP English students had four African American male teachers that year (AP Calculus, AP Government, Physics, and sports). As I have already stated, all the men were culturally sensitive and had positive relationships with their students. The male teachers, however, also found that the young men in their classes were not performing at the same levels as the young women. The race and gender of teachers did not explain the underachievement of my male students.

Factor 5: Economic Factors Cause
Lack of Resources in Urban Schools

According to the College Board (1995), many urban schools lack the necessary resources. It is true that our school as a whole experienced a shortage of books. However, these students were enrolled in a magnet program that had sufficient books for its students. In addition, we had computers in the classroom. Our program also had few problems with student mobility. All but three students enrolled in my AP English class on the 1st day.

The other three enrolled during the 1st week. No student left the school. All the young men except one had attended our school for 3 or 4 years.

Although there are schools that do have issues with resources and student mobility, my program does not. I eliminated this factor as one of the causes for the underperformance of my students.

Factor 6: Influence of Gangs and Violence

Some researchers point to the influence of gangs, violence, and other distractions in low-income communities. Even if students themselves lived in families that were not struggling financially, living in a neighborhood in which gangs are prevalent may have a negative impact.

The affect of gang activity on my students is not clear. None of these young men were affiliated with gangs. Nine of the 10 were members of varsity athletic teams. This took most of their free time and kept them involved in positive activities with other young men. The 10th student is an artist who spent the bulk of his free time drawing or playing computer games. Although it is possible that living in a low-income neighborhood and being exposed to gangs may have affected my students' attitudes toward high achievement, I could not determine the impact from the information I had gathered on the students.

REDESIGNING SCHOOLS AND CLASSROOMS

Having determined that these factors did *not* account for the underperformance of African Americans in my class, I decided that I would need to continue to look for ways to redesign my classroom to make learning more accessible for these young men. Knowing that I had parental support, a culturally sensitive staff of teachers, and sufficient resources, I felt that the next step was to make further changes in curriculum, teaching strategies, and attitudes.

Pedagogy, Athletics, and Attitudes: Exploring Other Factors

As I continued my research into African American male achievement, I began to look more closely at changing pedagogy, helping students balance academics and athletics, and improving student and teacher attitudes. Interviews, surveys, and observations of the young men in my class suggest that many African American males are bored and wish for more active learning opportunities. They also feel overwhelmed by the long hours they need to devote to both sports and homework. Many are complacent, feeling that lower levels of achievement are acceptable, and many are not pushed by teachers who also accept lower levels of achievement from African American males than from their other students.

African American Males Do Not Achieve Because They Do Not Have the Opportunity for Active Learning

Early on, I decided to make changes in my style of teaching in hopes of accommodating the needs of more students, especially African American males. I included more opportunities for small-group learning activities, literature circles, and projects. The young men reported that they liked working in groups. The products they created, however, were not of the best quality they could produce. For example, I allowed students to form their own groups for a magazine project due after the AP exam, with the freedom to write a poem, creative essay, and piece of fiction on virtually any topic. Two groups were exclusively male. Two other groups were of both genders, and two groups were females only. One young man decided to work alone. The boys-only groups had difficulties meeting intermediate and final deadlines. One of the magazines contained subject matter inappropriate for a high school audience. In the mixed-gender groups, the young men produced some of their better writing. The young man who worked alone produced the best work he had written all year. Its content was creative, deep, and original. He could have, however, benefited greatly from having had a peer editor.

I had thought that the freedom of choice in both what to write and whom to work with would inspire the boys to do their best work. That feature alone was not enough, however. Simply offering more opportunities for active learning is not enough. I needed to rethink the way in which I structured those opportunities.

Time Commitment to Sports

I know that I'm stepping onto the turf of controversy when I say that sports may actually hinder some young men from reaching their academic potential. I do believe that sports have contributed to the academic success of the young men in my class to an extent. Of the 10 young men, 9 were on varsity sports teams. They had all been involved in organized sports for many years. I believe that this activity gave them a chance to be around positive male role models and to interact with other young men who were generally engaged in positive behavior. Sports also gave them the incentive to earn decent grades, required for them to be eligible. Sports had probably kept them away from the negative influence of gangs and drugs.

But I am looking at high academic achievement, not at getting grades good enough for eligibility, typically only a 2.0. The young men in my AP class reported spending many hours after school at practices and games. Most said they arrived home after 7:00 or even 8:00 P.M. each day. After weeks of 14-hour days, they were physically drained and often did not have enough energy left to adequately prepare for class. In addition to my AP English class, most of the young men had AP Government, Calculus, and Physics. Each teacher required an hour of homework a night. There just were not enough hours in the day for school, practice, homework, chores, and sleep.

Compare these young men to the young women in the class. The girls were engaged in after-school activities too, but these activities often supported their academic growth. They were on the newspaper staff and active members of student government. Although they also stayed after school for activities, they did not do so every night of the week. Neither were they physically drained upon arriving home. Most of the girls devoted the necessary time each night to their studies. (Some girls did not, because of their own issues: One was a teen mother; two others worked long hours to help with the family finances.) The boys on average had a hard time competing with their female counterparts who had the time and physical energy to study.

I am not at all suggesting that young men should not be involved in sports. There is much to learn about collaboration from being on a team, about self-discipline by engaging in daily practice, about setting and achieving goals. Sports are a valuable part of the school curriculum and African American males need to be involved, but it is the extent of involvement that I question.

Student Attitudes Toward Achievement

The College Board report (1999) includes "cultural differences and peer influences" as factors that inhibit achievement among underrepresented minorities. The Writing Project fellows at the Urban Issues Conference also cited student attitudes as a major factor in lack of achievement. Because many African American males grow up in an environment in which their peer group does not discuss school, work together on homework, or share insights on how to achieve, they miss opportunities for advancement.

The culture of the school did not encourage young men to excel academically. In my non-AP classes I overheard students accuse others who were particularly enthusiastic about the class of "brown nosing." In AP classes it seemed safer to show one's intellect, but perhaps the outside forces of African American teen culture influence attitudes toward learning even in advanced classes.

Changing the culture of an entire school is a daunting task. Because our magnet program is a "school within a school," the staff has been more successful in getting students to have a more positive attitude toward achievement, but we need to continue to work in this area.

Teacher Attitudes

I wondered if the teachers these students had encountered, myself among them, were guilty of letting the boys do less than their best? I knew that these young men were varsity athletes who were challenged to do their best on the court and field. Like many other African American boys, they had learned early in life that their coaches, teammates, and parents had high expectations for them. Athletically, Black boys have permission to excel.

At my high school, most conversations about the achievement of African American males focus on their getting good enough grades to be eligible for sports or graduation. Too many young men are allowed to opt out of honors and advanced-placement courses. Many teachers are content to have young Black men sit quietly and obediently in their classrooms, earning Cs.

I shared my concerns with a Writing Project fellow who taught in the room next door to me. He recommended that I be more demanding and more direct with the students. He had taught several of the young men the previous year and was aware of their lackadaisical attitude toward their English work. "You've got to get in their face," he said. "Don't let them get away with it."

As the school year came to a close, I felt I had made only moderate progress toward helping the African American males in my class reach their academic potential. I had not succumbed to the temptation to remove any of them from the class, despite one grading period in which five of them earned Ds, which they later brought up to Cs. I had tried to be more demanding, letting them know I believed in their ability and that I would not accept less than their best. But in June the surveys they filled out showed that they knew they could have been better students. I wondered how they would fare in college.

YEAR 2: HEADED FOR THE STARS

As I began Year 2 of my study on African American males who were un-derperforming in AP classes, I ran into a major problem: I had no students to study. Six of the seven young men in my AP class that year were high-performing students. The seventh was a transfer student who came to our school because, he said, his previous school was not challenging enough. He desired to be in AP but did not have the academic background the other students had. One of the young men would go on to be the valedictorian. Another was our school's Berkeley scholar, whose high academic achieve-ment and 3-year participation in a special university program guaranteed him both admission and a scholarship to the University of California at Berkeley. A third young man would go on to receive the most scholarships of any senior that year.

In light of the new data, I shifted my research focus to try to discover why these young men were so successful. What was the secret to their suc-cess, and could these results be replicated?

The journey toward high achievement for these young men began well before their senior year. Through interviews and personal essays written for college admission, I was able to see some common experiences that had led to their success.

Faith in God

I videotaped an interview with four of the young men and asked each one, "To what do you attribute your success?" Three of the four young men stated that their faith in God was responsible for their success. Church played a prominent role in the lives of these students. Beverly Moss from Ohio State University has written about the importance of the church in the African American community and its "distinct role in education" (2000, p. 196). She states that "at the center of this instruction is the example that the minister set, as a literate person whose literacy practices and lit-erate behavior influence the majority of the congregation" (p. 196). The contemporary Black church continues to encourage education among its members. Some churches give small scholarships to their college students. College acceptances and graduations are sometimes mentioned during the announcement portion of the worship service.

While educators must be careful not to overstep the boundaries between church and state, we cannot ignore the powerful influence of the church on the lives of our students. Many students who are actively engaged in their church find it easier to avoid illegal drugs, gangs, and violence. For many students, faith in God is one factor in their success.

Choice of Friends

In a videotaped interview, the young men spoke of making the decision to have positive people as friends. My students sounded very much like the young men who wrote the book *The Pact* (Davis, Jenkins, Hunt, & Page, 2003). *The Pact* tells the true story of three young African American men who made a promise to support one another in their quest to become doctors. "We grew up in poor, broken homes in New Jersey neighborhoods riddled with crime, drugs, and death. . . . " But despite these challenges, two became medical doctors and one became a dentist. They write about the impact of friends in the lives of young people.

> The lives of most impressionable young people are defined by their friends, whether they are black, white, Hispanic, or Asian; whether they are rich, poor, or middle-class; whether they live in the city, the suburbs, or the country. Among boys, particularly, there seems to be some macho code that says to gain respect, you have to prove that you're bad. We know firsthand that the wrong friends can lead you to trouble. But even more, they can tear down hopes, dreams, and possibilities. We know, too, that the right friends can inspire you, pull you through, rise with you. (pp. 2–3)

My students spoke about "keeping the right people surrounding me" and "staying with the honors crowd." On the surface, this sounds elitist or snobbish, but what the young men meant, I believe, is that they chose to associate with students who went to class on time, who did their homework, who did not belong to gangs, who avoided the streets. Unfortunately, one of the young men in the class did choose to associate with a negative crowd. This association led him into risky behavior that later affected his education.

Support from Home

All four of the young men mentioned an adult in the home who had encouraged them and supported them in their quest for an education. In the interview, one spoke about how his mother is always on him about doing homework. Another spoke about what his father has done to support him. In their autobiographical essays for their college applications, one young man mentioned the positive influence his grandmother had had on his education; another mentioned his mother's influence.

It is hard to tell which came first, support from home or the individual desire to achieve. In either case, the individual choices the young men made were supported by an adult in the home. While the students did not mention other factors, I could see a pattern that could have been partly responsible for their success.

Prior Preparation

During Year 1 of my study, I spoke to Mike Johannson from the College Board about my concerns about my students' progress. He suggested that prior preparation might have been a factor. With this in mind, I thought about the preparation that the Year 2 boys had had and compared it to the preparation of the Year 1 students. The Year 1 boys entered high school just as our school district was reconfiguring junior highs to middle schools and sending ninth grades to high school. The Year 1 students were among our first ninth graders. Three of the young men had been in my ninth-grade English class. The others were taught by various teachers throughout the school. All of us were teaching ninth grade for our first time.

Three of the Year 2 students had also been in my English 9 class. I had told them and all the ninth graders I had that year about the AP program and encouraged them to make taking AP classes one of their goals. I also shared information from our college office about the opportunity for them to take college classes while in high school. One of the Year 2 students successfully completed a college course at a local community college while still a ninth grader.

During the time of the study my high school had come to the attention of the school district and media as one of the schools in the district that offered the least number of AP classes. We offered five courses; schools in some suburban neighborhoods offered three times as many. When the Year 2 students were juniors, our high school was given additional funds to start more AP classes. I decided to offer AP English Language, a course usually taught to juniors. Four of the Year 2 students took this class with me. One other student took the course with another teacher.

I believe that this early foray into AP had a positive effect on my students. While I was in the middle of my study with the Year 1 seniors, I kept comparing senior boys to the junior boys. The juniors were stronger writers and better readers. I wondered if this achievement was an anomaly, caused by an unusual concentration of good students, or if taking AP in the junior year might be a significant factor.

Teaching Practices

I became more aware of the need for AP students to engage in active learning and to have choices. The following list shows some of the activities I included to give students opportunity to active learning and choice.

1. Act out chapter of *The Scarlet Letter* (11th grade)
2. Generate the questions for the class discussion on an assigned book (11th and 12th)
3. Present polished papers and work-in-progress pieces to the class in author's chair (11th and 12th)
4. Participate in Oxford debates on a controversial issue (11th)
5. Choreograph and perform a dance as part of the Greek chorus in *Oedipus Rex* (12th)
6. Teach a chapter of the book to the class (12th)
7. Select from a poetry textbook the specific poems the class will study in depth (12th)
8. Work in a group to design, write, and publish a magazine (12th)

Outside Resources

Three of the students I interviewed mentioned at least one program or resource outside the classroom as one of the factors for their success. One mentioned "being in clubs." Another referred to the tutoring and work-experience programs at our school. Another simply said that "we have a lot of resources" in this school to help students.

I wondered about the impact of a university program on these students. The Year 2 students had been in an Early Academic Outreach Program through the University of California, Los Angeles (UCLA). An initiative to eliminate affirmative action in our state had just passed. With affirmative action eliminated for college admissions, the number of African Americans admitted to competitive public universities such as UCLA and the University of California (UC), Berkeley dropped dramatically. In response, the UC campuses were given money for intervention programs to help underrepresented minorities become not only eligible but also competitive for UC admission.

UCLA developed the Career Based Outreach Program (CBOP) for students in high schools that sent low numbers of students to the university. Four of the six young men in my class had participated in the program, once a week for about 15 weeks, during their English class in ninth grade.

UCLA sent undergraduates to our school to talk with the students about what it takes to be admitted to a UC campus. They showed students a completed college application and had students evaluate it as an admissions officer would. While the CBOP program was valuable, English teachers complained about giving up so much of their class time.

During the 10th-grade year, the program was offered after school. The group met in my room; UCLA students ran the meetings. We ran into an attendance problem early on. Almost none of the young men could come because they were attending athletic practices. In fact, only one of the young men in my Year 2 senior AP class had attended during 10th grade. I recall a conversation he had with a CBOP fellow.

> *CBOP fellow*: What grades did you get on your report card.
> *Student*: Five As and one B.
> The group applauded.
> *CBOP fellow*: What are you going to do to turn that B into an A?

She was responding to the reality that the typical UCLA student now has a weighted GPA of 4.0. Although I worried that CBOP students would focus too much on getting high grades and not enough on learning, I believed it was important to make students aware of what they must do to have access to major universities.

Because I attended the CBOP meetings, I was able to share the most important information with my entire class. For example, I attended a weekend retreat at the university, where a graduate student explained what readers wanted to see in the college essay. I would later use that information to help my seniors write much better college admissions essays. A professor explained to an audience of 9th and 10th graders how to write an argumentative essay, giving them a much more sophisticated structure than they generally learn in high school. Again, I incorporated that information in my classroom practice so that all my students wrote essays with more depth and insight than they had been producing.

Year 2 students also participated in other programs that shared the following characteristics:

1. *High Expectations*: Students who participated were held to high standards and the leaders in the program believed that the students could achieve these high standards.
2. *Knowledgeable Leaders*: The leaders brought in information not readily available on our campus.

3. *Caring Individuals*: The people who worked with our students genuinely cared about the students and their future.

FOLLOW-UP ON THE YEAR 1 STUDENTS

Ten out of the 11 young men in my senior AP class in the 1st year of the study chose to attend 4-year universities, and all successfully completed their 1st year of college. Two returned to speak to my classes to give advice to the juniors and seniors. They exhorted students to work harder while in high school. They also reported that they liked college and had received satisfactory grades. Both of the young men had opted not to play sports in their 1st year of college.

I spoke with three other young men when they returned for the homecoming football game in October. They also were successful in college and reported that they relied heavily on what they had learned in their high school AP classes. I heard about the progress of three others through younger siblings who still attend our high school and through the returning students. Once again, I was pleased to hear that the young men were still enrolled and successful in college.

The one young man who was not underperforming while in my class also returned to visit the school. He spoke to my senior English class, which included many varsity football players. The returning student had also been on the football team and had received a football scholarship for college. After answering questions about what it was like to be a student-athlete, he told the class, "My scholarship is for 5 years. I'm going to get a master's degree, since the university is paying for it."

I am in the process of getting more precise data, but these early reports indicate that being in AP classes helped prepare even the underperforming Year 1 students for a successful 1st year of college.

FOLLOW-UP ON YEAR 2 STUDENTS

Five of the six Year 2 African American male students attended 4-year universities. They, however, had more options than their Year 1 counterparts. These young men were accepted into several competitive universities. One is on the staff of a student magazine at UCLA. He returned to be a guest speaker at our annual Circle of Scholars. Sadly, one of the six committed a crime and was sent to prison. His decision to hang out with the wrong crowd temporarily derailed him. Instead of giving up, however, he kept in touch with the school and asked to borrow a graphing calculator so that he could continue his studies while incarcerated. He has since been released from prison and is now attending a 4-year university. As the study came to a close, I had only word-of-mouth information about one other. The valedictorian is doing fine at UCLA.

REFLECTIONS AS A TEACHER AND PARENT

At the end of my 2-year study I know that I am still far from finding all the answers to the questions I have on African American male achievement. I am beginning to see patterns for achievement and underperformance, but I realize that individual students may not fall within the pattern. The factors that led the five young men to achieve in Year 2 may not have the same positive impact on all African American males. Still, I think it is valuable to summarize how this study has shaped my beliefs and teaching practices.

I know not to assume that all African American males are underperforming academically. This misconception sets some young men up for low expectations from teachers and leads them to be placed in classes that do not challenge them sufficiently. I have learned that all African American males who are underperforming are not doing so for the same reasons. Using a combination of written surveys, talks with the student and parent, analysis of the student's work, and observation of the student, I now try to determine which factors may be affecting an individual student. I know how to eliminate those that don't apply so that I can focus on the real problem.

I constantly evaluate my attitude toward achievement among the African American males in my class. I know that regardless of race and gender, we can all hold attitudes that cause us to have lower expectations from some students than from others. Students can often detect these attitudes even if we say all the right words about having high expectations. At my school, I am working to communicate this message to counselors, teachers, and administrators. As a parent, I have learned to be more direct in talking with the adults who work with my sons.

To support students who are also athletes, I work to help them balance sports practice, homework, and the need for sleep. I have restructured my instructional practices to give students more lead time on assignments so that they can use the weekend to get ahead.

Most important, I have become even more determined not to give up on African American male students. Giving up usually comes in the form of excluding capable but underperforming students from advanced classes. Rather than exclude young men from honors and AP classes, I now do what I can to recruit them. I retain them, even if their mediocre grades do not seem to warrant it, and I require them to work.

Underachievement for some African American males begins early in their school career. I hope to one day see a study that follows African American boys from pre-K to college and examines what teachers, parents, and students need to do at each grade level to encourage African American male students to reach their potential. Perhaps we can invite young men to be coresearchers with us in finding solutions to this problem. As we find ways to better support our African American male students, we will have more opportunities to ask, "What is the secret of your success?"

REFERENCES

College Board. (1999). *Reaching the top: Report of the National Task Force on Minority High Achievement*. New York: Author.

Davis, S., Jenkins, G., Hunt, R., & Page, L. F. (2003). *The Pact: Three young men make a promise and fulfill a dream*. Riverhead Books: New York.

Ellison, R. (1952). *Invisible man*. New York: Random House.

Finn, P. (1999). *Literacy with an attitude: Educating working-class children in their own self interest*. Albany: State University of New York Press.

Harris, J. L., Kamhi, A. G., & Pollock, K. E. (Eds.). (2000). *Literacy in African American communities*. Mahwah, NJ: Lawrence Erlbaum Associates.

Hrabowski III, F., Maton, K., & Greif, G. (1998). *Beating the odds: Raising academically successful African American males*. New York: Oxford University Press.

Kunjufu, J. (1987). *Countering the conspiracy to destroy Black boys* (Vol. 3). Chicago: African American Images.

Ladson-Billings, G. (1997). *The dreamkeepers: Successful teachers of African American children*. San Francisco: Jossey-Bass.

Moss, B. (2000). From the pews to the classrooms: Influences of the African American church on academic literacy. In J. L Harris, A. G. Kamhi, & K. E. Pollock (Eds.), *Literacy in African American communities* (pp. 195–211). Mahwah, NJ: Lawrence Erlbaum Associates.

Perry, T., Steele, C., & Hilliard, A. (2003). *Young, gifted, and Black: Promoting high achievement among African-American students*. Boston: Beacon Press.

Rose, M. (1995). *Possible lives: The promise of public education in America*. New York: Penguin Books.

Smith, M., & Wilhelm, J. (2002). *"Reading don't fix no Chevys": Literacy in the lives of young men*. Portsmouth, NH: Heinemann.

CHAPTER 14

The Gap Is in Our Expectations

Joan Kernan Cone

Sixteen years ago I taught low-track ninth-grade English/reading classes. These began with lessons on sentence structure, paragraphing, and spelling, and when I felt students were ready, I assigned personal narratives. I taught literature through short stories and short, easy-to-read novels and checked students' understanding with multiple-choice and short-answer questions and an occasional essay. I administered an easy-to-correct comprehension test to assess reading levels and then assigned individual exercises from large boxes of programmed learning kits. My students sat in straight rows facing the chalkboard. They worked quietly and alone. I avoided group work and class discussions out of a need to set a serious tone and to keep control.

Often as many as 80 to 85% of the students in these classes were African American males—even though fewer than half the students at our school are African Americans. The castelike placement of students in remedial classes and the huge racial imbalance inspired me and other English teachers to redouble our efforts to teach the basic reading and writing skills that we believed would help get them into the academic mainstream.

Yet the students did not seem to improve in any appreciable way in our classes or throughout high school; most programmed into low-track 9th-grade English classes were still in low-track English classes in 12th grade. Why this happened, despite all our good intentions, was a revelation.

In the mid-1980s, four ninth-grade English teachers signed on to do a 2-year collaborative research study with University of California professor Rhona Weinstein, investigating ways to create success for low-achieving students. That collaboration revolutionized our theory and practice.

Reprinted with permission from the author. "The Gap Is in Our Expectations" originally appeared in *Newsday.com*, May 26, 2002, at http://www.newsday.com/news/opinion/ny-vpcon262720105may26.story.

As we analyzed our expectations for low-track ninth graders, we came to see that in giving them less challenging texts and programmed writing exercises, and in shying away from essay assignments and having them work quietly and alone, we were telling our students: "You are not thinkers, readers, and writers; your behavior needs to be controlled; you are not ready for exciting, challenging curriculum. You need to be separated from students who want to learn." We saw from our students' low attendance rate, disruptive classroom behavior, and poor school work ethic that they understood our messages and had learned to fulfill our expectations.

As veteran teachers who saw ourselves as caring women and progressive thinkers, it was painful to accept our complicity in our students' failure. We had not become teachers to create failure or to be co-conspirators in perpetuating the racial and social-class inequities that divide American society.

Our first response was to phase out tracking. Instead of being separated into low, average, fast, and honors classes on the basis of test scores, all 9th and 10th graders were programmed into heterogeneous classes, each with clusters of high, middle-, and low-achieving students. Eleventh and 12th graders could choose honors classes (many for advanced-placement college credit) or less demanding college-prep courses, but the separation went no farther than that. We also broke down the old system in which the most prestigious teachers taught the most elite classes.

While this required some program juggling, the most important changes occurred inside the classroom. Early on, I found that placing low-achieving students in a class with high achievers was not enough; I had to learn to teach differently, to meet the more varied needs of students in the same classroom. I did not come to this awareness on my own. Paula, one of the few Latinas in my first untracked advanced-placement class, pointed it out. After only a few days, Paula told me she wanted to transfer out of the class. "I can't stay," she told me, "I don't talk like these kids." This made me realize that I needed to make Paula and students like her comfortable discussing academic work: making meaning of complex texts, asking questions, sharing writing, working in groups. That was the beginning of what I call my "pedagogy of talk," in which I encourage students to get to know each other and participate in social talk so that all will feel more comfortable taking part in academic discussions later. Now they sit facing each other, not the blackboard.

The heterogeneous classes also have forced me to position myself not as a teacher of books but as one who teaches students to read books. Now I take time to teach skilled and unskilled readers, both of whom need the lesson, that reading is a social, cultural, and cognitive act that requires their active involvement. My focus is on strategies for entering a text, making meaning of it, and connecting it to life. Non-fiction works and magazine and newspaper articles help students to make these connections, as do works by writers who reflect their now more diverse cultural and racial backgrounds.

It remains a daily struggle to avoid giving in to the temptation to conclude that a student's lack of skills indicates lack of ability or that a student's lack of energy or enthusiasm means that we are failing. It helps to have colleagues who believe in what we are doing, but also the evidence is that in struggling to maintain high expectations for all students, we are succeeding in the vast majority of cases.

While English teachers have not kept quantitative data, we see a connection between untracking and the increasing percentages of our school's African American and Latino students who are meeting University of California and California State University admissions requirements. From 1991 to 1997, qualified African Americans went from 25% to 58%; Latinos went from 30% to 60%.

We see results in students like Michael, who came to ninth grade below grade level and 4 years later, bolstered by a 3.0 average and academic confidence, easily chose to work with the most high achieving students in his psychology class. Or in students like Hui who, as a ninth grader transferred out of an ESL class into an untracked ninth-grade class and as a senior enrolled in AP English and earned a 4 on the national AP examination. Or Jorge, who saw the difference between his untracked ninth-grade English class and his low-track physical science class and petitioned to get out of the science class—an experience he recounted in a moving college application essay.

We know our work is not done. Enrollment in advanced-placement classes still does not reflect the racial diversity of our student body; numbers of seniors still struggle with reading and writing and don't see themselves as students; some teachers continue to resist the idea that all students can learn with and from each other. While most departments in our school praise our work, they continue the less complicated separation of "achievers" from "nonachievers."

Unfortunately, across the country, and even in our own school system, the winds are blowing in their favor. New York and a number of other states have begun reporting standardized test scores by race. It seems that this can only lead to the segregation of low-achieving students into skills classes where their teachers can focus on improving test-taking skills. Indeed, a few months ago, our superintendent called for the reinstatement of tracked classes in 9th- and 10th-grade English. Already students are calling the classes the "smart" class and the "dumb" class or "honors" and "ghetto."

Administrators also are planning to begin remedial English/reading courses for students who score low on state tests and plan to purchase a state-approved literature series that will standardize the entire language arts curriculum.

When English teachers argued against the changes, which threaten to undo all that we have achieved, we were told that "dramatic" changes had to be made to improve district test scores. The parallels between what will happen to our students and what will happen to us are chilling: We both are to be controlled and given prepackaged materials so we can improve our test scores.

Sadly, the days are numbered in which in our English classes "gifted and talented" students sit side-by-side with social-promotion students and native English speakers next to students newly out of ESL classes, and together read *Animal Farm* and learn lessons about power.

NOTE

To learn more about Joan Kernan Cone's teaching, see Constructing Urban High School Students as Achievers" at her website, http://www.goingpublicwithteaching. org/jcone/

CHAPTER 15

"And Justice for All": Using Writing and Literature to Confront Racism

Griselle M. Diaz-Gemmati

I was beginning my 10th year as an educator. I smile as I remember entering this school for the first time; my very first teaching assignment. I recall my apprehension. A Latina teacher in an Anglo neighborhood, hired to teach a handful of bused kids in a Spanish bilingual program that spanned Grades 1 through 8. The school's community is in a White neighborhood at the edge of the Chicago city limits. It is a place that borders and looks like the suburbs, but is within the city limits and gives the city's police and firefighters the job's required city address. I was insecure and inexperienced, but determined.

I overlooked the often inadequate and sometimes nonexistent materials, the makeshift classroom, and the school clerk's bigoted rudeness. Resourcefulness soon replaced my fears. My bilingual program became a working reality of a multiage, student-directed curriculum.

I dreaded the moment when my kids left my classroom and entered the mainstream student population; it was then that I saw a rekindled look of apprehension and fear in their eyes. I taught them how to stand, but I could not follow through to watch them run.

Three years after I first walked into the school, I told the principal that I would be interested in the newly vacated eighth-grade teaching position, and he agreed to place me in a regular classroom. But the old feelings of uneasiness assaulted me once more. What would the community think? What would they say about a Latina teacher taking over the eighth-grade class?

"And Justice for All: Using Literature to Confront Racism" by Giselle M. Diaz-Gemmati originally appeared in *Inside City Schools: Investigating Literacy in Multicultural Classrooms* by Sarah Warshauer Freedman, Elizabeth Radin Simons, Julie Shalhope Kalnin, Alex Casareno, and the M-CLASS Teams, 1999, Chapter 3, pages 57–76. Reprinted with permission.

Surprisingly, it was not the community that had misgivings about my ability, but my own faculty, the people I considered my colleagues. They were a group of very traditional Anglo teachers who had about 100 years of teaching experience among them. Some were bold enough to ask me outright if I was qualified to teach typical subjects in a "regular" classroom.

My apprehension developed into a passion for success. Their trepidation became my motivation. That was 6 years, 12 teachers, and 3 principals ago. Again I had withstood challenge and did not fail.

I was awakened from my ruminations by my eighth graders sauntering into the classroom. Although it was the 2nd day of the new school year, I knew each of them well. I had been their seventh-grade teacher the previous year. My new principal and I were concerned about this group. They had been subjected to a parade of teachers during their fifth and sixth grades. They were not cooperative; they lacked motivation, and they took no initiative. We decided that I should follow them for 2 years to see what impact, if any, I could have on them academically and emotionally. The risk paid off. This class was becoming a cohesive group of adolescents who were well liked by the entire faculty. I had grown attached to them and was glad that my opportunity to embark on a research project included this particular group.

THE QUESTION AND THE CONTEXT

I began my research by asking a specific, and I thought noncontroversial, question: What happens when adolescent students begin to explore the themes of racism and prejudice as they discuss and write about literature? Specifically, can they separate how they feel from what they have heard from their family, friends, and communities?

Before I relate our story, I would like to share some information about my kids. My class consisted of 33 students—19 girls and 14 boys. Of this total, 21 were bused from inner-city schools. The class's median age was 13.8. The ethnic demographics of my group were 15 African Americans (of these, 1 had a Latino parent and another had a European American parent), 10 European Americans, 6 Latinos, 1 Asian American (who had 1 European American parent), and 1 student of East Indian heritage. I used a combination of school records and student's self-labels to identify them ethnically. The class's reading abilities, according to standardized test scores, ranged from the latter part of 4th grade to the beginning of 11th grade.

My class was part of a unique school of 260 students, with one grade per class and one class per grade. The school is a microcosm of the idealistically integrated community of the future. Our realm encompasses students in a beautiful blend of colors and cultures, including a small number of special education and physically challenged students.

We are an urban school set in an open nine-acre campus on the northwest edge of the city. All of our students love the sprawling grass playgrounds where softball, soccer, football, and basketball games are played simultaneously. For our bused children, who make up about 48% of the school population, the setting contrasts sharply with the black-topped, gang-ridden, fenced-in playgrounds of many schools in their neighborhoods. I enjoy the opportunity to watch the students play with their schoolmates on self-chosen teams during the daily 15-minute morning recess or 45-minute lunch break.

Of three neighborhood public schools in this northwest area of the city, ours is the only one that is truly, and according to federal law, desegregated. The immediate neighborhood at first did not look at our integration with favor. Yet our nine acres were our sheltered zone, our paradise. It seemed to work. The kids were getting along. Their fights seemed to be the minor rumblings of dubiously scored points, ignored rules, or rowdy games of "Johnny Tackle" rather than directed racial instances.

As the eighth-grade teacher, I relish the task of putting the finishing touches on all who graduate from our school. I try to assure my students that their final year of elementary school will be not only enlightening and challenging, but memorable. It's a teacher's utopia. I consider it an advantage to be able to work with these ethnically diverse children from varying socioeconomic levels, with different children brought together in one place to work, study, play, and coexist during their grammar school years.

I embarked on my journey of teacher research with a single focus. I wanted to showcase my kids—a group of 33 fabulous adolescents who had responded enthusiastically to a literature-based, student-directed curriculum. Before me, I had all the ingredients of a thousand success stories. I initiated my research certain that it was going to be effortless. I actually believed that all I would need to do was state what I thought was the obvious. I held fast to the belief that all children can overlook their physical, ethnic, and cultural differences, if all the conditions for learning are just so. I truly believed that if they were provided with a nonpartisan, caring, and safe environment anything was possible. As I look back to the beginning of my study, I wonder, was this my reality, or was it all an illusion?

The rude awakening that my students and I experienced as a result of my research caused havoc in our classroom, on our playground, in our homes, in our communities. I find it difficult and agonizing to talk about our transition. Truthfully, the mere thought of committing the story to paper leaves me raw and emotionally depleted. I could not begin to narrate our experience without first admitting to feeling like an imbecile. How could I not have detected the snags in this magical, imaginary fabric I had woven? What was I thinking? Seeing? Ignoring?

LITERATURE CIRCLES

I'll begin by providing some information about how my classes work. First, to establish a student-directed reading environment, I organize an individualized literature program. All students are responsible for selecting their own novels. They keep a log of what they have read and a journal in which they react to and critique what they are reading. They also are responsible for reporting their reading progress to the members of their literature group. Because our school offers its teachers extended class periods, I can provide a daily 20- to 25-minute sustained silent reading time. We have a reading rug where students can sit or lie down on throw pillows they have brought from home, as they read silently. I want them to get comfortable and relaxed when they read. I believe that this atmosphere fosters a pleasant and inviting attitude toward what the students once believed was a tedious task.

Literature discussions usually take place two to three times a week. The literature groups consist of five to seven members of varying reading abilities. I make sure that the members of each literature circle contain both boys and girls, from different ethnic groups, with varied reading skills and interests. Sometimes I choose their groups, and sometimes I help them with their choice. Each circle is responsible for selecting a scribe and a leader. The scribe records in the group's journal what each of the members is reading and the group members' reactions to each piece of literature. The leader prompts each member to talk about different literary aspects of the book, such as character analysis, setting, plot, and the like.

The literature leader keeps everyone's comments to a specific time limit, usually no more than 3 to 5 minutes, and briefs the entire class on the discussions that have taken place during his or her meeting. Responsibilities shift every 2 weeks or so to assure that everyone gets an opportunity to be a leader and a scribe. Since five literature circles meet at once, I go from one to the next as an observer and as a member, not as a supervisor. I really get a charge from listening to my students discuss literature from different perspectives and watching them attempt to substantiate their opinions with passages from their novels. When I am part of the group, I share my reactions to whatever novel I happen to be reading and relate my reactions to the author's writing. My students feel empowered by the ability to choose what they read.

Once the independent reading workshop becomes part of our daily routine, I initiate class novels into the program. The routine for reading a class novel is the same as for independent reading, except that now everyone reads the same novel. Reading the same piece of literature helps the class build an intellectual community as we share common reading experiences. We get to know and discuss characters we all are familiar with. Together we interpret the same dialogues and discuss the structure of a commonly known plot. I still assign independent reading for homework. The record keeping for both readings remains entirely the responsibility of the individual student.

To assist the students with the choice of a class novel, I present them with a list of prospective paperbacks on the same general theme as well as a brief synopsis of each of the suggested titles. The students then select the novel by a majority vote. Usually they elect to read something I recommend, but there are times when they negotiate with me to select a book they've heard about that isn't on my list.

To understand what happens when my adolescent students explore themes of racism and prejudice as they discuss and write about literature, I wanted my class to read two novels, *To Kill a Mockingbird* (Lee, 1960) and *Roll of Thunder, Hear My Cry* (Taylor, 1978), both of which deal with racial prejudice, but from different perspectives. I had read *To Kill a Mockingbird* years before and was haunted for weeks by its poignancy. Scout, the main character and narrator, is a prepubescent girl who is not afraid to speak her mind. Her relationship with her father is unique, and at several junctures in the novel, she flagrantly opposes her father's opinions. Scout is one of two children in a one-parent family, something I felt many of my students could relate to. I was also intrigued by the subtle understanding that the nucleus and mother figure in this White family was their Black maid, Calpurnia. I planned to use class discussions, student journals, audio recordings of literature circle discussions, student writing assignments, and written reflections of what I observed in class as the data for my research.

READING *TO KILL A MOCKINGBIRD*

I first initiated a strong campaign to kindle interest in *To Kill a Mocking-bird*. I lobbied for my choice by announcing to the class, "There's this novel I've read about a man who gets accused of rape. At his trial, all evidence points to his innocence. It becomes increasingly obvious to the reader that this accused man is physically incapable of committing this horrendous act of violence."

"What happens to him?" asked Nick.

"Well," I answered, "I'd rather you read the book to find out."

The class emitted a mixture of moans and chuckles.

"Mrs. Gemmati!" smiled Melissa, "Why do you do us like that? OK, I'm curious, where's this book?"

After 2 years with the same class, I felt that I had a good understanding of their group dynamics. Still, I did not want the students to feel as if they were forced into reading the novel, so I had an alternate plan. Had I felt strong resistance, I planned to organize a group of interested students to read the novel and derive my research data from their responses and reactions. I knew that the ideal situation was to have the entire class participate, but I would not have compromised my integrity or risked the students' trust. Fortunately, though, the whole group was eager to begin with *To Kill a Mockingbird*. After the paperbacks were distributed, I let the kids skim through them for a while, encouraging them to read the back cover. Some asked me questions about the time in history when this story takes place. We talked informally about the South, especially after the Civil War. We discussed mockingbirds. We reviewed and shared our general knowledge about Alabama.

I deliberately focused at first on injustice rather than on racial preju-dice. I wanted my students to arrive, if they ever did, at the topic of racism by themselves.

After their initial reading assignments, the students' enthusiasm to read *To Kill a Mockingbird* varied. Some were hesitant to start such a "fat" book; others waded through its heavy metaphoric descriptions as if trying to sprint through water, but ultimately, the animated discussions that started coming from the literature circles were well worth these early difficulties.

Initially, everyone was on equal footing. Everyone seemed to pick apart the literal meaning of the words and phrases in the reading assignments. During class discussions, we explained the descriptions of Maycomb to each other. Some of the metaphors Lee uses were taken quite literally by some students. When we discussed the description "tired old town," I was amused to discover that some children envisioned a town of elderly people.

The Race Issue Surfaces

Then something altered the discussions. I happened to be sitting in on a circle discussion when a major disagreement erupted between two of my top students. The word *nigger* offended the White students in the circle much more than the Black students. Shelly, who is White, brought up this point in the discussion. In not so many words, she let her circle know that it was one of those words everyone knew, but did not use. Nancy, who is Black, resented Shelly's taking offense.

"I don't see what your problem is," she sarcastically responded to Shelly. "No one ever called you guys nothing but 'Master.'"

Shelly insisted, "Doesn't it bother you to see that vulgarity in print?"

"No, why should it?" retorted Nancy. "We know where we come from."

At this point I asked Nancy if she or people she knew addressed each other by the term *nigger* and how she felt about it.

"It don't bother us. We know we mean no harm by it."

"Then why does it tick you off when I get offended by it?" Shelly persisted.

"It takes on a different meaning coming from you," Nancy snapped.

I was perplexed. I felt that it was one of those things that many people wondered about, yet never vocalized for fear of being misinterpreted. Shelly did not possess the inhibition I felt. I asked Nancy to explain what she meant by her remark, "It takes on a different meaning coming from you."

She thought for a moment before she replied, "Mrs. Gemmati, it's like different. If my mama is complaining about her boyfriend and calls him an ass, that's OK. But if I call him an ass, she gets all over me. It's like that."

Still, Shelly refused to give ground. "It's like using a swear word."

"It depends who's doing the swearing!" Nancy shot back.

The battle lines were drawn. Others joined the fray. Soon the group was talking at rather than to each other. The rest of the discussion volleyed back and forth around the conjecture that the word *nigger* was a White man's way of ensuring the imposed lower status of the Black man. It also touched upon how some Blacks refer to each other as *nigger* without offense because they share common ground. I sat back dumbfounded. Being neither Black nor White, I felt inept at defusing the mounting tension. Yet I knew exactly what Nancy was talking about. I too used nuances with relatives and close friends that would take on an abrasive tone if used by someone other than a Puerto Rican.

The bell reverberated in the hallway, but no one paid attention. The discussion was becoming a heated argument. I felt that I had to intervene. I knew the issue was unresolved, but there was no getting them past this one point without appearing to side with one person or the other. I uneasily shooed them out to recess. A heavy tension lingered in the room for the rest of the morning. The final entry in my journal that day was, "God, what have I gotten us into?"

My drive home felt unusually long that evening. The discussion from Nancy and Shelly's literature circle was on constant replay in my mind. I couldn't drown it out. My resolve to do something about it was over-whelming. A strong part of my personality consists of being nonconfronta-tional. This was uncomfortable territory, and I didn't enjoy finding myself in this predicament. I wanted to discuss my situation with someone and thought of contacting some of my teacher friends but was apprehensive about their reactions. After quite a bit of deliberation, I decided to keep this incident to myself.

I arrived at school early the next morning. The previous night's fitful sleep did nothing to enhance my usual grouchy morning disposition. I lis-tened to my voice making the morning announcements. It sounded terse. The students seemed edgy. Was I imagining this tension, or was it really still there?

The morning's opening activities went on as usual. Larry collected the lunch orders, Maria passed out journals, José took attendance, Freddy watered the plants, Shelly vacuumed the reading rug. The rest of the stu-dents talked among themselves as is their custom. When the chores were done, we quieted down to start writing in our personal journals. Twice I attempted to write. Nothing came. The stark white page dared me to write about my inner turmoil. I couldn't. I said a silent prayer and stood up to start the class.

"Today I'd like you to help me do a word cluster." The exercise was not new to the class. I often use this procedure to introduce new vocabu-lary. I find it can help the kids understand words or phrases in context and individually. The students' stirrings told me that they were fishing in their desks for their thesauruses and dictionaries. "Put them away," I an-nounced over my shoulder as I turned toward the blackboard. "You'll only need your honest opinions and beliefs for this cluster." I printed the word *stereotype* on the board. The class sat strangely still for a few moments. The members of Nancy and Shelly's literature group silently stared at the word. Other hands around them shot up.

"A belief about something."

"A notion."

"A judgment."

The chalk in my hand tap danced as I hurriedly wrote their responses on the blackboard.

"Is a stereotype good or bad?" I prompted.

"Bad!" was their chorused reply.

"Why?" I attempted to look directly at each of them in turn as I spoke.

"Because," Nancy spoke for the first time that morning, "it's like saying all blondes are dumb." Shelly's head flew up and her icy blue glare bore into Nancy's face.

Fearing a repeat of yesterday's heated discussion, I quickly wrote the word *prejudice* next to our first cluster.

"OK, now let's cluster this word." Did my voice sound as tense as I felt?

"White."

"Black."

"Hispanic."

"Hindu."

"Chinese."

Again I hurriedly wrote on the board. After a moment, I stood still, with my back toward the class. I ignored the names of the other ethnic groups that were shouted out. Ultimately, the room settled into an uneasy silence.

"What," I asked, still facing the blackboard, "do any of these ethnic groups have to do with the meaning of the word *prejudice*?" I slowly turned to face a group of kids I thought I knew.

"Blacks hate Whites."

"Whites hate everyone," someone abruptly countered.

"The word in question is not hate!" I snapped harshly. Again I tried to look directly into each of their faces. The strained tone of my voice did not elicit any other comments or responses. I felt they had plenty to say, yet I knew that the general tone of their answers was not conducive to a productive discussion.

Thinking I might be able to diffuse some of the tension by stopping the whole-class discussion, I said automatically, "Get in your literature circles, and cluster the word *prejudice* with your groups." Divide and conquer. Was that what I wanted to do?

As was my usual practice for my teacher research when students worked in groups, I went around to each group to set up tape recorders. The last thing I wanted to do was interfere or disrupt their discussions. I did not want my presence to infuse their answers with whatever responses they'd think I would want. As I later listened to the tapes of their circle discussions, I felt like an intruder. I felt as if I were eavesdropping on something confidential, something personal.

Their discussions that morning bounced back and forth for nearly half an hour. I asked each group to instruct its scribe on precisely what the members wanted to report to the whole class. I hoped that this impromptu system of channeled reporting would harness some of the negative energy that threatened to ignite my classroom.

Issues on the prejudice of gender, age, religion, race, and roles surfaced in these class reports. In a fervent circle discussion, Allen, a Black student, helped everyone realize a very important truth.

"Today's society," he reasoned, "makes us be prejudiced against each other." He stood up to emphasize his point when the others in the circle told him he was way off base.

"If you see a big guy," he directed his comments to the girls in his circle, "with a black, bulky leather jacket, face not shaved, funny-looking eyes, earrings on, hands in his pockets, walking over in your direction when you on a street, and it's getting dark and you alone, don't tell me you ain't going to be scared. You going to imagine the worse, and you going to try to get out of his way. Right?"

The group did not respond.

"Hell," he continued, "even the cops say we should report stuff like that . . . call if we see anybody suspicious. Who gets to define suspicious? Our prejudices!"

Not one person countered Allen's argument. They felt he had a valid point.

For a while the scribes, holding true to our literature circle procedure, kept personal attacks at bay. Although the intensity of the students' convictions ebbed slightly during our attempts at proper classroom etiquette, it flowed just as profusely beneath the surface of our decaying facade.

BACK TO THE NOVEL, AND THE ARGUMENT

In *To Kill a Mockingbird*, the attitude of White townspeople toward Blacks and those who helped Blacks sparked heated exchanges in literature circles. I tried to put everything in a historic perspective by having my students research the Jim Crow practices. I also attempted to explain the social, economic, and moral climate of the South after Reconstruction. I by no means tried to assuage the feelings of frustration the class felt when they realized the way the Blacks were regarded and treated. The students could not comprehend the flagrant disregard for human dignity the White townspeople displayed toward the Blacks.

Alas, common ground! Everyone agreed that the treatment of Blacks in the South during that period of history was deplorable. The students of color felt angry and vengeful. Their journals and writings reflected one common underlying theme—pent-up resentment. The White students felt defensive and their writings told me that they were angered and confused about their feelings.

I convinced myself that if I prompted my students to channel their energies into their reading logs and journals, I could help them deal with their anger. My strategy helped, and I watched their writings take on a new, sharper hue. They exposed themselves to me in a way that was personal, sad, and confidential. They shared dismal chunks of their lives through the silent monologue of their pens. They pressed their secrets between the sacred pages of their personal writings.

Mary, an African American girl, confessed to being afraid of fights, arguments, and confrontations. She related that her literature circle forced her to take stands on issues through combinations of unrelenting stares and uncomfortable silences. Her opinions were carefully neutral; she was afraid of being wrong. Her pent-up rage exploded several times during circle discussions, and she completely lost control. Her question to me in one journal entry will plague me forever: "Why you have to bring all this garbage into the classroom? This was the only place I could be without being made to think about stuff like who don't like who. Why you doing this to us?"

Her question pelted me with regrets. "Why was I doing this to one of the best classes I had ever had? What was I doing to them? What was I doing to me?" I wanted to cancel my commitment to the research at this juncture. After long periods of reflection, I knew I couldn't. I had pushed too far. We had heard too much. The students and I would never—could never—go back to the place we were before the project started. We needed to finish what I had started to obtain some sort of closure. It would have been cruel of me to evoke these feelings in my students and then abruptly try to reestablish the relationships we had before the research began. I continued the research, but was anxious about it.

The Gender Issue Surfaces

The accusation of rape in the novel was another burning issue during circle discussions. Once again my class divided itself into separate camps—this time the dividing factor was gender.

The issue was not whether the character Luella was raped. Obviously she wasn't. The problem was the attitude of several males in the classroom:

"If she wanted Robinson that bad, he should have done it. After all, he was convicted of the crime anyway."

This viewpoint made me seethe. The girls were angrier still. It was difficult to keep my emotions from interfering in their discussions. Many times I abruptly left a circle whenever a comment I passionately disagreed with was made. The girls brought up the issue of prejudice again.

"If a girl talks or dresses a certain way, it's your belief that she's asking to be raped if she doesn't agree to a man's advances?" Nancy was livid.

Violence Erupts

A student with a police officer in his family brought in a graphic description of a rape from an actual police report. Slowly and carefully, I tried to steer these boys clear of the ignorant, but generally accepted, assumption that rape is a crime of passion. I quietly reminded the class of the number of innocent children, including boys of all ages, who are violated or molested every year. Some male students defended their belief that the punishment for rape depended on who the victim was.

Discussions continued to volley back and forth. Shelly sarcastically reminded the boys that all female victims were someone's mother, sister, daughter. "Pray it never happens to anyone you love." Her words were tainted with acid. Some boys started mumbling among themselves.

Nancy commented that Black men in the old days were done away with for looking at a White woman, and those stupid ones who went with White women were "killed like dogs in the street." But any White man could do what he wanted to a Black woman.

I don't know what prompted Larry to say, "Joe's mother's White."

Before I knew it Larry and Joe were exchanging blows in the middle of the classroom. I watched frozen with shock as they rolled over each other on the floor. Once I could get to where the melee was taking place, I found myself incapable of separating them. Nancy appeared, as if from nowhere, and grabbed one boy from behind. They got to their feet and continued exchanging blows. Nancy somehow got one of the boys into a full Nelson while I pressed the other to the wall with all my strength.

"Go ahead," she yelled, "Kill each other off. Isn't that what we doing to ourselves? Isn't that why we have no Black brothers hanging around? How many of you got your daddy home? Black men can't discuss nothing without killing each other. No wonder we in such a sorry state."

A hush fell over the classroom. I was shocked. No one except Nancy had tried to stop the fight. I was so disappointed. Holding back tears, I barked commands at the students. Everyone was to sit absolutely still at their own seats until the bell rang. In a choked voice I told the students to ask themselves why they did nothing to help Nancy and me intervene. During the final 15 minutes of that day not one student met my furious gaze.

In the quiet aftermath of a classroom left in utter disarray, long after I heard the buses pull away from the curb, I wrote in my journal: "The violence of today's society has permeated our classroom."

A Discussion of Prejudice

The novel was finished, much to my relief. I sat and pondered the ramifications of our discussions on our class. I knew that the kids' feelings were still raw. Yet they seemed hesitant to let the issue go. I asked the class if there was some unresolved sentiment about the novel that we had not explored. One question that stirred up an animated discussion was "Were the children in the novel prejudiced?"

All in the class agreed that they were not. The students observed that the kids in the book saw the town recluse more as a mystery than anyone to be shunned. They also realized that the children believed in Robinson's innocence and supported their father's defense of him.

"Why then," I asked, "do you think that these particular children in the novel were not prejudiced when most of their neighbors and school friends were?" Subsequently, most agreed that it had to do with the children's father and upbringing. I prompted their circle discussions with questions such as "Have you ever been discriminated against?" "If so, when and why?" The obvious responses of color, nationality, and religion surfaced. When I suggested they write whatever they did not feel comfortable talking about, other responses started to trickle in.

"Some people don't like me on their team, I'm kind of slow when I run."

"Some kids say I'm ugly, my brothers do too. When they have their camera in school they don't want me in the pictures."

"Some of my friends make fun of me cause I go to LD [learning disabilities] classes. They think I'm dumb and don't want me on their science team."

Kathy, a child of White South American and Black Caribbean heritage, usually sat inert and despondent during class discussions about racial issues. No matter what type of peer pressure was exerted, she refused to comment and countered the group's questions with stony silence and hostile glares. She also wrote journal entries that carefully skirted the issue of racism, but concentrated frequently on injustice. It wasn't until I asked for this writing that I was to find out the source of Kathy's misery:

My aunt had all the family over for Easter a few years ago. When it came time to take pictures of the kids with their baskets, she asked me, my brother and my sister to step out of the way. She don't like my dad 'cause he's Black. I guess she don't like us 'cause we're not White. My cousins on my dad's side say he had to marry my mom. They make fun of me too. My mom's always depressed. My stupid sister is going with a White boy. I guess I don't ever feel like I'm going to fit anywhere, and it's not my fault. It's not fair.

"I can't be part of their group," another student wrote. "Everything they do costs money. My parents can't just hand over money for the movies or the mall. So I make believe I'm not interested in their activities. They'd make fun of me if they thought I was poor. My mom and dad would kill me if I said to someone we had to count our money twice before spending it. No one in this neighborhood is supposed to be poor."

Another student who has an Asian father and a White mother tells me, "My mom acts real cool when I have my friends come over. She even drives them home. But afterwards she says, 'Why don't you have more White friends from our own neighborhood?'"

It surprised me that this particular student checked "White" on his high school application form. I never had the courage to ask him why. Later that semester, I proofread a description of himself in a letter he wrote to a prospective mentor. He stated that he looks "slightly Asian."

I read the students' comments and saw the ugly shreds of our social fabric that are woven into their personal lives and that destroy their self-confidence. That day I saw my students as vulnerable children, carrying on their shoulders the ills of our civilized world.

The class concluded the novel with new insight and raw feelings. The general consensus was that people are taught to be prejudiced and that racism and injustice have their roots in the home. Our frank discussions and open writing, I think, helped them air some of their previously hidden feelings and helped them begin to separate their opinions from those of their parents. Some of the students told me about a commercial that they had seen on television. In it, the first scene is of bassinets with newborns of different ethnic origins. Then the camera fades into a panorama of a graveyard. The narrator at this point says: "In our world, these shouldn't be the only two places where people don't care who's next door. Stop racism now." The students continued to worry, however, that there really were few cures. To quote Kathy, "Words are cheap. Actions come too late after the hurt has been done."

I asked the children to explain if affirmative action and civil rights have helped ease the division of the races. All agreed they had to a great extent, but that there is still much to accomplish. Most concluded, however, that they were just kids and were subjected to following rules and not making them. They had no choice but to accept the fact that their parents and the adults in their lives constantly exposed them to preconceived beliefs about racism and prejudice.

One journal entry states: "It is not easy to tell my dad not to call some of my friends Spics. He's my dad. He gets mad when I tell him not to say things like that. He's the boss. What he says goes."

I knew that I would never be able to answer their questions, or assuage their fears. Their pain was real and intense. They were hesitant to drop the issue, and I was terrified to continue. Yet I wanted this decision to be their call. I felt as if I no longer was directing the orchestra, but that the music was directing us.

Reading *Roll of Thunder, Hear My Cry*

The next novel I had in mind, Mildred Taylor's *Roll of Thunder, Hear My Cry*, was a mirror image of *To Kill a Mockingbird*. It was set at approximately the same time and also dealt with racial conflicts. *Roll of Thunder*, however, presents the racial conflict from the point of view of a Black child subjected to the horrors of racism in the South during the Depression, not from the point of view of White children. Taylor is a wonderful children's writer and her stories reflect the realism of a historical perspective. I proceeded with the same selection process as before, only this time the students immediately voted unanimously in favor of reading *Roll of Thunder*.

Again we started the literature circles by redefining the words *prejudice* and *racism*. This time the students' answers were not so hostile, not so combustible. I think the initial shock and reaction of talking about something that's always present, yet avoided, had worn off. They logically concluded, in one circle, that prejudice "is the result of preconceived judgments dictated by certain behaviors in the home and society." I was not only impressed; I was proud.

Issues of discrimination again surfaced, catapulted by certain issues in the novel. One of these issues surfaced when the Black children in the novel received used textbooks from the White schools; the textbooks were tattered and torn. One of the Black children in the story questioned why they had to learn from these old used-up books. We learned that it was the accepted practice in the South to give unusable materials to the "Nigra" schools. This fact brought on a new discussion of the "separate but equal" ruling.

We researched and examined the *Brown v. Board of Education* case and dissected and discarded the separate-but-equal practice as a Band-Aid cure for a social malignancy. We reviewed and applauded Rosa Parks's courageous and nonviolent stand against bigoted laws.

Some children asked older relatives if they remembered the "Whites Only" drinking fountains and rest rooms. Recollections of these times lived by grandparents and great-aunts were the topic of discussion for the entire morning. Horror stories of midnight lynchings and cross burnings were told again and again. Allen told a story he had heard about a neighbor of his great-aunt's in Mississippi who had been set on fire for supposedly stealing something from a White man's field. Allen's story made *Roll of Thunder* more real, more atrocious.

One part of the novel graphically describes the physical condition of a Black man set on fire by a posse of Klan members because he had allegedly looked at a White woman with a "degree of undisguised lust." The students compared this incident with Tom Robinson's trial in *To Kill a Mockingbird*. The circumstances and outcomes were similar, but as Allen put it, "Robinson had a White lawyer protecting him. It did nothing but buy him some time. This guy here had nothing but his words, and a Black man's word ain't worth nothing."

Nancy continued, "He was set on fire to set an example and make others afraid. I'm sure that if they wanted him dead they would have lynched him in the woods. They needed to send a message to the other Black folk that this could also happen to you. They had to spread fear, to intimidate."

All my students were disturbed by the fact that the Black children in the novel were expected to walk miles each day to school, while daily they were passed by a bus full of White kids going in the same direction. Their walks to school included being the object of humiliation as the White bus driver tried to run the children off the road and into muddy embankments.

Desegregation and Busing

At this point I asked the students to try to identify the improvements that they felt have occurred in public education since that time. I asked them how they would try to ensure that all children received a similarly effective public education. The majority of their answers revolved around the need for the improvement of school facilities and the communities that surround them. Busing and integration, however, were the issues that reopened the proverbial can of worms. I was once again faced with an explosive issue with my classroom of both bused and neighborhood kids.

"Now minorities can get into colleges and jobs first just because of what they are." Shelly spoke without malice. The bused students, I detected, took offense at her statement.

"And if they are the token, they better watch their back, and they got to work twice as hard as their White peers." Nancy's words were spat out like rounds from a machine gun. Their target was obvious. Shelly seemed to gear up for another confrontation.

"Whites are just trying to play catch-up for all the years of inequality. They owe us." Kathy reasoned out loud, before Shelly could answer.

Larry commented next,

> Who's kidding who? Yeah, so we come to this nice clean school in a White neighborhood. Who are the ones standing on the street corner in the early morning, in the rain and the snow and in the cold to catch the bus while most of the kids from around here are still in bed? You ever heard of a White kid being bused to our neighborhood? The Whites gave us rides to school all right, away from our own. Every time we try to get a piece of what the Whites got, it backfires on us. They fix it so we are pissed, and then they can say, "Hey, ain't this what you wanted?" We always gonna be wrong, no matter what we get.

All the bused kids nodded their heads in agreement with Larry's comment. Not one of them had been spared the frustration of waiting for late buses during inclement weather.

Allen spoke slowly, deliberately, "Yeah, we come here and see all the stuff our neighborhood ain't. It's just like the textbooks that the Black kids got in the book. Our neighborhood's like that. We get the leftovers, the areas no one else wants."

I asked the group, "Do you feel that the environment here or the environment of your home school is more comfortable for you?" I wanted them to be specific, and I wanted substantiated answers. I did not want the class discussion to turn into an "Oh I'm so grateful I'm here" testimony. I asked the class to name specific examples of the pros and cons of busing, on the students' being bused and on the schools' receiving them. As I expected, the cons outweighed the pros. Some of the most indisputable reasons were the following:

"All our neighborhood friends are scattered all over. We all go to different receiving schools. The kids from here stay together. They grow together."

"I leave this place at 3:15, so I guess this place is integrated from 9:00 to 3:15, Monday to Friday, September to June, excluding all holidays."

"If the neighborhood kids want to stay for the after-school programs and social center, they just walk back to school. If we want to stay we need an act of Congress, a way to get home after dark, a White family that will take us home with them until the activities start and three notes from our momma. It ain't worth all that."

"It is fine if one of the neighborhood kids learn to speak Spanish. Wow, how smart! How intelligent! But we're expected to learn English. Our Spanish ain't so smart. If we don't learn to speak like them, we're dumb."

One of the neighborhood kids asked if the bused kids felt just a little safer here, rather than in their neighborhood schools.

"Sure, but you better run like hell when those buses let you off in front of the home school. Then we got to walk the rest of the way to our house. Sometimes the gangs are there waiting for us to beat us up. At times it's like we're delivered right to them. It ain't all the time but it happens often enough."

The issues they mentioned as pros were touching:

"I've made some good friends."

"I see the kind of neighborhood I want my kids to grow in."

"I met Mrs. Gemmati."

"We do stuff like this—reading novels that kids in other schools don't do. We kinda have a say in things here."

One neighborhood student spoke up. "We don't have it all so great here. Some of the kids from this neighborhood that go to private schools won't talk to us because we talk to you."

Another neighborhood kid continued. "Yeah, they chase us and throw rocks at us, and if we are caught around their house, they try to beat us up because we go to this school. Because there's minorities at this school."

"The people around here don't care how good you are or what you do, and it ain't only the kids; they'd hate Mrs. Gemmati too because she's Puerto Rican."

The moment this was said, a hush permeated the classroom. All eyes turned toward me. I tried to remain unfazed but I felt yanked out of my neutral zone. I now was categorized, labeled, seen differently. I was no longer just the teacher. I was not one of the "sides" I had so desperately tried to stay out of. I hoped that this was the wedge necessary for me to help them realize that they needed to look at a person's qualities first and foremost.

I tried to ask for reasons for their persecution other than being members of our school. None were offered. The bused kids promised to help the neighborhood kids "show these bigots a lesson." I saw a subtle change in the kids toward the end of that particular discussion. I saw them bond, if only temporarily, against a common enemy.

Back to the Novel

The theme of inequality again was analyzed and cast as a result of racial prejudice. They discussed the fact that in *Roll of Thunder*, Cassie's family was targeted more than others because they had the distinction of being landowners. The students arrived at the conclusion that the Whites were uncomfortable with Blacks who had the potential for material equality—especially as landowners. Ultimately, at the end of the book, the students felt torn. They realized that Cassie's father had deliberately set his crop on fire to distract and ultimately stop the lynching of a neighbor's son. They knew that this crop was the only thing the family counted on to pay the taxes on their land. The students concluded that the family would either have to sell part of their land or lose it outright. They also knew that the boy who was saved from the lynching would now stand trial for the murder of a White man and would be convicted because of the improbability of a fair trial due to his color.

The children had a hard time dealing with the author's decision at this juncture. They compared the ending of *To Kill a Mockingbird* to this one and agreed that it was possible in *Roll of Thunder* for the Black family to keep the land their White neighbors so desperately wanted. "Their decision was a poor one," most maintained. "The kid couldn't be saved anyhow. What was the point?"

"Cassie's dad was faced with choosing between his beliefs and convictions, and the land that had been his since birth. He chose what he believed in," I announced quietly.

"Is that what you want from us, Mrs. Gemmati?"

"What's that?" I asked Shelly.

"You know, to let go of the stuff we see at home and make up our own minds about prejudice?"

Shelly's assumption took me by surprise. I literally had no idea that this was what I had unknowingly conveyed. I smiled at this group of students that I loved unconditionally.

"No," I responded. "What I want is not the issue. It's what you feel is right that's important. If I ask you to follow my convictions, I am doing no better than the person who tells you to believe that all Blacks are bad, that all Whites are racists, or that all Hispanics are ignorant and loud. I strongly believe that the way to end prejudice is to stop taking another's judgment as your own. Don't let someone else prejudge for you."

The abrupt ending to the novel left them wanting answers and solutions to the problems we discussed. The novel tied no loose ends.

I attempted to explain that society's ills nowadays were the same yet different. One of the kids brought up the case of the Rodney King beating, and the subsequent beating of the truck driver during the ensuing riots in Los Angeles. Another student brought up the Jeffrey Dahmer case. All his victims were minorities.

"I wonder if the police would have returned that last Asian boy to Dahmer if the kid was White and Dahmer was the minority." Larry's comment surprised everyone.

An animated discussion on many "what ifs" followed. I sat back and listened. Their logic was, I thought, beyond their years.

CONTINUING TENSION

My eighth graders have read their novels. The discussions, writings, and responses to literature in the format I established for the research dramatically changed our class.

Our feelings are still somewhat coarse, our nerves still exposed. These kids no longer tiptoe around issues of race. In many cases, the issue of race became the stated reason for even the most inconsequential verbal exchanges. Unfortunately, the following type of conversation became quite common in our classroom:

"Let me have a pen."

"Don't have another one."

"You won't let me have one 'cause I'm White. You think I should have my own pen. If I were Black, you'd lend me one. You're a racist."

"I don't care what color you are, girlfriend, I ain't got another pen."

"Why," I asked Nancy's literature circle a few days later, "haven't you ever discussed how these racial differences bothered you before?"

"They always were there, Mrs. Gemmati," she answered, "we just never acted on what we thought."

"Explain."

"It's like how do you act in church? Or in a library? Or when your mamma has company over? You don't act the same as when someone's there watching you, or when you're home and your mamma ain't there."

I knew exactly what she meant. I've become very sensitive about bringing up issues in class that could eventually lead to further rifts among what I once thought was a close-knit group of kids. Ignorance seems to be bliss and safe, but can I truly affect the lives of my students by reciting prerehearsed lines on a make-believe stage? Do I want to defer these discussions of race and prejudice to dark alleys that are constantly punctuated by the sound of gunfire? Do I let the neighborhood children continue to be steeped in the smog of superiority that is so choking and prevalent? It was an armor of racism that my students had been dressed in during their years of upbringing, one that was difficult to dent. I did find clues, hints maybe, that the confusion, frustration, and ordeal of adolescence was bleeding into another issue—the questioning of their parents' beliefs about different nationalities, races, and religions. As the year progressed, they wrote in their journals:

"I don't know how long he's [Dad's] felt that way [about others], but lots of things he grew up with ain't even around anymore. The movies ain't a dollar, and damn ain't considered a swear word."

"So what if I bring home someone who isn't Black. If that person loves me and respects me and doesn't do me wrong, why should I refuse him for a Brother who sells on the corner and is a player?"

"Why does she [Mom] call them rag heads? God, that pisses me off. How would she of felt if her Jewish grandfather married another Jew instead of her grandma? She isn't the puritanical Protestant she acts on Sunday all the rest of the week."

"I don't care if my dad says we have to stick to our own. If someone doesn't try to move into more decent places and show other people we ain't the loud and dirty Spics they say we are, how are they going to know different? Someone has to cross over to other neighborhoods and show that we want the same things they do."

The year was ending and I still did not feel closure with my students on these issues of prejudice. Their attitudes were shifting but their sense of one another was still fragile. I believed that the children felt this way too.

COMING BACK TOGETHER

We were slated to go on the eighth-grade school trip to Washington, and after our difficult year, the trip began to seem more of a necessity than an option. A few days away from school, parents, teachers, books, and students in other grades seemed like the perfect cure for what felt like a nagging cough. I figured if we didn't bond after being on a bus for umpteen hours and sharing sleeping quarters, there would be no hope.

Interestingly, the tension seemed to dissipate the farther we got from Chicago. As some kids dozed off, others left their groups to form new ones with those who remained awake. We talked about everything and nothing. The boundaries that identified us as people from specific places and with distinct roles got fuzzier and fuzzier. By the time we reached Philadelphia, we seemed to be one group of people, from Chicago, eager to spend uncurfewed time with one another. We cared about each other's luggage, comfort, and likes. We cared.

The tours of Washington were important, yes, and of course educational. But what I was looking at was more than the monuments that mark our country's growth. I was seeing in my students the behavior that is displayed when children are allowed to follow their basic friendly instincts—without worrying about approval or criticisms of whom they speak to or whom they hang around with.

On the last night before our long bus ride back to Chicago, my student teacher came banging on my door late at night. She was on the verge of hysteria, and it was a good long minute before she could inform me that a group of the kids had not returned to their rooms yet. She had fallen asleep and some of the kids had sneaked out. Just as I was about to dial the hotel security, Melissa ran into my room yelling that Nancy wouldn't answer the door, no matter how hard she banged on it. I dropped the phone and hurried down the hall. I yelled, I screamed, I kicked, but no one answered the door. I had my student teacher run down to the lobby to get a master key. I shuddered as the security guard opened the door.

The scene inside the room was incredible. Pop cans and popcorn were scattered everywhere, the TV was blaring, and about 15 of my students were asleep fully clothed, minus their shoes, which were piled up in a corner, fermenting. The kids were in an array of sleeping positions. Multicolored legs and arms were tangled everywhere. Nancy slowly opened her eyes and saw Shelly, Larry, Joe, and Maria sleeping on the same bed she had happened to crash on. Slowly they started to waken. They looked around and seemed surprised to find themselves in such a noisy, overcrowded room, with their teacher and a security guard standing in the doorway. I started laughing. Freddy took one look at my faded Garfield sleeping shirt, my one sockless foot and tangle of hair, and he started laughing. Pretty soon everyone was giggling at someone's sock, pointing at whomever with their thumb in their mouth, the drool coming from a half-open mouth, the weird look of half-closed eyes or disheveled hair.

The security guard looked at us as if we were truly nuts. "These your kids, Miss?"

"Yep," I answered. "Each and every one of them."

I would be lying to myself if I pretended to be the teacher I was before I had initiated this project. If anything, this research has taught me that hard talk on candid issues can take place within the safety of classroom walls. I know that a society that is free of prejudice is many, many years away, but it's something I hope to keep striving for—even if it's only the microcosm of life that constitutes my classroom.

REFERENCES

Lee, H. (1960). *To kill a mockingbird*. Philadelphia: Lippincott.
Taylor, M. (1978). *Roll of thunder, hear my cry*. New York: Bantam Books.

CHAPTER 16

Ma-Lee's Story

Gerald Campano

Long before children have any acquaintance with the idea of nation, or even of one specific religion, they know hunger and loneliness. Long before they encounter patriotism, they have probably encountered death. Long before ideology interferes, they know something of humanity.

—Martha C. Nussbaum, "Reply"

Ma-Lee was initially introduced to me as a student with low standardized test scores, in the lowest quintile band for reading, and therefore as a child in need of some form of remedial literacy intervention.[1] During the 1st month in class, Ma-Lee's silence was a felt presence. She rarely spoke, even in small groups, and when she did speak in response to questions, I felt it was out of deference to authority. She only whispered inaudibly to a classroom friend, Kari, who was also Hmong. There were several uncomfortable instances when visiting instructors mistook Ma-Lee's lack of participation as defiance and consequently reprimanded her. She would just turn her head down, cover her mouth, and fall more deeply into herself, into her silence.

On September 30, still early in the year, Ma-Lee put the following essay on my desk. We had been having some initial class discussions about the idea of culture, and this was her response, in her own words:

> My family were in Thailand for 15 years. My mom and dad were embroiders in Thailand. I was born in Thailand. I didn't know about the Thai people, but my dad said Thai people were bad. We lived in the camp, but we had U.N. serve food for my family.
>
> My parent were from Laos to Thailand. Their lives in Thailand were very hard because they had no money and enough food for us.

> My family came here because my country wast war. Vietnam took
> over so my parent can't stay there. My family immigrant in 1992.
> My family lives in U.S.A. It was very nice and so much different
> from my country,
> I feel aboutr culture is difficult for me maks me confused. I don't
> know what to be But think that I want to be both cultures.

It became immediately obvious that Ma-Lee is a thoughtful child. Far from
having a deficit, she reflects profoundly upon her family's experiences and
its implications for her present situation. Her autobiography becomes a
means of gaining a critical distance from the past while making sense of
the present. She writes and discusses with the humble (and humbling)
authority of a 10-year-old about a life that I couldn't even begin to
understand. For me, the scale of hunger, malnutrition, disease, torture,
and violence is necessarily abstract. For Ma-Lee and her family, there
is no "outside" the border, no relatively autonomous safe space, except,
perhaps, her immediate home and community. The United Nations refugee
camp becomes synecdoche for her world. She is a "foreigner" wherever
she goes; every place is a potential site of conflict and threat. Nevertheless,
under conditions of sustained duress, Ma-Lee invokes her past with
judiciousness and clarity.

The last few sentences of her essay register a note of ambivalence about
her most recent migration to *Hmong America*, a note that is not uncommon
in much of my students' work. She is grateful for the ways in which the
United States is *nice*, but at the same time feels *confused* about existing
in both cultures. I think Ma-Lee's growth in my class involved transforming these confused and ambivalent sentiments into new, more empowering
emotions and experiences. This process began with informal discussions.
I invited Ma-Lee to join an open, and flexible group of current and former
students to talk in more depth about "multiculturalism," or really any issues that were relevant to their lives.

Sometimes these occurred during regular class time, but more often we met at lunch, during recess, and before or after school. In the
liminal spaces and marginal times of the official school day, Ma-Lee
began to participate regularly. She spoke openly about her experiences
in an ongoing dialogue that I believe had a profound impact on the other
students. Together, they gained a deeper understanding of the particu-
larity of one another's stories while at the same time coming to a more
comprehensive view of their common vulnerabilities. Or rather, *through*
shared insight into suffering and struggle, they could begin to hear and

learn from one another and I from them. Toward the end of the school year, Ma-Lee began to write something surreptitiously. She did this on her own time, during whatever we were supposed to be working on. I would pretend to sneak over to take a peek, and she would cover her paper or hide it in her desk. Eventually, she handed in the following piece, fully typed and edited:

Autobiography of a Hmong Girl

I was born in Thailand. My family was not rich. They worked hard just to make us grow and survive, but they were happy to stay how they were. We lived in Lao. My mom and dad were born in Laos. That time I was not born yet. One day Vietnamese came and took over Laos. My family migrated to Thailand because they had hoped there would be no more war and poverty. My family stayed there not long. Then I was born. I remember my cousin bought me candy. She also tried to take me to school with her, but she couldn't. It was forbidden to let anyone in school until they're 8 or 9 years old. That's why I didn't go to school.

We stayed in Thailand about three years. I had 4 brothers when we were still in Thailand. When my sister was born she died; she was supposed to be the biggest in our family. When I was 3 years old we immigrated to the United States. My dad tried to take me to school, but they said, "you're too little to go to school." I was too small to go to kindergarten. So when I was five years old I went to school. I liked that school. It was the best school I ever went to. I had good friends. Their names were Ma-Lee, Jennifer, Ma-Lee, and Jennifer. My friend's names were like a pattern.

I stayed in school about five years because I started kindergarten and stayed until 4th grade. Then we moved here. When I first came to this school, I didn't like it. I said this school doesn't look like my old school. I liked my old school better. When I came to this school everyone always made fun of us and always said we were Chinese people. So I felt bad about myself. I couldn't wait to go to fifth grade. When I came to 5th grade in Mr. Campano's class I think I was very fortunate. He always made people get better or feel better about themselves. So I think my culture is the right way to be.

No matter what people said about my culture, I pretended not to hear. Now it's May 4th, 2000. I'm going to sixth grade. I'll miss my teacher. We only have about four weeks to spend time and have fun together.

Now I will tell you a little bit about my people. In our Hmong
culture we have to wake up very early to go to our garden. Even a
little girl like me has to go. You also have to sew your own clothes.
You can put red, blue, yellow or you can put any color you like. You
can go to the store to buy it, but it costs a pack of money for just one
dress, so we prefer to sew our Hmong clothes. We sewed clothes for
ourselves, but we didn't even have shoes to wear.

I want everyone to know about my life and know how to respect
my culture to make our Hmong people full of freedom. I know
someday if no one wants to go out there and talk what they believe, I
will because I don't want people to make fun of me and my culture. I
know everyone wants to live in freedom. If someday my dreams come
true, the world that I live in will always be radiant and never be dim
with prejudice.

This is what I believe in my heart.

Ma-Lee's story articulates what is deep in her heart and asserts her
desire to be heard; her autobiography demonstrates the ways in which
she organized "inchoate or confused feelings to produce an emotion that
is experienced more directly and fully" (Mohanty, 1997, p. 206). This
experience is both theoretical and political.[2] Ma-Lee achieves a more
focused and accurate understanding of the continued relevance and value
of her culture as a source of insight that could guide action. She evalu-
ates what has been meaningful to her, such as the friendships she culti-
vated in her old school, her family's former work embroidering, and her
preference to make clothes and grow food in the garden. She also discusses the obstacles of coming to the United States and is able to name
specific forms of marginalization, including the experience of having her
ethnicity be rendered invisible in the majority's eyes. At the same time,
Ma-Lee points toward a more universalistic need for everyone to *live in
freedom.*

Ma-Lee's growth in my class was at least partially predicated on our
ability to create a classroom community that would encourage the children to recognize the value of their own experiences. I also needed access
to a scholarly community that could help me interpret these very experiences. The students' narratives, and my own act of reflecting on them, have
enabled me to better "imagine," as Elaine Scarry might say, individual
children in their full "weight and solidity" (1996, p. 98). In the process, I
become more mindful of their presence under teaching and learning conditions that can be described, in all fairness, as daunting and at times dehu-

manizing. These imaginings ideally lead to alternative ways of structuring classroom space and time, different means of evaluation, new frameworks from which to recapture the past to create meanings for the present and act toward the future. Sometimes this type of work has a ripple effect outward into the school, maybe even the neighborhood, allowing the children's voices to become more audible and empowering. It was striking to me how the migrant narratives of the children were also ineluctably educational narratives, reflecting their deep cultural and emotional investments in schooling. The following year, in sixth grade, Ma-Lee's test scores rose substantially and she earned medals in a highly competitive academic pentathlon. Her story of achieving a more fully realized cultural identity was coextensive with her academic success.

But I think it's important to stay sober. There is no finality to the stories of Ma-Lee and the other children. Theirs is a ceaseless struggle. I also think about the students who remain shrouded in the mystery of their own particular histories, students who have left my class as well as the new students to arrive in the fall. These are the ones who are silent or "defiant," the ones who are disciplined or just ignored because their value is unintelligible and foreign, whose mouths remain covered because we haven't learned how to listen. Until we can work more critically and imaginatively beyond our own insular institutional and cultural boundaries, it may be best to heed one of Ma-Lee's final observations: "There is more to a person's life than can fit on paper"—and I would add, especially when these papers are our own representations of a child's success, or failure.

NOTES

1. I am writing a book and creating a web page provisionally titled *Dancing Across Borders: Creating Community with Children from Immigrant, Migrant, and Refugee Backgrounds*. It is grounded in my work as a fifth-grade teacher in a multi-ethnic neighborhood school in Stockton, California. By taking an inquiry stance into my practice, I investigate how school literacy may be deeply inflected with the students' own cultural values and put in the service of their own cares and interests. This particular narrative is from the chapter "School Literacy as Bearing Witness," where I describe how students use autobiography as a means of working through trauma.

2. For a fully developed account of the cognitive nature of "experience", see Satya P. Mohanty's foundational essay, "The Epistemic Status of Cultural Identity: On Beloved and the Postcolonial Condition," in *Literary Theory and the*

Claims of History: Postmodernism, Objectivity, and Multicultural Politics (1997) and the introduction to *Reclaiming Identity* (Moya & Hames-Garcia, 2000).

REFERENCES

Mohanty, S. (1997). *Literary theory and the claims of history: Postmodernism, objectivity, multicultural politics*. Ithaca: Cornell University Press.

Moya, P., & Hames-Garcia, M. (Eds.). (2000). *Reclaiming identity: Realist theory and the predicament of postmodernism*. Berkeley: University of California Press.

Nussbaum, M. C. (1996). Reply. In M. C. Nussbaum (Ed.), *For love of country: Debating the limits of patriotism* (pp. 131–144). Boston: Beacon Press.

Scarry, E. (1996). The difficulty of imagining other people. In M. C. Nussbaum (Ed.), *For love of country: Debating the limits of patriotism* (pp. 98-110). Boston: Beacon Press.

CHAPTER 17

Because You Like Us:
The Language of Control

Cynthia Ballenger

This chapter is the result of a year spent in conversations about teaching: difficult conversations in which I, a seasoned teacher and fledgling sociolinguist, was only rarely the informed party.[1] Mike Rose, in *Lives on the Boundary* (1989), uses the metaphor of "entering the conversation" to describe the process of learning to participate in academic discourse. In my case, there was a multitude of different conversations I was trying to enter, and in each I had a different role to play.

During that same time, I was teaching preschool, as I have done for most of the past 15 years. The school was in the Haitian community in Dorchester, Massachusetts, and primarily served the children of Haitian immigrants. I went there because in my previous work as an early childhood special education teacher I had noticed that more and more Haitian children were being referred to my class. These children were arriving attended by all kinds of concerns from the educational professionals: they were "wild," they had "no language," their mothers were "depressed." There were certainly some children I saw who had genuine problems, and yet time and time again I found that, after a period of adjustment, they were responsive, intelligent children; their mothers were perhaps homesick and unhappy in a strange, cold country, but generally not clinically depressed. During that period, however, we did make many mistakes, and I became interested in learning the Haitian culture and language in order to see the children more clearly. After a period at graduate school studying sociolinguistics, I took a position as a preschool teacher in a bilingual school where both Haitian Creole and English were spoken and where, as I came to understand, Haitian culture was quite central. I was the only teacher at this school who was not Haitian, and although by this time I spoke Creole, I was still getting to know the culture.

During that time I was one of two instructors of a course in child development that a local college offered for Haitian people who wished to work in day-care centers. My Haitian coinstructor and I designed this course based on the model of a conversation about child rearing—a dialogue between Haitians and North Americans about their attitudes on the subject. I was also a new member of the Brookline Teacher-Researcher Seminar (BTRS), a group of public school teachers and academic researchers who are attempting to develop a common language and a shared set of values with which to approach classroom issues (Michaels & O'Connor, in press; Phillips, 1991). As a graduate student in sociolinguistics, I had done research; as a teacher, I had thought about teaching; I was now involved in trying to approach issues in ways that incorporated both of these perspectives. The work that I will report on here was part of these conversations. I will try to let the reader hear some of the different voices that I heard.

In this chapter, I will discuss the process I went through in learning to control a class of 4-year-old Haitian children. Researchers who regard language as the principal vehicle by which children are socialized into their particular family and culture have consistently regarded control and discipline as central events—events where language patterns and cultural values intersect in visible ways (Boggs, 1985; Cook-Gumperz, 1973; Watson-Gegeo & Gegeo, 1990). When, as in my case, the adult does not share the same cultural background and the same experience of socialization as the children, one becomes very aware of learning how to enter and manage the relevant conversation. Although it can be argued that my participation in the events I relate here was in some ways informed by sociolinguistic theory, I present this more as a story than as a research report. This is my attempt to discuss this experience in a way that will not deny access to the conversation to those who helped form my understanding of it. I must stress, however, that all of these conversations would not have been possible if there hadn't been room in the preschool day for talk—the school was run jointly by the teachers and we spent considerable time each day together—and if there had not been some financial support for the Brookline Teacher-Researcher Seminar (Phillips, 1991). This support, in the form of small stipends, xeroxing, money for an occasional day off to reflect, and a sense of being valued, combined with the nature of the school where I was teaching, made my situation luxurious compared with that of many teachers faced with problems similar to mine.

THE PROBLEM

Having had many years of experience teaching in early childhood programs, I did not expect to have problems when I came to this Haitian preschool 3 years ago. However, I did. The children ran me ragged. In the friendliest, most cheerful, and affectionate manner imaginable, my class of 4-year-olds followed their own inclinations rather than my directions in almost everything. Though I claim to be a person who does not need to have a great deal of control, in this case I had very little—and I did not like it.

My frustration increased when I looked at the other classrooms at my school. I had to notice that the other teachers, all Haitian women, had orderly classrooms of children who, in an equally affectionate and cheerful manner, *did* follow direction and kept the confusion to a level that I could have tolerated. The problem, evidently, did not reside in the children, since the Haitian teachers managed them well enough. Where then did it reside? What was it that the Haitian teachers did that I did not do?

The group of Haitian preschool teachers whom I was teaching in the child-development course recognized the problem in their own terms. As part of the course, they were all interning in various day-care centers, some with me at the Haitian school, the majority in other centers. Many of the teachers in the other centers were extremely concerned about behavior problems. What they told me and each other was that many of the children in their centers were behaving very poorly; many felt that this was particularly true of the Haitian children. They felt that the way in which they were being instructed as teachers to deal with the children's behavior was not effective. One woman explained to me that when she was hit by a 4-year-old, she was instructed to acknowledge the anger he must be feeling, then to explain to him that he could not hit her. She told me that, from her point of view, this was the same as suggesting politely, "Why don't you hit me again?"

When I talked with Haitian parents at my school, I again heard similar complaints. From the point of view of many of the people I talked with, the behavior tolerated in their neighborhood schools was disrespectful; the children were allowed to misbehave. A common refrain in these conversations was, "We're losing a generation of children"; that is, the young children here now, who were not brought up first in Haiti, were not being brought up with the same values. However, when I asked for specific advice about things I might do to manage the children better, the teachers and I could never identify any behaviors of mine that I could try to change.

I took my problem to the Brookline Teacher-Researcher Seminar. The members of BTRS have come to share a focus on language—the language of instruction; children's language in a wide variety of situations; the language of science talk, of book talk, of conflict; and so on. Thus, in our conversations, the BTRS group encouraged me to approach my problem by discovering what it was that the Haitian teachers *said* to the children in situations where directions were being given. The seminar members have also come to believe that an important part of a research project is examining where a particular research question comes from in one's own life—why it seems important, what its value is to the teacher-researcher. In many cases, this is a matter of investigating one's own socialization, a kind of self-reflection that became an important part of my investigation.

SITUATIONS AS TEXTS

I began to write down what the Haitian teachers said to the children in situations where the children's behavior was at issue. I then carried these texts to the various conversations of which I was a part: the Haitian teachers in the child development course, the North American teachers in the Brookline Seminar, and the parents and teachers at the school where I was teaching. I will present here some texts that I consider typical in their form and content, and then share some of the responses and the thinking engendered by these texts among the people with whom I had been conversing.

I present first Clothilde's account of an event at her day-care center. Clothilde is a middle-aged Haitian woman and a student in the child-development course. She has a great deal of experience with children—both from raising her own and from caring for other people's—and many of her classmates turn to her for advice. The text below is from a conversation in which she had been complaining to me about the behavior of the Haitian children in the day-care center where she was student teaching. She felt that the North American teachers were not controlling the children adequately.

One day, as Clothilde arrived at her school, she watched a teacher telling a little Haitian child that the child needed to go into her classroom, that she could not stay alone in the hall. The child refused and eventually kicked the teacher. Clothilde had had enough. She asked the director to bring her all the Haitian kids right away. The director and Clothilde gathered the children into the large common room. The following is the text of what she told me she said to the children:

Clothilde: Does your mother let you bite?
Children: No.

Clothilde: Does your father let you punch kids?
Children: No.
Clothilde: Do you kick at home?
Children: No.
Clothilde: You don't respect anyone, not the teachers who play
    with you or the adults who work upstairs. You need to respect
    adults—even people you see on the streets. You are taking good
    ways you learn at home and not bringing them to school. You're
    taking the bad things you learn at school and taking them home.
    You're not going to do this anymore. Do you want your parents to
    be ashamed of you?

According to Clothilde, the Haitian children have been well behaved ever
since. Other Haitian teachers with whom I have shared this text have confirmed that that was what the children needed to hear. However, they also
said that Clothilde will have to repeat her speech because the children
won't remain well behaved indefinitely without a reminder.

The next text involves an incident at my school. Josiane, who has
taught for many years both here and in Haiti, was reprimanding a group of
children who had been making a lot of noise while their teacher was trying
to give them directions:

Josiane: When your mother talks to you, don't you listen?
Children: Yes.
Josiane: When your mother says, go get something, don't you go get it?
Children: Yes.
Josiane: When your mother says, go to the bathroom, don't you go?
Children: Yes.
Josiane: You know why I'm telling you this. Because I want you to
    be good children. When an adult talks to you, you're supposed to
    listen so you will become a good person. The adults here like you,
    they want you to become good children.

Finally, we have Jérémie's father speaking to him. Jérémie is a very
active 4-year-old, and the staff had asked his father for help in controlling
his behavior:

Father: Are you going to be good? (Jérémie nods at each pause)
Are you going to listen to Miss Cindy?
Are you going to listen to Miss Josiane?

Because they like you.
They love you.
Do it for me.
Do it for God.
Do you like God?
God loves you.

REFLECTING

The content and the form of these texts are different from what I, and many other North American teachers, would probably have said in the same circumstances. I shared these and other texts and observations with many parents and teachers, both Haitian and North American. I asked them to reflect with me on how these conversations were different and what underlay them. What follows is a blend of many people's observations and self-reflections, including my own. Here I want to note that I am assuming that the North American teachers, including myself, shared similar training and enculturation. Although we differed in many ways, I would characterize our culture— as Heath does in *Ways with Words* (1983)—as "mainstream culture." The Haitian teachers also shared some, although not all, values and assumptions. Although I am trying to distill these conversations in order to identify "typical" practices of Haitian or North American teachers, I do not mean to imply that all North American or all Haitian teachers are the same.

The Haitian preschool teachers had clear insights into behavior characteristic of North American teachers. Clothilde commented that the North American teachers she knows frequently refer to the children's internal states and interpret their feelings for them; for example, "you must be angry," "it's hard for you when your friend does that," and so on. Clothilde pointed out to me that in her speech she makes no reference to the children's emotions; other Haitian teachers I have observed also do not do this as a rule.

Rose, another Haitian teacher, also commented that North American teachers often make reference to particular factors in the child's situation that, in the teacher's opinion, may have influenced his or her behavior. For example, Michel, whose mother had left him, was often told that the teachers understood that he missed his mother, but that he nevertheless needed to share his toys. When a child pushes or pinches another child sitting next to him or her, many North American teachers will suggest that, if the child does not like people to sit so close, he or she should say so rather than pinch. Rose felt, and from my observation I concurred, that Haitian teachers rarely do this. Josiane suggested further that if she were concerned about an individual child and his or her particular problems, instead of articulating them for him or her, her goal would be "to make him or her feel comfortable with the group." If the child were misbehaving, she felt she would say, "You know I'm your friend," and then remind him or her that "we don't do that." In fact, I have seen her do exactly that many times, with excellent results.

These examples suggest to me a difference in focus between the North American and Haitian teachers. It seems that North American teachers characteristically are concerned with making a connection with the individual child, with articulating his or her feelings and problems. On the other hand, Clothilde, Josiane, and the many other Haitian people I spoke with and observed, emphasize the group in their control talk, articulating the values and responsibilities of group membership. For example, we have seen that both North American and Haitian teachers make reference to the family, but in different ways. North American teachers are likely to mention particular characteristics of a child's family, characteristics that are specific to that family and are seen as perhaps responsible for the child's individual actions. The Haitian teachers emphasize instead what the families have in common. The families do not differ in their desire that the children respect adults, that the children behave properly, and that their behavior not shame them. The children's answers, when they are given in unison as in Josiane's text above, present a vivid enactment of the sort of unity the Haitian teachers' approach may engender.

Another difference the Haitian teachers noted is the use of consequences. North American teachers typically present the particular consequences of an act of misbehavior. For example, I often say something like, "He's crying because you hit him," or, "If you don't listen to me, you don't know what to do." Haitian teachers are less likely to differentiate among particular kinds of misbehavior; they condemn them all, less in terms of their results than as examples of "bad" behavior. Clothilde is typical of the Haitian teachers in that the immediate consequences are not made explicit; she does not explain why she is against biting or punching. She instead refers to such behavior as "bad," and then explains to the children of the consequences of bad behavior in general, such as shame for the family. Jérémie's father simply tells Jérémie to be good, to be good for those who love him. Josiane, too, tells the children to be good because the people who like them want them to be good. I have heard other Haitian teachers refer to the impression that bad behavior would create in a passer-by, or to the necessity of modeling good behavior for younger children. But Haitian teachers rarely mention the specific consequences of particular acts, a clear difference from North American teachers.

In the Haitian texts, one has the impression that the children share the adult's understanding of what bad behavior is. Clothilde's series of rhetorical questions, like "Do your parents let you kick?" is an example of the form that many Haitian teachers adopt when addressing children about their behavior. The children understand their role without difficulty; they repeat the expected answers in choral unison. The choice of this form— that is, questions to which the answer is assumed—emphasizes the fact that the children already know that their behavior is wrong.

In the North American control situation, on the other hand, the child often appears to be receiving new information. If there is a consensus about behavior—certain behavior is bad, certain other behavior is good—we don't present it this way. North Americans frequently explain the consequences of particular actions as if they were trying to convince the child that there was a problem with his or her behavior. As presented in school, misbehavior is considered wrong not because of anything inherent in it, but because of its particular consequences, or perhaps because the behavior stems from feelings that the child has failed to identify and control.

These differences, as I came to recognize them, seemed significant enough to account for some of the difficulties I had been experiencing in my classroom. But what to do about them?

PRACTICE

With the overwhelming evidence that these children were used to a kind of control talk other than what I had been providing, I have since begun to adopt some of the style of the Haitian teachers. I assume that I am not very good at it, that I have no idea of the nuances, and I continue to include many of the ways I have typically managed behavior in my teaching. Nevertheless, I have developed a more or less stable melange of styles, and my control in the classroom has improved significantly. In addition, I find that I love trying out this Haitian way. I was struck by an experience I had the other day, when I was reprimanding one boy for pinching another. I was focusing, in the Haitian manner, on his prior, indisputable knowledge that pinching was simply no good. I also used my best approximation of the facial expression and tone of voice that I see the Haitian teachers use in these encounters. I can tell when I have it more or less right, because of the way that the children pay attention. As I finished this particular time, the other children, who had been rapt, all solemnly thanked me. They were perhaps feeling in danger of being pinched and felt that I had at least been effective. This solemn sort of response, which has occurred a few other times, gives me the sense that these situations are very important to them.

The following anecdote may suggest more about the way in which these interactions are important to the children. Recently I was angrily reprimanding the children about their failure to wait for me while crossing the parking lot:

> *Cindy*: Did I tell you to go?
> *Children*: No.
> *Cindy*: Can you cross this parking lot by yourselves?
> *Children*: No.
> *Cindy*: That's right. There are cars here. They're dangerous. I don't want you to go alone. Why do I want you to wait for me, do you know?
> *Claudette*: Yes, because you like us.

Although I was following the usual Haitian form—rhetorical questions with "no" answers—I had been expecting a final response based on the North American system of cause and effect, something like, "Because the cars are dangerous." Claudette, however, although she understands perfectly well the dangers of cars to small children, does not expect to use that information in this kind of an interaction. What, then, *is* she telling me? One thing that she is saying, which is perhaps what the solemn children also meant, is that, from her point of view, there is intimacy in this kind of talk. This is certainly the feeling I get from these experiences. I feel especially connected to the children in those instances in which I seem to have gotten it right.

THE LARGER CONTEXT

North American teachers generally think of reprimands—particularly of young children who are just learning to control their behavior—as put-downs, and are reluctant to give them. North American preschool teachers, in particular, will take great pains to avoid saying "no" or "don't." In contrast, I have learned from working with Haitian children and teachers that there are situations in which reprimands can be confirming, can strengthen relationships, and can, in a sense, define relationships for the child, as seems to have been the case for Claudette in the example given above.

Such an opportunity may be lost when we go to great lengths to avoid actually telling a child that he is wrong, that we disagree or disapprove. When we look at the difference between the ways in which things are done at home and at school, and the negative consequences that may result from these mismatches for children coming from minority cultural backgrounds, the area of misbehavior and the way it is responded to seem particularly important because it affects so directly the nature of the relationship between child and teacher.

I was not unaware when I began that this subject was a hotbed of disagreement: North Americans perceive Haitians as too severe, both verbally and in their use of physical punishment, while Haitians often perceive North American children as being extraordinarily fresh and out of control.[2] Haitian immigrant parents here are at once ashamed and defiantly supportive of their community's disciplinary standards and methods. In order to represent the views of Haitians I spoke with independent of my process of understanding, I asked them to reflect again on our two cultures after they had heard my interpretations.

People, of course, offered many varied points of view, yet everybody emphasized a sense of having grown up very "protected" in Haiti, of having been safe there both from getting into serious trouble and from harm. This sense of being protected was largely based on their understanding that their entire extended family, as well as many people in the community, were involved in their upbringing. Haitian families in the United States, some pointed out, are smaller and less extended. The community here, while tight in many ways, is more loosely connected than in Haiti. This change in social structure was bemoaned by the people I spoke with, especially with reference to bringing up children. They attributed to this change their sense that this generation of children, particularly those born here, is increasingly at risk. They are at risk not only of falling away from their parents' culture, but also, and consequently, of falling prey to the drugs, crime, and other problems of urban life that they see around them.

And yet everyone I spoke with also recalled some pain in their growing up, pain they relate to the respect and obedience they were required to exhibit to all adults, which at times conflicted with their own developing desire to state their opinions or make their own choices. This pain was nevertheless not to be discarded lightly. For many of the Haitian people with whom I spoke, religious values underlie these twin issues of respect and obedience; respect for parents and other adults is an analogue for respect and obedience to God and God's law.

Many people seemed to agree with the ambivalence expressed by one Haitian lawyer and mother who told me that, while she had suffered as a child because of the uncompromising obedience and respect demanded of her in her family, she continued to see respect as a value she needed to impart to her children. She said to me, "There must be many other ways to teach respect." She was one of many Haitians who told me of instances where a child from a poor family, a child with neither the clothes nor the supplies for school, had succeeded eventually in becoming a doctor or a lawyer. In these accounts, as in her own case, it is in large measure the strictness of the family that is regarded as the source of the child's accomplishment, rather than the talent or the power of the individual.

Presumably, there is some tension in all societies between individual and community. In these accounts is some suggestion of the form this tension sometimes takes within Haitian culture. For my part, I am struck and troubled by the powerful individualism underlying the approach I characterize as typical of me and many North American teachers. It appears that North Americans do speak as if something like the child's "enlightened self-interest" were the ultimate moral guidepost. In comparison to the language used by the Haitian teachers, North American teachers' language seems to place very little emphasis on shared values, on a moral community.

The process of gaining multicultural understanding in education must, in my opinion, be a dual one. On the one hand, cultural behavior that at first seems strange and inexplicable should become familiar; on the other hand, one's own familiar values and practices should become at least temporarily strange, subject to examination. In addition to the information I have gained that helps me to manage and form relationships with Haitian children in my classroom, I also value greatly the extent to which these conversations, by forcing me to attempt to empathize with and understand a view of the world that is in many ways very different from my customary one, have put me in a position to reexamine values and principles that had become inaccessible under layers of assumptions.

I am not teaching Haitian children this year, although I continue to visit them. Next year I expect to have a classroom with children from a wide range of backgrounds. It is difficult to say how my last experience will illuminate the next—or, analogously, how my experience can be of use to teachers in different kinds of classrooms. I do believe that teachers need to try to open up and to understand both our own assumptions and the cultural meaning that children from all backgrounds bring to school. It seems to me that accommodation must be made on all sides so that no group has to abandon the ways in which it is accustomed to passing on its values. I have been fortunate that the knowledge and collaboration of so many people, Haitian and North American, were available to help me begin to understand my own experience. All of these conversations have been their own rewards—I have made new friends and, I believe, become a better teacher.

NOTES

1. Earlier versions of this work have been presented at the Penn Ethnography in Educational Research Forum in February 1991 and the Brookline Teacher-Researcher Seminar in June 1990. My research was carried out as a member of that seminar with teachers and children at my school. In this chapter, all teachers' and children's names have been changed.

2. It must be stated that the consequences of this disagreement are, of course, vastly more painful for the powerless. Contact with schools, with social service institutions, with the police, is in many cases highly problematic for Haitian families. The Haitian family, in these situations, is frequently met with a lack of understanding that leads easily to a lack of respect. Mainstream assumptions about "proper" ways of talking and dealing with children's behavior often stand in the way of distinguishing a functioning family, for example, from a dysfunctional one, in distinguishing a child whose parents are strict in order to help him or her succeed from one whose family simply does not want to deal with the child's problems. Such assumptions often stand in the path of appropriate help as well. The school where I taught was often called upon to discuss cultural differences with social service groups, hospitals, and other schools. Occasionally, we were asked to provide some assistance for particular cases. But, of course, there were countless instances in which Haitian families were involved with these various powerful institutions and the families were without such aid.

REFERENCES

Boggs, S. (1985). *Speaking, talking, and relating: A study of Hawaiian children at home and at school*. Norwood, NJ: Ablex.

Cook-Gumperz, J. (1973). *Social control and socialization*. London: Routledge & Kegan Paul.

Heath, S. B. (1983). *Ways with words*. Cambridge, Eng.: Cambridge University Press.

Michaels, S., & O'Connor, M. C. (in press). *Literacy as reasoning within multiple discourses: Implications for policy and educational reform*. Newton, MA: Education Development Center.

Phillips, A. (1991, February). *Hearing children's stories: A report on the Brookline Teacher-Researcher Seminar*. Paper presented at the Penn Ethnography in Educational Research Forum, Philadelphia, PA.

Rose, M. (1989). *Lives on the boundary*. New York: Penguin.

Watson-Gegeo, K., & Gegeo, D. (1990). *Disentangling: The discourse of conflict and therapy in the Pacific Islands*. Norwood, NJ: Ablex.

PART IV

Negotiating the Dilemmas of Teaching

This section casts the challenges that teachers face—including those of pedagogy, shifting school contexts, educational policy, and teacher research—into high relief. For these teachers, the "problems" of teaching bring both struggle and opportunities for learning. Brown, a secondary special education English/language arts teacher in Philadelphia, provides a narrative case (and an associated video case on a website) that describes the clash between her students' realities and her beliefs about social action and the resulting growth for both the teacher and students. Martínez explains how Proposition 227—a proposal to eliminate bilingual programs in California schools—coupled with high-stakes testing and prescriptive reading programs, curbs his ability to improve and empower his first-grade students' language facility in his Los Angeles classroom. Using ideas from chaos theory to frame the complexity of classroom teaching, Maas, an elementary teacher in Wisconsin, outlines five principles that have guided him in building a culture for learning amid the unpredictability that comes with an extremely challenging class of students and shifting school contexts. Moving back and forth between the world of practice and the world of research through an exploration of her work in a fifth-grade math class, Lampert argues that teachers cannot resolve the dilemmas of teaching, but they can make thoughtful choices and develop new solutions that take those dilemmas—and the ever present tensions that come with them—into account.

CHAPTER 18

Human Agency, Social Action, and Classroom Practices

Vanessa Brown

I have been teaching in Philadelphia since 1974. I transferred to Germantown as a special education learning support teacher in 1993. At G-Town, I have taught adapted English/Language Arts, world history, American history and a School to Career course for seniors.

This project focuses on the students and classroom practices of my ninth-grade English/language arts classes.[1] It grew out of the tensions that arose when my beliefs about the juxtaposition of social action and classroom practices collided with the realities of socioeconomic status, personal agency, social and emotional stability, and student choice and voice.

THE SCHOOL

Many of the teachers at Germantown have taught there for their entire teaching careers. Several teachers and staff members attended the school during its "glory days" of high student enrollment; high student achievement; athletic programs; marching bands; vibrant student government; choirs and choruses; and academic, vocational, and technical course offerings. Those teachers are now retiring or preparing for retirement, having watched the school shift from "glory to the near grave" as a combined result of unconscionable budget slashing, high unemployment, drugs, housing-pattern shifts, and systemwide neglect. The student body is predominantly African American, 1% Latino, and perhaps .5% Asian and .5% Caucasian. Most students have scored at basic or below basic on national and local standardized tests. While it is not considered a Title I school, most students are from low- to lower-middle-income families. Our freshman class has experienced a retention rate of over 50% for 4 years in a row.

Under the leadership of its fourth principal since I arrived in 1993, the school has purchased a research-based whole-school reform model called Talent Development. It is hoped that this program will guide Germantown forward to its dreams of new glory days.

MY BELIEFS ABOUT
TEACHING AND LEARNING

Because this school was built in an area that is so richly entrenched in its history, and because it has been witness to an area that has seen integration, toleration, industrialization, and social activism at its best and worst, it seemed a perfect place to use the curriculum to bring forward a legacy of social justice and action as an integral part of the culture of the community. I did not have to be at Germantown very long before I realized that a more thoughtful and purposed approach to education was in order for this school or at least for the students whom I met.

Consequently, this project/inquiry has been grounded in my belief that young people of this generation have an obligation to carry out this legacy so as to ensure a life of opportunity and access for themselves and for those around them. No less important than a reverence for this history is my own experience of growing up in a nearby north-central Philadelphia neighborhood in the 1960s and 1970s.

I was a young teen at a time when many adults shuddered at the sound of the word *relevant*. Education had to be relevant. Religion had to be relevant. Morals and mores had to be relevant. Parenting and sexual orientation were all measured by this relevancy. I attended, with pride, the Black Panthers Constitutional Convention. We were going to remake America; construct a more relevant government for the people and by the real people. When I walked out of my high school to protest the absence of African American history classes in the general curriculum, I joined others in demanding a curriculum that was holistic, truthful, and relevant to my existence as an African in America. Action, as I saw it, was an integral part of being American. I had the right of expectancy and school/education had become my most valuable tool to apprise me of those rights. Now, almost 4 decades later, those beliefs provide the framework for the pedagogy I promote in the classroom.

Through the stories of two urban high school youth who actually represent hundreds of others with similar stories, I hope to contribute to and challenge the discourse regarding critical pedagogy in urban education.

MAY

"Knowledge is power." You have to know and understand all kinds of things in this world. If you want people to pay attention to you, you have to be intelligent. (An entry from May's journal, October 1999)

May is a short, round, dark-skinned ninth-grade female in my special education English class. Her eyes are dark and penetrating even through her thick eyeglasses, which were prescribed as a result of the havoc that lupus had wrought on her youthful body. She has puffy, thick, pink lips made even more prominent by her illness. Despite her tenuous health status, May is strong, resourceful, and determined. She, Eisha, and another friend from our class tried out for and won spots on the JV cheerleading squad. She helped out in the library at lunchtime and requested after-school tutoring, which is not exactly the popular thing to do among her special-class peers.

She is keenly sensitive and intuitive, as shown in her long, lingering glances, which she follows with a slant of an eyebrow and a tilt of her head, signaling to me, "I know, Mrs. Brown, I know" when a student does something that she and I both quietly agree is inappropriate. She will sometimes, without hesitation, pronounce to the class, "Some of you are only doin' that, 'cause you want Mrs. Brown to help you and you scared to ask her." May was feisty and not easily pushed around. She spoke her piece loud and clear—"I ain't takin' that stuff from 'im, Mrs. Brown" or "Mr. K—ain't teachin' us what we need—I want my class changed."

May was on a mission during her ninth-grade year, and "Knowledge is power" became her battle cry.

She fit ever so neatly into my teacher plan of creating a teaching and learning environment that challenged and supported students to find critical connections between literacy and social action. She invited instruction and eagerly participated in activities. She was both engaging and supportive of the plan I wanted to set in motion.

So when I announced that our class had an opportunity to apply for a local grant to support student projects, she led her class in a positive and enthusiastic response. She volunteered to write student ideas on the board when I asked for suggestions for a project theme and helped to keep order when we began the process of narrowing the themes down to one. When I asked each person who suggested a theme to tell why they felt the theme was important to explore, she imitated my mannerisms of nodding, smiling, and affirming each speaker. When she heard something she thought was off track, she would look at me with that "I know, I know" look and wait for me to say or do something. She was relentless in convincing her classmates to accept "Knowledge is power" as the most applicable to our thematic project, which we agreed would have a school-to-career focus, using the historical context of our school community as a foundation for the inquiry.

May had great difficulty with spelling, organizing written information, and reading comprehension—and she knew it. Her strengths were in oral expression and listening comprehension, and she knew that, too. She was adamant about finding a way to market her strengths. She felt that a good teacher had the responsibility to help her use what she brought to the teaching and learning community to achieve academic success.

She was the student whom most teachers would pray for. She would study my voice, my intonations, my graphics on the board, and especially my shared journal entries. She seemingly studied everything about me as a teacher with a peculiar intensity, forever looking for clues, looking for an open door to knowledge and power.

She clearly and quickly recognized the significance of using a historical context for approaching our project and later worked with other students on social-action initiatives that grew out of the research (such as writing letters to the city council and the mayor about vacant lots and abandoned buildings along G-Town Avenue and the lack of diversity of businesses in the area).

Midway through the school year, we started the short novel, *The Watsons Go to Birmingham* (Curtis, 1995), which takes place at the time of the burning of the Sixteenth Avenue Baptist Church in Alabama. May became a key player in pushing forward a fire-prevention initiative after hearing a radio news report regarding the number of reported fires in our surrounding school community. G-Town had the largest number of reported fires and fire fatalities of any area in the city. She made a connection between that stark reality and a chapter in the book in which a major character was discovered playing with matches after several warnings.

May's classmates were not far behind her. As a matter of fact, all the students were pretty much walking alongside one another. They had slowly evolved into a real community, nudging one another forward and making allowances for individual strengths and weaknesses. There was room to take risks and room to fall and plenty of room to move on.

So when we planned a fire-prevention project that grew out of May's sharing of the radio reports, the class embraced the idea with such fervor that even I was taken aback. I became a resource person and they quickly became the fuel for what now seems to be an unquenchable flame, colored by energy and enthusiasm.

They had found the intersection of school, career, and community, and together they teased out connections in literature about Malcolm X, Frederick Douglass, Toni Morrison, Maya Angelou, and Gwendolyn Brooks and that of Christopher Paul Curtis, bell hooks, Sonia Sanchez, and even the children's author, Pat Palacco. Dr. Seuss's *Hooray for Diffendoofer Day!* (1998) had a significant impact on their thinking about the power of thinking together and believing in one's abilities. Sandra Cisneros's "Those Who Don't" in *The House on Mango Street* (1991) led us into a most moving talk about how we represent ourselves and how others read our representations. We used a writers' workshop format to refine these pieces and hung them on the bulletin board with candid shots of ourselves working together both in and outside the classroom. It was great!

Oh, was I pleased. Literacy and activism were merging in a most natural manner. No, we weren't ready to picket the city council or form a human blockade across G-Town Avenue. But we were recognizing the need for action and using what we were learning to fuel our shared passion for intervention and change.

DJ

I can remember that DJ had a rapid-fire manner of speaking to everyone. His words could dart past you with such swiftness you would hardly know they were directed at you. His daily greetings almost always foreshadowed the upcoming tenor of our next 52 minutes together. I would have to move fast to catch the words, the tone, the message, and its implications for teaching and learning in Room 226.

DJ is an impressive yet average-sized ninth grader who is dark and handsome. He has deep brown eyes that never rest on any one subject for any length of time. He moves with a frantic, but consistent, gait as if always on his way to somewhere else—his speech already gone on the journey. DJ might say, "Good mornin', Mrs. Brown"—"Fuck you, bitch"—"Oh, I didn't mean to say that," all in what seemed like one long breath.

He could grab his journal, work in it, and throw his books on the floor in a matter of minutes—"I'm tired today!"

However, DJ could be thoughtful, kind, and deeply sensitive. Having been raised by his religious grandmother, he also had an abiding awareness of right and wrong, of justice and injustice. On rare, but cherished, occasions his spirituality would pervade the classroom—"My soul is at peace today, Mrs. Brown."

At those times, he would stand close to me and inquire about my weekend, my family, and an engagement about which we had talked or what the journal-writing topic was for the day.

DJ was an anomaly. In spite of his unyielding level of energy, his impulsivity, and his frantic behaviors, he was eager to be a part of a supportive community. One might initially surmise that his indiscriminate use of profanity, his verbal and physical threats to me and the students, and his assaults on students were attempts to circumvent teaching and learning in our class. However, closer examination, albeit painful at times, revealed some other impetus for this madness—power and control.

When DJ was in a "mood," he was a powerful and controlling force to be reckoned with. More than a few times, only the presence of a school security officer could calm him down. Yet he rarely wanted to actually leave the classroom. With tears streaming down his face, he would sometimes plead, "I'll stop! I'll change! Just let me stay!!" Unfortunately, I learned rather early on that it would serve no one's purpose to let him stay after an attack. He would have to leave. He would have to pay for his indiscretions. Needless to say, chance meetings with him in the halls later on those days would be characterized by his angry retorts about my unfairness.

By the onset of winter-like weather, DJ was writing and sharing aloud very short journal responses to daily prompts designed to help create and support a community of reading, writing, teaching, and learning. DJ and his classmates required much more time for this part of the lesson plan than for other classes on my roster. Each day, for weeks, we repeated the same journal-writing ritual.

DJ eventually took great pride in having an opportunity to command the attention of this audience. He would often-times embellish his entries during the sharing, ensuring a lasting impression on his listeners and cursing the nonlisteners. He savored my connections and comments on his writing, especially when I or another student acknowledged, "Your entry makes me think of . . . or this reminds me of . . ."

DJ was not too different from several boys and a few of the girls who came to my class burdened with social and emotional challenges. Despite the obviously increasing joy that DJ and others felt during the journal sharing, this burden hovered over them like an albatross.

Nonetheless, we started a familiar Philadelphia Writing Project activity, a three-part interview to foray into the realm of community building. I wanted to get students to talk about and listen to stories about themselves.

DJ and his classmates conducted peer interviews and then produced illustrations to depict the impressions left by the individual interviewees. I prepared sample interview questions beforehand and cleared the final four questions with the group the day before actually doing the project.

The illustrations became the first student work to adorn the walls of the classroom and the first pronouncement that we were on our way to building a community. We had started the process of creating a safe place to ask questions and/or show confusion, to reveal understandings and struggles, sources of joy and areas of pain (Schoenbach, Greenleaf, Cziko, & Hurwitz, 1999).

My pedagogical beliefs were grounded in the intersection of social action, service learning, political acts of change, and reading-and-writing-intensive classrooms. I imagined that the words of the political and literary giants we discussed in class would catapult the students into a different way of thinking about their world and their roles and responsibilities in it. I challenged students to critically examine conditions in their own families, neighborhoods, and schools; to look closely at what problems most prominently affected their communities; and to make suggestions on ways to confront and remedy problems while encouraging community assets. Through the journal writing, creative writing, letter writing, and sharing and literature responses and weekly newspaper activities, DJ and others were asked to find the connections to political and social action. I thought that I could use the literature and writing to ease our way into our becoming a community of politically and socially conscious and active teachers and learners.

While DJ actually did begin to write with increasing ease, neither he nor his classmates showed any sign of a willingness to directly confront issues that they identified. In fact, DJ was often impatient with these topics and hostile when I would try to push the idea of taking responsibility for our communities and enlisting the aid of others to make change—"Fuck dem, they ain't goin' ta change . . . What we keep talkin' bout dis for?" At other times, he wouldn't write at all.

Months later, a widely publicized, horrific, drug-related murder that claimed the lives of six people and wounded three others occurred in a neighborhood near our school. I asked students to talk in small groups about their feelings about drug activity in our communities and how we might get young people to stay away from drugs. Two students suggested that we develop fliers and put them up around our school and in student lockers. I thought, "Well, this is a start."

Surprisingly, DJ drew a very detailed flier on which were the words "We want you alive, not dead—Don't do drugs." Immediately after school,

I drove to a local copy shop and had five copies made of each child's finished flier. We stuffed them in student lockers and hung them on walls around the building the following day, within a limited, 10-minute time frame while other classes were still in session. DJ actually helped us decide who would cover which area of school.

This was our turning point. The students had decided on and implemented an action and I had entrusted them to do what they said they would do. Again, I had served as the witness, observing that students could and would do what they said they would.

DJ started taking advantage of the power embedded in the processes of the classroom. A particularly interesting example of this was when DJ's class was scheduled to take a written exam covering the details of *The Watsons Go to Birmingham, 1963*.

On the morning of the exam, another male student was acting out, actually threatening to disrupt the entire exam process. Just as I moved in to calm the student by talking slowly and softly, touching his shoulder and drawing his attention to parts of the test that I thought he would be comfortable with, DJ took charge of the others and initiated a move that surpassed my wildest dreams.

DJ whispered to the students in his row in front of the windows to turn their desks around to face the window, thus turning their backs to Kev (the disruptive student) and me, as we struggled to find a point of focus. DJ further instructed the students to engage in a modified writers' workshop to complete the literature-response sections of the test.

I was floored. Here was DJ taking on the role of leader at a crucial moment and there were his peers respecting and responding to his leadership in the most natural way.

The establishment of community and frequent opportunities to exercise action in the classroom, undergirded by reading, writing, talking, and listening with caring others, had been critical. We had moved from square one, but at the students' own pace.

CONCLUSION

Some children walk into a classroom ready to be presented with a finished agenda. All one need do is point to the path and they commence walking. This was the case during a large part of my career. When I got on my soapbox to teach—or preach, as some children called it—about the power of the people to make change in our communities, students would often be overcome by my passion. Connections between literacy and social action were made often and easily.

However, for a large and increasing number of students, this accommodation to my agenda was not to become their status quo. They were not developing their own rhythms and strategies, because either they were controlled by mine (Calkins, 1986, p. 183) or they spent inordinate amounts of time resisting that control.

So, while I continue to value predictability in the classroom, there is now more room for student voice and choice. There are multiple entry points and opportunities to acknowledge for establishing and achieving personal milestones and inserting *self* into *self-determination*. And there are new access routes to "create themselves as new subjects" when needed (Mohamed & Abdul, 1994, p. 242).

Because educators must recognize the broad interpretations and manifestations of social agency and action in the classroom, we must revisit over and over again how we see our students, how we describe their work, and how we assess it.

This particular work in progress, then, may contribute to the scholarship of teaching and learning by

- disrupting the discourse that supports the status quo of trapping children in preset boundaries;
- encouraging the discourse around equitable education;
- examining further how leadership, agency, and action evolves in teachers and students; and
- raising critical questions about the implicit and explicit effects of teacher behavior and pedagogy.

We owe these conversations to our children, and our children have an inalienable right to expect these conversations to occur, with their active participation.

NOTE

A video version of this narrative accompanied by contextual information, strategies, and student work can be viewed at http://www.goingpublicwithteaching. org/vbrown/

REFERENCES

Ackerman, M. (1996). Can I speak Gussak? In A. Peterson, J. Check, & M. Ylvisaker (Eds.), *Cityscapes: Eight views from the urban classroom* (pp. 1–13). Berkeley: National Writing Project.

Anson, C. M., & Beach, R. (1995). Purposes for using journals. In C. Gordon (Ed.), *Journals in the classroom: Writing to learn* (pp. 21–52). Norwood, MA: Christopher-Gordon.

Baldwin, J. (1988). A talk to teachers. In R. Simonson & S. Walker (Eds.), *The Graywolf annual 5: Multi-cultural literacy* (pp. 3–12). St Paul, MN: Graywolf Press.

Ball, A. F. (2000). Empowering pedagogies that enhance the learning of multicultural students. *Teachers College Record, 102*(6), 1006–1034.

Ballenger, C. (1995). Because you like us: The language of control. In G. Noya & G. R. Capella Noya (Eds.), *Shifting histories: Transforming education for social change.* Cambridge, MA: Harvard Educational Review.

Black, I. S. (1968). *The little old man who could not read.* Chicago: Albert Whitman.

Calkins, L. M. (1986). *The art of teaching writing* (4th ed). Portsmouth, NH: Heinemann.

Christensen, L. (2000). *Reading, writing, and rising up: Teaching social justice and the power of the written word.* Milwaukee, WI: Rethinking Schools.

Cisneros, S. (1991). *The house on Mango Street.* New York: Vintage

Curtis, C. P. (1995). *The Watsons go to Birmingham–1963.* New York: Bantam.

Freire, P. (2000). *Pedagogy of the oppressed.* London: Continuum Press.

Giroux, H. A., & McLaren, P. (Eds.). (1994). *Between borders: Pedagogy and the politics of cultural studies.* New York: Routledge.

Haley, A. (1964). *The autobiography of Malcolm X.* New York: Ballantine Books.

hooks, b. (1993). Eros, eroticism, and the pedagogical process. In H. Giroux, P. McLaren, & L. Grossberg (Eds.), *Between borders: Pedagogy and the politics of cultural studies* (pp. 114–118). New York: Routledge.

Lowry, L. (1979). *Anastasia Krupnik.* New York: Bantam Books.

Mohamed, J., & Abdul, R. (1994). Some implications of Paulo Freire's border pedagogy. In H. A. Giroux & P. MacLaren (Eds.), *Between borders: Pedagogy and the politics of cultural studies.* New York: Routledge.

Schoenbach, R., Greenleaf, C., Cziko, C., & Hurwitz, L. (1999). Motivating students to take control of their reading. In *Reading for understanding: A guide to improving reading in middle and high school classrooms.* New York: Jossey-Bass.

Seuss, Dr. (1998). *Hooray for Diffendoofer Day!* New York: Alfred A. Knopf.

CHAPTER 19

Proposition 227, Stanford 9, and Open Court: Three Strikes Against English Language Learners

Ramón Martínez

For the past 4 years, I have taught first grade at Utah Street Elementary School in the Boyle Heights section of East Los Angeles. During my teaching experience at Utah Street, I have learned a great deal about teaching and learning. In particular, my students, who are all English-language-learners, have taught me the importance of language and culture as factors that influence their experiences with schooling. Understanding my students' particular sociolinguistic environment has enabled me to adopt approaches to teaching that contribute to their empowerment. Unfortunately, recent trends in educational policy have seriously limited my capacity to continue empowering my students in the classroom. The passage of Proposition 227, the statewide focus on student accountability through high-stakes testing and the Los Angeles Unified School District's rigid implementation of the Open Court reading program have all made it increasingly difficult for me to provide my students with the instruction that they need and deserve.

PROPOSITION 227

When it was approved by voters in 1998, Proposition 227 effectively ended bilingual education in the state of California. Before the passage of this proposition, I taught my students English, while at the same time providing instruction in the core content areas (mathematics, social studies, and science) in my students' native language–Spanish. Currently, I teach what is called a "Model

Reprinted with permission. "Proposition 227, Stanford 9, and Open Court: Three Strikes Against English Language Learners" by Ramon Martinez originally appeared in the online journal *Teaching to Change LA*, Democracy 2001, Winter 2000/2001, Vol. 1, No. 1, at http://tcla.gseis.ucla.edu/democracy/politics/prop227.html.

B" class, in which I am expected to instruct my students in English, while providing any support that they might need in Spanish. Although I do my best to meet the language needs of my students within the parameters of the Model B program, I have become convinced that this program has resulted in my students receiving an unequal education. Indeed, bilingual education was first established on the grounds that a student cannot receive an equal education, if she does not understand the language of instruction.

In addition to limiting educational access, Proposition 227 also represents an attack on students' language rights. The Model B program teaches my students that Spanish only has value insofar as it serves to help them learn English. My students are encouraged to "transition" out of Spanish and into the language that is valued by the dominant culture in society. Whereas, before 227, Spanish was recognized as a meaningful, valuable, and legitimate means of expression, it has since been relegated—both implicitly and explicitly—to a substandard and subordinate status on our campus.

STANFORD 9 EXAM

While the passage of Proposition 227 has resulted in an unequal education for English-language learners, the use of the Stanford 9 to measure student achievement has served to perpetuate these inequalities. In an attempt to appear "serious" about educational reform, Governor Gray Davis has focused his efforts on holding students accountable. The cornerstone of his accountability program is the Academic Performance Index (API), which ranks schools based on their Stanford 9 scores. Unfortunately, the content of the Stanford 9 has been shown to be culturally biased, as it draws from the experiences of predominantly White, middle-class students. Moreover, the exam is administered in an unequal educational context, since schools in wealthier areas often have more resources and better-qualified teachers than do schools in low-income areas. In addition, the Stanford 9 is a norm-referenced exam, which means that half of all students tested will always score at or below the 50th percentile. It should come as no surprise, then, that the students who score below the 50th percentile are students, such as mine, who speak little or no English.

Having been stripped of their home language, my students are now expected to take a norm-referenced, standardized exam, which, in addition to being inherently biased, is administered in a language that they do not understand. Obviously, the Stanford 9 does not provide me with an accurate indication of my students' progress in the various subject areas. The only thing that it does show me is that which I already know—that my students are limited English proficient. Under the API scheme, the results of this unfair and inaccurate assessment are used to determine the allocation of funds to schools, thereby punishing those students who are already at a disadvantage. English-language learners and other students of color who attend schools in low-income communities will undoubtedly suffer, as their schools fail, in disproportionate numbers, to improve their test scores.

OPEN COURT READING PROGRAM

Because the Stanford 9 is being used as the sole measure of student achievement, teachers have consequently been under a great deal of pressure to "teach to the test." Indeed, this emphasis on test-readiness has been driving curriculum within Los Angeles Unified. The most recent example of this is the district's implementation of the Open Court reading program. In a nutshell, Open Court is a scripted reading program that ignores the instructional needs of English-language learners and teaches reading skills in isolation, detached from meaningful texts and students' lived experiences. Some elements of the program are effective and could conceivably be incorporated into a balanced literacy program for English-language learners. Unfortunately, most teachers in Los Angeles Unified (myself included) are not being given the discretion to decide how best to teach their students. Rather than being able to pick and choose components that work for their students, "low-performing" schools are being forced to rigidly implement the entire Open Court program, while schools with high test scores are allowed to continue providing their students with rich, varied, and meaningful learning experiences. Needless to say, this policy is serving to perpetuate existing educational inequalities.

Proposition 227, the Stanford 9, and Open Court represent three strikes against English-language learners. With each successive strike, the educational inequalities between English-language learners and their English-speaking counterparts have increased. Proposition 227 condemned my students to an unequal education, while the Stanford 9 and Open Court have worked together to perpetuate that inequality. It is clear that policymakers at the state and district levels are more concerned with implementing accountability programs than they are with working to ensure educational justice. Critical educators must, therefore, step up and take a stand. In defense of educational justice and sound pedagogy, we must begin to engage in forms of individual and collective resistance. If we truly seek to empower our students, we must begin to challenge the educational policies that serve only to harm them.

CHAPTER 20

Principled Practice:
New Science for the Classroom

Jeffrey Maas

> Chaos turns out to be far subtler than the commonsense idea that it is
> the messiness of mere chance—the shuffling of a deck of cards, the ball
> bouncing around in a roulette wheel, or a loose stone clattering down a
> rocky mountainside. The scientific term "chaos" refers to an underlying
> interconnectedness that exists in apparently random events. Chaos science
> focuses on hidden patterns, nuance, the "sensitivity" of things, and the
> "rules" for how the unpredictable leads to the new. (Briggs & Peat, 1999)

Chaos in the world of old science has connotations of disorder, randomness,
and destruction. As an educator, my principal would be greatly disturbed if I
told him my children had a chaotic day or that my teaching was currently in
chaos. But there is now a new set of new connotations developing.

Chaos is not randomness. It is not reality falling apart into nothingness and disconnectedness. The new science of chaos theory tells us that
complex systems are *held together by relatively simple principles*. When a
system moves to the edge of chaos the principles act as a universal gravity
to hold the pieces together so that it can adapt and reemerge in a new form.
For me, this new science definition of chaos echoed a growing reality of
my teaching experiences.

OPENING THE DOOR TO CHAOS

As I write these words, I have completed my 2nd year of teaching second
grade. I have also finished my 2nd year at my current school. After 10

years in the same school teaching the same grade, I wanted to test the validity and strength of the educational approaches I embraced. So once again I chose chaos, changing grade level, changing schools and the neighborhood it served, and changing school culture.

My new school is racially and economically mixed, typical of most schools in Madison, Wisconsin. It could be labeled a school in transition, with student ethnic diversity and poverty levels increasing dramatically over the past 7 years. My 1st year of teaching second grade was filled with new realities. I was surprised at how the continuity of the learning community was continually disrupted by institutional realities. The school instituted a pull-out program for all students who received supplemental instruction, which included English as a Second Language, Title I, and Reading Recovery; all students with Individual Educational Programs (IEPs) were also in the program. The net effect on the classroom was a constant disruption. There was little effort spent building continuity between the various programs.

My 1st year also brought a new principal. This principal valued inclusion over the fragmentation created by pullout programs. Inclusion and collaboration became the institutional agenda for the 2nd year. For that 2nd year, I agreed to collaborate with the special education teacher. While I agreed with the philosophical underpinnings of his agenda, I was also hoping to limit the number of disruptions in my classroom. While I did manage to limit the number and the effect of institutional disruptions, I experienced a very different, profound kind of disruption that 2nd year.

Because of a state program, I had 15 children in my room. Five of the children came to the class with an IEP. They were classified as either learning disabled or emotionally disabled. Some had demonstrated severe emotional/antisocial behavior in the past. By the midpoint of the year, I had 14 children, 7 of whom were receiving special education instruction. Of these 7, 4 were especially disruptive to the community and the work we were trying to accomplish. During the course of the year, they engaged in violence, destruction, profanity, crime, and intimidation.

But while there have been so many new facets to the contexts of my teaching, some things have remained constant. When entering my new school, I carried with me *five guiding principles* that form the foundation of a *learning theory*.

Learning is more powerful when it is

1. owned by the participants of the community.
2. a social activity.
3. reflective.

4. inquiry–based.
5. based on standards.

The principles helped me understand, organize, and manage the learning in my classroom. These principles were found in the 1st minute of the 1st day to the farewells on the last hour of the year, from the small assignment to the grandiose project.

The First Moments of the 1st Day

Those first few moments when a community comes together are fragile. Like particles orbiting in space, members of the community are thrust into proximity by the gravity of the school. All teachers want the new classroom to get off on the right foot. All teachers establish a community, creating norms and expectations. Some spend time on school rules or make a classroom contract. Others create opening day ice-breaking activities. ("What did you do on your summer vacation?") But no matter the learning theories and subsequent practices, all communities must establish a working protocol, a way to go about the business of the community.

My goals for those 1st hours of the 1st day of the new year were certainly no different. However, I wanted those moments of "first contact" to be imbued with the five principles. So floating among the typical 1st-day events was the language of my guiding principles. Embedded within that language were the processes, attitudes, and dispositions that would guide our work for the entire year.

On that 1st morning, children entered the room packing school supplies, which they deposited on their tables. No seats had been assigned, so they gathered wherever they chose. After supplies were dropped, they all sat down, waiting to be told what to do. Their schema of traditional schooling became immediately apparent. Some of them were good at playing the roles that were delineated within that schema. Some were not.

But I knew that the protocols and processes we would use throughout the year were not traditional. I knew that those initial moments were just as powerful as any other moment during the year. As facilitator, my language was laced with words that reflected the guiding principles. The principles were activated with the first "Hello. We have much to do today."

I asked the kids to leave their seats and to join me in another area of the room where we could sit in a circle, a more socially conducive setting for conversations. Because we would be engaged in many conversations over the year, both large and small, the discussion format was entered into our community's tool kit and immediately became one way that we "went about our business." Some of them were good at playing the social roles required for meaningful conversation. Some were not.

We took care of administrative necessities and began to get organized as a community. I began to make the implicit processes of the community explicit. They emerged as we talked. The word *system* was introduced and defined. Implications (end states) of classroom systems were discussed. I deliberately labeled us a "team" and conveyed an attitude that said, "We are in this together," that the classroom was not "mine," but "ours."

As facilitator, I led the children into a discussion about how to best operate as a team. Children's ideas and behaviors became the topics and curriculum of our first conversation together. Behavioral disruptions evolved into minilessons on group dynamics. A seating-arrangement system was created and the fairness discussed. In order to foster ownership of the classroom, the team's first project was to decorate the classroom.

All this took place within the countless interactions of the first 30 minutes of the school day. I took my discourse cues from the activities and actions of the newly forming community. All the interactions were guided by the five principles. Even situations that could be labeled as negative, were filtered through the lens of the principles.

T's Story

As the children entered the room on that 1st day, some came in quietly, some noisily. Everyone had his or her own memories of first grade. Everyone had a schema. Along with their school supplies the children had brought with them the roles they had created for themselves within that schema. I knew T would be in my room. I also knew that he had a violent past, spending much of his first-grade year suspended from school for disruptive behavior.

T entered the room that morning with everyone else and immediately sought out a friend. They sat next to each other and began to catch up on news. They took out their supplies and were ready to begin school. When I asked everyone to leave their seats and join me at the carpet, T refused. He waited for my response. His buddy waited with him. The rest of the class was waiting for my response as well.

School had not officially started. The bell had not yet tolled and we had already reached a critical moment in the new life of our community. T was testing his schema. He had given me a choice. I could ask T to join us. I could demand that T join us. I could move into the world of reward and punishment and establish that world as the norm of our community. I could send a message to the entire community that said, "I am in control. My will will dictate."

But the principles guided me. I wanted children to buy into and be part of our emerging community. I knew that my reactions to this first small moment could have unforeseen, major implications in the life of our community, implications that could ultimately undercut the learning I wanted to undertake. So when T said that he did not want to join us, I said, "That's your choice. But don't bother the rest of us, 'cause we have work to do."

That simple message is packed with significance. I gave T a choice, just as he had given me one. He had received his response. I would now gauge his. I had also set the stage for all members of the community. They would all be given choices during that 1st day and for every other school day of the year. I sent the message to T and the rest that a member's choices must not interfere with work of the community, thereby establishing a basic relationship between the individuals in the community and the community as a whole.

As the rest of the class moved to the carpet to proceed with the business of the morning, T sat at his table, reading from a piece of paper that he had brought with him. His voice filled the room as he read "words" about a teacher. As we sat on the carpet, T's voice booming in the background, I had to make another choice concerning T, a choice that was just as vital as my first.

It was clear to me that his actions were an attempt to establish his dominance in the group. Again he was gauging my reaction to verify his schema for school. He escalated his behavior, expecting me to punish him. But I was establishing a new way of doing school. T did not get the response he expected. And once again, all children in the community witnessed a response that foreshadowed their developing reality.

I validated T's need to be noticed and at the same time I turned the situation into a social inquiry. I asked the group, "Why do you think T is doing that?" The answers of the children turned into a quick minilesson on social/group dynamics, with the ultimate message being that all humans need to be noticed, that the emotions and needs of all group members are to be respected and understood. My comments were designed not only to establish social-inquiry processes in the community, but also to show that the students' social realities had a place in our culture, thus increasing the ownership of that culture.

All this took place within the first 10 minutes of the day. T chose to join our group, sitting in a chair behind me rather than in the circle on the carpet. During the ensuing conversation, he continued to reach into his bag of school-tested tricks, testing my response to each. Each time, I continued to turn his choices and behavior into positive learning for the group. While he never fully dropped his role as "the misbehaving boy," he did manage to participate in the remainder of the activities.

C's Story

As we sat in the circle, sharing stories, joking, getting to know one another, I pointed out that I had not completed decorating the room. While I had made the environment tidy and appealing, several bulletin boards were untouched, displaying only a simple question mark. That question mark appeared in several spots around the room, on our door, and in the hallway outside our room. The first activities and projects of the year were imbued with the same principles that would guide all our work. I wanted the children to own not only the work of the room, but the environment as well. We would decide together on the decor of the workplace through inquiry processes that were reflective and social in nature. And we had standards. We wanted the outcome of our work to "look good."

Before we could leave our circle and begin the work of the day, we had to talk about a seating arrangement. I had not assigned seating. I told the children they could sit wherever they wished, but a "system" had to be discussed first. T asked what the word meant. "It's a way of doing things," I replied. The simple act of finding a seat became connected to one of the most important words in our community. A focus on "systems" helped make the implicit processes of the classroom explicit. Once invisible systems are visible, they become a topic of discussion and a tool for children to use. Once used, the systems also become objects of reflection.

We discussed several systems for finding a seat. We discussed the "outcomes" of each of the proposed systems. "Was the system fair? What will happen if a problem arises?" After a brief yet important discussion, the children scurried to find a seat, alliances of friendship being formalized in transit. Within 4 minutes, everyone had a seat that pleased. Except C. The only seat that remained was across from T and his friend. She did not want to sit there.

As I had done with T, I framed C's dilemma as a choice. As I facilitated her decision-making process, her problem was made public. C said that she sat next to the boys in first grade and their talking was a distraction. While the boys denied the accusations, I replied that I understood her dilemma.

I had no solution to the problem in mind. I probably would have moved some children around to accommodate C's request or I would have asked her to sit across from the boys against her wishes. Either decision would have been worse than the solution C proposed. She broke my mindset on the way I had placed the chairs and asked if she could squeeze between two friends. There was room. It was a perfect solution. I said, "Sure." The work of the morning progressed.

While sensitive dependency on initial conditions helps us understand the power of even the smallest event in a complex system, an understanding of fractals, self-similarity across scales, reveals the connections between those little, day-to-day pieces of classroom culture and the larger, grandiose projects that can dominate weeks. With an understanding of fractals serving as a management model in the classroom, teachers are grounded. Seemingly disparate experiences are connected. Children experience coherency and continuity.

The Fall and the Halloween Play

The range of academic skills my children brought into the community was staggering. Several kids were grappling with basic understandings of multiplication, while others could barely count past 50. Some were through with the major struggles of decoding and were beginning to delight in aspects of literature. To others, letter-sound relationships were a mystery, one they were nearly ready to abandon.

But even more amazing than the breadth of academic skills was the mismatch in emotional health. After a relatively smooth beginning, the disabilities that caused several children to be unavailable for learning began to eat away at the edges of our community. During the 1st month of school, several children had to be physically removed when their violent outbursts became physical, threatening the safety of others. Chairs were thrown. Wastepaper cans kicked. Work destroyed. One girl refused to do any work. When encouraged and cajoled to do so, she would explode into a diatribe of profanity, punctuating her anger with slamming doors. T missed 20% of his schooling because of suspensions.

I had agreed to teach an inclusion classroom because I wanted to limit the disruptions that were created by pullout programs. The disruptions I saw unfolding before me were more disturbing. I was concerned that the type of learning I valued and the open-ended projects that had been the foundation of that learning could not take place within our community.

The fall was a series of evaluations, reflections, and soul searching. I wanted to understand and manage chaos. I had no idea that chaos could take the form that it did.

The choices I grappled with during the fall were similar to the choice T presented to me on that 1st day. The voice of my traditional training kept telling me to abandon student-centered projects. They were laced with the problems of individual choice and contributed to the complexity of the learning environment. But just as I had embraced my principles to manage T's behavior and facilitate C's dilemma, I decided to hold firm in the chaos of the fall.

I felt that many of the special education students did not have an emotional or intellectual connection to the community. Their skill level and their behaviors isolated them from their peers. While I had talked about "the team," by the end of September we had not really done work as a team. Those students on the fringes had not been given an opportunity to show their worth, other than "being good" during workshop assignments. My emotional and intellectual energy had been focused on stabilizing individuals at their emotional and intellectual levels. The needs of the larger community had gone unmet. Without addressing that piece, the principles lacked their influence.

So, on top of the everyday classroom assignments, I created a major team project. We began to write a play for Halloween. At precisely the moment at which the special education teacher was advising me to narrow the complexity of the classroom, I chose to engage in theater performance, a tremendously complex endeavor. I knew the project had a built-in motivation. The project was designed to tap into that motivation and reaffirm the principles that governed our culture.

Writing the play took more than 3 weeks. For each daily writing session, all children sat for extended periods of time, listening to the idea of others and adding their own. Ownership was high. Kids who could not sit still for a 5-minute lesson on weather bought into the creating of the play. Since the play was a creation of the community, it was an inquiry-based, social endeavor. Since we were inviting others to see the performance, our standards were high. We rewrote, each writing session beginning with a reflection on our words to see if it "sounded right." The kids rehearsed and followed directions. The play was an overwhelming success. Despite the children's often deliberate attempts to undermine "the team," our community held tight, grew, and flourished. The team now had a successful event in their history to build upon.

CHAOS

Chaos is not randomness. It is not reality falling apart into nothingness and disconnectedness. The new science of chaos theory tells us that complex systems are *held together by relatively simple principles*. When a system moves to the edge of chaos, the principles act as a means of universal gravity to hold the pieces together so that the system can adapt and reemerge in a new form.

For me, this new definition of chaos echoed the reality of my teaching experiences. This basic concept of chaos theory added a new reality to the five guiding principles I had found embedded within creative processes: Learning is more powerful when it is owned by the participants of the community, when it is a social activity, when it is reflective, when it is inquiry-based, and when it is based on standards.

The Butterfly Effect

> Because weather is a chaotic system full of iterating feedback, it is nonlinear, which makes it incredibly sensitive to tiny influences. This sensitivity comes from the fact that even small increases in temperature, wind speed, or air pressure cycle through the system and can end up having a major impact. (Briggs & Peat, 1999)

Sensitive dependency on initial conditions is an effect of complex systems that has been dubbed "the butterfly effect." It basically means that the smallest event can have profound, unpredictable effects somewhere in the system's future. It also means that each isolated event is the start of other possible events. And conversely, each current event is connected to a history of prior events.

Like any other teacher in any primary grade around the country, my first moments with the kids were important. But one main difference existed. I was working from a chaos theory perspective. *Sensitive dependency upon initial conditions* told me that the first moments in the life of a complex system are filled with a power that influences the future of a complex community. Small beginnings point to the future and connect to the past.

As teachers, we understand that working with children is not solely about academic subject matter. The smallest event can trigger very unexpected events, both positive and negative. A child's restless night, the visit of a puppy, or a sudden thunderstorm can lead a community on countless paths.

With the metaphor of the butterfly effect, classroom events can once again be connected in ways that were not possible within the reality of the old sciences. Within chaos theory, there are no isolated, unimportant events. All events are weighted with a power that influences and guides the future. Each single event is a learning event, connected to the whole learning of that community. A greeting of "Good day!" at the start of the day is directly connected to a lesson on fractions.

Fractals

> A coastline is produced by the chaotic action of waves and other geological forces. These act at every scale to generate shapes that repeat, on smaller scales, a pattern roughly similar to the one visible at the larger scale. In other words, chaos generates forms and leaves behind tracks that possess what chaos scientists refer to as *self-similarity at many different scales*. (Briggs & Peat, 1999)

On that 1st morning of school, the children engaged in several small-scale activities and projects. A system for seating had to be invented and discussed. Lockers had to be assigned in a fair and equitable way. Lockers had to have name tags that reflected team colors. A process to design and decorate our room had to be introduced, discussed, and implemented. The processes we engaged in that 1st day were guided by the five principles.

But these principles were enacted time and time again throughout a variety of scales, through daily, weekly, and monthly activities and projects. The first conversation on that 1st morning was similar to the discussions we engaged in to create and perform the play.

Because the fractal pieces are connected by the principles, my role as teacher had to evolve. In traditional learning theory, the pieces of the curriculum are disconnected and static, organized and managed before interactions with children. But in this new learning reality, the connections that hold the pieces together emerge through the learning of children. I needed to be actively involved in the emerging conversations, making on-the-spot connections between the pieces of knowledge the children provided. All connections were guided by the five principles.

While *sensitive dependency on initial conditions* helps us understand the power of even the smallest event in a complex system, an understanding of *fractals, self-similarity across scales*, reveals the connections between those little, day-to-day pieces of classroom culture and the larger, grandiose projects that can dominate weeks. With an understanding of fractals serving as a management model in the classroom, teachers are grounded. Seemingly disparate experiences are connected. Children experience coherency and continuity.

THE JOURNEY'S CIRCLE

During this 1st year at my new school, I was caught between two opposing forces. The traditional science of my training told me to isolate the pieces, to remove the complexity. But new science told me to hold true to those things that I believe in, to the principles that have made my teaching a joyous profession. The new science of chaos theory has given me a language with which to understand the pedagogy I practice. And with that language has come concepts, knowledge, and methodology that help put theory into practice. I can now create a new educational reality that not only makes a place for complexity, but also embraces it.

NOTE

This chapter brings together excerpts from a longer article available on the Web at www.carnegiefoundation.org/castl/k-12/goingpublic/.

REFERENCE

Briggs, J., & Peat, F. D. (1999). *Seven life lessons of chaos: Spiritual wisdom from the science of change.* New York: Perennial.

CHAPTER 21

How Do Teachers Manage to Teach?: Perspectives on Problems in Practice

Magdalene Lampert

In the classroom where I teach fourth-, fifth-, and sixth-grade mathematics, there are two chalkboards on opposite walls. The students sit at two tables and a few desks, facing in all directions. I rarely sit down while I am teaching except momentarily to offer individual help. Thus the room does not have a stationary "front" toward which the students can reliably look for directions or lessons from their teacher. Nevertheless, an orientation toward one side of the room did develop recently in the fifth-grade class and became the source of some pedagogical problems.

The children in my classroom seem to be allergic to their peers of the opposite sex. Girls rarely choose to be anywhere near a boy, and the boys actively reject the girls whenever possible. This has meant that the boys sit together at the table near one of the blackboards and the girls at the table near the other.

The fifth-grade boys are particularly enthusiastic and boisterous. They engage in discussions of math problems with the same intensity they bring to football. They are talented and work productively under close supervision, but if they are left to their own devices, their behavior deteriorates and they bully one another, tell loud and silly jokes, and fool around with the math materials. Without making an obvious response to their misbehavior, I developed a habit of routinely curtailing these distractions from the lesson by teaching at the blackboard on the boys' end of the classroom. This enabled me to address the problem of maintaining classroom order by my physical presence; a cool stare or a touch on the shoulder reminded the boys to give their attention to directions for an activity or to the content of a lesson, and there was no need to interrupt my teaching.

But my presence near the boys had inadvertently put the girls in "the back" of the room. One of the more outspoken girls impatiently pointed out that she had been trying to get my attention and thought I was ignoring her. She made me aware that my problem-solving strategy, devised to keep the boys' attention, had caused another, quite different problem. The boys could see and hear more easily than the girls, and I noticed their questions more readily. Now what was to be done?

I felt that I faced a forced choice between equally undesirable alternatives. If I continued to use the blackboard near the boys, I might be less aware of and less encouraging toward the more well behaved girls. Yet if I switched my position to the blackboard on the girls' side of the room, I would be less able to help the boys focus on their work. Whether I chose to promote classroom order or equal opportunity, it seemed that either the boys or the girls would miss something I wanted them to learn.

This first-person account of a particular pedagogical problem is an unusual way to begin an analysis of the work of teaching. Commonly, such inquiries begin with general observations based on a consideration of several instances of teaching practice or with assertions about what teaching can or should be. I have taken a different tack, however, not because I believe these approaches cannot offer useful insights into what it is that teachers do, but because I believe they are incomplete. Efforts to build generalized theories of instruction, curriculum, or classroom management based on careful empirical research have much to contribute to the improvement of teaching, but they do not sufficiently describe the work of teaching.[1] Such theories and research are limited in their capacity to help teachers know what to do about particular problems such as the one I have just described. My intention, however, is not to build another kind of theory which can more adequately guide practice but to describe those elements of practice which are unconsonant with theoretical principles. To do this, I shall use both my experience as a classroom practitioner and the tools of scholarly inquiry.

The special and salient value of descriptions of teaching from the practitioner's perspective has been recognized by scholars and supported by researchers.[2] Moving back and forth between the world of practice and the world of scholarship in order to inquire into the nature of practice fosters in the inquirer a useful sort of deliberation; it enriches and refines both the questions one can ask about teachers' work and the attempts one can make to answer them.[3] In this essay, I shall present two cases which first describe teaching problems from the teacher's point of view and then examine, from the scholar's point of view, the work involved in facing them.

The teacher's emphasis on concrete particulars in the description of a classroom problem distinguishes the perspective of practice from the perspective of the theory-builder. This distinction has received considerable attention in the literature on teaching.[4] Another fundamental though less familiar difference involves the personal quality of teaching problems as seen through the eyes of a practitioner.[5] Who the teacher is has a great deal to do with both the way she defines problems and what can and will be done about them.[6] The academician solves problems that are recognized in some universal way as being important, whereas a teacher's problems arise because the state of affairs in the classroom is not what she wants it to be. Thus, practical problems, in contrast to theoretical ones, involve someone's wish for a change and the will to make it.[7] Even though the teacher may be influenced by many powerful sources outside herself, the responsibility to act lies within. Like the researcher and the theoretician, she identifies problems and imagines solutions to them, but her job involves the additional personal burden of doing something about these problems in the classroom and living with the consequences of her actions over time. Thus, by way of acknowledging this deeply personal dimension of teaching practice, I have chosen not only to present the particular details of two teachers' problems but to draw one of these problems from my own experience.

In addition to recognizing the particular and personal qualities of the way teachers understand problems in their work, I would like to consider another distinction between practice and theory building in education. Some of the problems the practitioner is required to do something about might be defined as unsolvable. The work required to manage such problems will be the particular focus of my inquiry. It is widely recognized that the juxtaposition of responsibilities which make up the teacher's job leads to conceptual paradoxes.[8] I will argue further that, from the teacher's point of view, trying to solve many common pedagogical problems leads to practical dilemmas.[9] As the teacher considers alternative solutions to any particular problem, she cannot hope to arrive at the "right" alternative in the sense that a theory built on valid and reliable empirical data can be said to be right.[10] This is because she brings many contradictory aims to each instance of her work, and the resolution of their dissonance cannot be neat or simple. Even though she cannot find their right solutions, however, the teacher must do something about the problems she faces.

Returning to my own classroom at this point will serve to explicate more clearly these qualities of a teacher's work. One might think it possible to monitor the boys' behavior in my fifth-grade math class in a way that does not reduce my attention to the girls, or to involve the girls more in the math lesson without reducing my capacity to monitor the boys' behavior. But teaching dilemmas like this are often not so easily resolved in practice. For example, if I were to assign seats mixing the boys and the girls, it might be possible to give equal attention to everyone no matter which blackboard I use, but the silliness that results from proximity to the opposite sex in the fifth grade might then take so much away from the lesson that there would be less of my attention to go around. If I were to leave the boys and the girls where they choose to sit, and walk around the room to spread my attention, then the walking around might cause even greater disruption because it would take me away from the boys who need my presence. It might be possible to use desks instead of tables and seat everyone facing in the same direction as a way of monitoring behavior, but that might make the students' valuable problem-solving discussions with one another impossible. All these possible "solutions" lead to problems. I felt I could not choose a solution without compromising other goals I wanted to accomplish. Yet I knew that not implementing a solution would have negative consequences too. I was convinced that some action had to be taken.

When I consider the conflicts that arise in the classroom from my perspective as a teacher, I do not see a choice between abstract social goals, such as Excellence versus Equality or Freedom versus Standardization. What I see are tensions between individual students, or personal confrontations between myself and a particular group of boys or girls. When I think about rewarding Dennis's excellent, though boisterous, contributions to problem-solving discussions, while at the same time encouraging reticent Sandra to take an equal part in class activities, I cannot see my goals as a neat dichotomy and my job as making clear choices. My aims for any one particular student are tangled with my aims for each of the others in the class, and, more importantly, I am responsible for choosing a course of action in circumstances where choice leads to further conflict. The contradictions between the goals I am expected to accomplish thus become continuing inner struggles about how to do my job.

A PEDAGOGICAL DILEMMA
AS AN ARGUMENT WITH ONESELF

The solutions I imagined to restrain the boys' boisterous behavior and to encourage the girls' involvement in class activities were contradictory. I could do neither without causing undesirable consequences, yet both were important to me. One way to think about the dilemma that I faced is to see it as a problem forcing a choice between equally undesirable alternatives. In this view, my job would be to grit my teeth and choose, even though choosing would bring problematic consequences.[11] Another way to think of a dilemma, however, is as an argument between opposing tendencies within oneself in which neither side can come out the winner. From this perspective, my job would involve maintaining the tension between my own equally important but conflicting aims without choosing between them. It may be true that some teachers do resolve their dilemmas by choosing—between excellence and quality, between pushing students to achieve and providing a comfortable learning environment, between covering the curriculum and attending to individual understanding; but I wish to argue that choosing is not the only way to manage in the face of self-contradictory alternatives. Facing a dilemma need not result in a forced choice. A more technical definition of a dilemma is "an argument that presents an antagonist with two (or more) alternatives, but is equally conclusive against him whichever alternative he chooses."[12] This definition focuses on the deliberation about one's alternatives rather than on a choice between them. The conflicted teacher is her own antagonist; she cannot win by choosing.

As I presented my case for leaving the boys' area of the room to be nearer to the girls, my argument for taking such an action was conclusive against me because my students and I would be distracted from our lessons by my need to control overtly the boys' behavior. If I argued, on the other hand, for continuing to teach from the boys' side of the room, I would also lose the argument because I would not be giving the girls at least equal amounts of my attention. Instead of engaging in a decision-making process that would eliminate conflicting alternatives and lead to a choice of which problem to solve, I pursued a series of such losing arguments with myself as I considered the consequences of various alternatives. One element of the teacher's work is having an argument with oneself—a speculative argument that cannot be won. The thinking involved in this sort of work is quite different from the kind of thinking that might go into concluding that one can make the correct choice between dichotomous alternatives. My arguments with myself served to articulate the undesirable consequences of each of my alternatives in terms of potential classroom confrontations. In order to hold the conflicting parts of my job and myself together, I needed to find a way to manage my dilemma without exacerbating the conflicts that underlay it.

PEDAGOGICAL DILEMMAS AND
PERSONAL COPING STRATEGIES

My argument with myself resulted from a desire to do contradictory things in the classroom. My ambivalence about what to do was not only a conflict of will, however; it was a conflict of identity as well. I did not want to be a person who ignored the girls in my class because the boys were more aggressive in seeking my attention. I think of myself as someone who encourages girls to become more interested and involved in mathematical thinking. At the same time, I did not want to have a chaotic classroom as a result of turning away from the boys' behavior. But neither did I want to appear to have such a preoccupation with order that I discouraged enthusiasm; standing near the boys enabled me to keep them focused without attending to their misbehavior directly. Working out an identity for this situation was more than a personal concern—it was an essential tool for getting my work done. The kind of person that I am with my students plays an important part in what I am able to accomplish with them. Figuring out who to be in the classroom is part of my job; by holding conflicting parts of myself together, I find a way to manage the conflicts in my work.

The self that I brought to the task of managing this classroom dilemma is a complicated one. My personal history and concerns contributed to the judgment that it would not be wise simply to make a choice in this case. I felt sympathy for the girls who were seated in what had inadvertently become the "back of the room" because of the many pained moments I had spent with my raised hand unrecognized at the back of my own predominately male trigonometery class in high school. But I was not of one mind about that experience. Competing for attention with the more aggressive boys in my math class had not been wholly negative; a significant amount of the satisfaction which I derive from my work in mathematics is based on the knowledge that there are few women who are successful in this area. Although I believe girls are entitled to special encouragement in learning mathematics, this belief is entangled with my feeling of accomplishment from having developed an interest in the subject myself despite discouragement. Now, as part of my job, I had to accomplish a balance between these conflicting influences in what I chose to do about this classroom dilemma. There were similarly divergent personal concerns behind how I understood the actions I might take in relation to the boys in the class. In my teaching relationship with them I had to balance my own conflicting yet simultaneous desires for freedom and order.

My capacity to bring disparate aspects of myself together in the person that I am in the classroom is one of the tools that I used to construct an approach to managing my dilemma. Because a teacher is present to students as a whole person, the conflicting parts of herself are not separable, one from another, the way they might be if we think of them as names for categories of persons or cultural ideals, like child oriented versus subject oriented, or democratic versus authoritarian.[13] A teacher has the potential to act with integrity while maintaining contradictory concerns. I did not want to be a person who treated girls unequally, as my high school trigonometry teacher had done. Nor did I want to be someone who gave special attention to girls just because they were girls. I did not want to be a person who had such a preoccupation with order that I discouraged enthusiasm. Nor did I want to try to do my work in a disorderly classroom. The person that I wanted to be—this ambiguous self-definition—became a tool to enable me to accomplish my pedagogical goals.

CONSTRUCTING SOLUTIONS
IN THE FACE OF UNSOLVABLE PROBLEMS

When I met my class the morning after recognizing my dilemma, I had not resolved any of the arguments with myself about what to do, but I did have some sense of who I wanted to be. And that made a difference.

It happened that two of the more offending boys were absent that day, so I was able to leave everyone seated where they were, walk to the other side of the room, and do most of my teaching standing at the blackboard near the girls' table without any major disruptions occurring. I used this hiatus to construct a strategy for managing the conflict that did not involve stark choices.

While I taught the class, my thinking about the boys and the girls merged with my thinking about some other currently pressing matters in the classroom. I was about to begin a new instructional unit which involved using manipulative materials and had been wondering about how to organize the students' activities with those materials. I had also been talking with my student teacher, Sandy, about ways in which she might take on responsibility in the class. We had planned the next unit together, and she was prepared to do some of the teaching. So I divided the class into four small groups (two of girls and two of boys) and put Sandy in charge of instructing and managing one group of boys and one group of girls, while I took responsibility for the other two groups. This strategy depended heavily on specific elements in the context of my classroom. It enabled me to cope with the surface of my problem while keeping its more general conflicts submerged. It was not a general solution nor a permanent one; it was an act of improvisation, a product of adjusting my ambivalent desires to the particular circumstances in which I was working.

I moved one group of boys to the area near the girls' blackboard and one group of girls to the other side of the room. This helped to avoid the distractions that would result from grouping the boys and girls together, but without geographically dividing the class along gender lines. Furthermore, because there were now two groups of boys and two of girls, both the class and I could identify other criteria for group membership besides gender. Instructing in small groups also meant that neither the teachers nor the students would be performing in front of both boys and girls at the same time, so my attention would be less likely to be judged as preferential toward either the boys or the girls. Paradoxically, because I would be teaching boys only in the company of other boys, and girls only in the company of other girls, I would be able to respond to the children more as individuals than as members of one sex or the other, as I had done when I taught them all together while they were seated at opposite ends of the room.

What can we learn from this case about how a teacher works? I did not choose this strategy because it would solve problems. I managed my dilemma by putting the problems that led to it further into the background and by bringing other parts of my job further to the foreground. Although this meant that the problems remained, my strategy gave me a way to live with them, a temporary respite that would prevent the underlying conflicts from erupting into more serious, distracting discord.

A SECOND CASE:
CONFLICTS OVER THE NATURE OF KNOWLEDGE AS ANOTHER SOURCE OF CLASSROOM DILEMMAS

The adversity in my situation arose because of contradictory social goals in my teaching. One might imagine that if I had been able to put problems of social organization aside and had defined my job only in terms of whether my students learned the subject matter, then the dilemmas I described would have disappeared. In fact, some scholars have argued that by using an impersonal "technology of instruction" (more often called a curriculum) teachers can produce subject matter knowledge in students without concern for social problems in or out of the classroom.[14] Others, who understand knowledge as a construction of the individual learner, leave social problems aside and focus on the teacher's work in fostering an individual child's understanding.[15] It may be true that if teaching and learning occur in a one-to-one encounter outside the classroom, the sort of dilemma I have described may not arise, but it is not possible in schools to separate social problems from subject-matter knowledge. In the teacher's job, at least as it is now understood, a clear distinction between tasks related to social organization and tasks related to instruction is unachievable. The following case study is intended to illustrate this point. Neither it nor the preceding case, however, is intended in any way to illustrate good or bad, skillful or skill-less, teaching. Both cases presume a value in studying common teaching practice, however it may be evaluated, whatever its effects.

Rita Cerone is a fourth-grade teacher in a small, urban public school.[16] In the situation I am about to describe, she was faced with a set of problems which arose out of her use of a workbook to instruct students in science. Her concern for solving these problems led her into a pedagogical dilemma, and what she did to manage her dilemma raises issues about teachers' work that are similar to those already described.

Science lessons in Rita's classroom often consisted of students reading their workbooks, looking at the drawings and diagrams in them, and then answering questions and checking their answers with the teacher. The topic of one such exercise was "The Cycle of Water." The workbook presented the students with a picture of a cloud, and next to it a question: "Where does the water come from?" Rita said it seemed obvious to her from the illustration that the answer was "clouds," and so she had "marked it right" when students gave that answer. (She checked other answers which were not so obvious to her in the teacher's guide before she judged them right or wrong.) Rita was, therefore, a bit perplexed when one of the girls in her class, Linda, came up to have her work corrected and declared with unusual confidence that "the answer to where water comes from is *the ocean*." Rita indicated on the girl's paper that this answer was incorrect, but Linda was surprised by this judgment and insisted that she was right.

Rita was hesitant to contradict Linda because the girl was so confident about her answer. Although Rita disagreed with her, she sensed a conflict brewing and wanted to avoid it. So she tried to understand more about what Linda was thinking. "I said to her: `Well, I don't understand. Explain it to me.' I was fumbling around and I was trying to figure out what she meant. It finally turned out that she knew, but she couldn't verbalize it for quite a while. After asking her questions and having her look at the workbook page, [Linda] said, `The clouds pick the water up. I don't know how, but it puts the water from the ocean back in the clouds.'" Rita decided in this exchange that Linda "knew" what she was supposed to learn from the lesson even though her answer did not match the answer in the teacher's guide.

The potential conflict between perspectives on what it means to "know" something was momentarily resolved when Rita agreed with Linda that her answer was indeed correct. The equilibrium between Linda's understanding and the textbook's standards of knowledge was short-lived, however, when the other students in the class took an interest in Rita's judgment. As Rita recalled, "Linda went running back to the rest of the group and told them she wasn't wrong. The other kids started arguing with Linda because they saw it the way I saw it *and* the way the answer book saw it. But Linda could prove she was right." Rita had exacerbated an underlying contradiction in her classroom when she told Linda that her answer was correct. The conflict came to the surface because Linda was a member of a group of students studying the same material. Moreover, they had all been using the teacher's guide as the standard by which to judge the correctness of their answers. Their complaint was that Rita had applied a familiar standard to judging their answers but had used another standard to evaluate Linda's. Unless Rita did something to manage this conflict, it threatened to become a more difficult classroom problem.

One student, Kevin, confident that *his* answer was right because it matched the answer in the teacher's guide and because Rita had told him it was right, led the class in an argument with Linda and, by implication, with their teacher. In Rita's words: "One of the kids, Kevin, said Linda was really dumb because the ocean was where the water started out, and it ended up in clouds just before it rained. It wasn't that he didn't get her explanation, but he just dismissed it because I had told him earlier that his answer was right and he also knew that was the answer the book wanted. That's why she came up to me in the first place: to get confirmation that she was right because Kevin had said she was wrong." Like Rita, Kevin "got" Linda's explanation. Yet her individual understanding of the matter was not his concern. He "dismissed" Linda's explanation (as Rita herself had done at first) because it did not match what the book and his teacher said was "right," and he began an argument in order to settle the matter. If the teacher and the textbook were to be taken seriously, he argued, Linda could not also be right.

Rita's job here, as in my situation, might be viewed as requiring a choice between dichotomous alternatives. If she were to practice "child-centered"

teaching, she would favor defending Linda's way of thinking while reject-
ing the textbook's authority. If she were to practice "curriculum-centered"
teaching, she would judge Linda's knowledge using the written curriculum in the teacher's guide as the standard. Those students whose answers
agreed with the book's answer were pushing her toward the latter, while
Linda was pushing her toward the former.

Rita's Argument with Herself

Rita did not represent her work in this situation as making such a forced
choice, however. Instead, she reviewed a series of complicated arguments
she had with herself on the issues involved. She contended on the one hand
that the question in the workbook was not very clear; its ambiguity made
her less inclined to trust the answers in the teacher's guide. In addition,
by reflecting on her conversation with Linda, she recognized that the girl
really understood the "cycle of water," whereas those students who put
down "clouds" might only have looked at the illustration in the book. Rita
articulated this skepticism about impersonal measures of students' knowledge in a conversation she had with some other teachers about the incident: "I think too often kids get marked wrong for things that really aren't
wrong. I mean, if you corrected Linda's paper and she wasn't around to
explain her answer, she would never have had the chance to defend herself
or say that this is the way I think. I mean, that's what happens on those
Stanford Achievement Tests. They're not given any room for individuality
of thought." Rita accepted Linda's answer as a valid representation of the
girl's understanding. Yet she also thought that both she and Linda should
concur with the answer in the book. Rita related her thinking about this
incident to her first year of teaching; she had read the teacher's guides very
carefully that year and "tried to stay one step ahead of the kids" because
she was trying to teach material she had not learned before. Even later she
relied heavily on the teacher's guide; she typically referred students directly to the "answer book" to check their own work so that she could spend
time on helping others who were slower to finish their assignments. Rita
argued that if she let Linda "get away with" her nonstandard interpretation
of the question in the science book, she might be undermining her students' trust in these books as well as her own ability to guide her students'
learning. For this teacher and her students, textbooks carry a great store of
meaning about the nature of what is to be learned. So Rita was torn: She
could produce good reasons for accepting Linda's answer as correct and
she could also produce good reasons for marking it wrong.

Rita could not win this argument with herself about how to evaluate Linda's answer; like me, she was her own antagonist. Whether she announced to the class that Linda was right and thus implied that what the book said did not matter, or that Linda was wrong because she had interpreted the "cycle of water" in her own way, the consequences would be more overt conflict. While some might see such additional conflict as educationally productive, Rita, in her circumstances, clearly did not.

Rita's Inner Tensions as a Tool of Her Trade

Rita drew on her own conflicted concerns to arrive at her decision about what to do in this situation. Her conviction that she should not choose between Linda and the textbook was based on her personal capacity to value different, potentially contradictory kinds of knowledge. This was part of the "person she wanted to be." She had begun teaching and had been reasonably successful at it without much understanding of science. She had also grown up believing that the people who write books are smarter than she—even smarter than her teachers. The public knowledge she learned in school from books had allowed her to achieve the position of teacher. So she had reason to trust the "rightness" of the knowledge represented by the standard curriculum. At the same time, however, she believed that much of what she knew could not be contained in books or measured by tests. She knew that she understood things she had figured out for herself, and sometimes she saw these ideas more clearly than those she had read in books. Rita was, therefore, concerned about the limitations of standard measures of knowledge, but her concern was not unconflicted.

Several months later Rita expressed the same ambivalent view of knowledge that formed the basis of her deliberations in this case in a conversation about the way a standardized test had been used to assess her own knowledge. She thought the test was not a very good tool for measuring what would make her a successful learner, but she also recognized that the test had some meaning to people who did not know her. She believed it would be "unfair" to deprive students of the instruction they might need to do well on such tests, even while she argued that the tests do not necessarily measure one's capacity for understanding. "If they don't have a serious attitude about tests," she said, "they're never going to make it in college. They have to have some respect for this information because it's controlling where they are going to go in life. I realize that society is not going to change before they get out of my classroom, and I don't want to put my burdens on the kids. You have to respect these tests, as I do, because I had to take them too. It's a ticket for the next place you want to go." Because Rita had not resolved her own feelings about the value of the sort of knowledge represented by scores on standardized tests, she had been in an effective position to use herself to mediate the conflict betwen conventional knowledge and individual understanding in the situation with Kevin and Linda. Her personal conflict about the value of standardized knowledge was a resource she drew upon in order to do her work in this classroom situation.

As the person responsible for settling disputes among her students about who is right, Rita represented the possibility of bringing these potentially contradictory ways of knowing together in the public arena of the classroom. Rather than siding with Kevin or Linda, she told them they were both right. She improvised. "I finally said to Kevin and Linda that they were both right. And I left it at that, and I let them handle it from there. (But I was kind of listening to what they would do.) Linda understood exactly what she was trying to get across. Kevin understood it also. But they understood on two different planes. I understood on a third one. I don't think there was any need for clarification, but there was a need for them to know they were both right."

Rita made no stark choices. She did not throw out the textbook and tell Kevin and Linda it didn't matter, nor did she tell Linda that she was wrong because she did not conform to the book's expectation. She accepted both of their answers on "two different planes" while putting herself on a "third plane," where she could value both Kevin's standards and Linda's divergence from them.

Coping Rather Than Solving

Rita constructed a way to manage the tension between individual understanding and public knowledge without resolving it. Since she had some authority as the teacher in this situation, Kevin and Linda took her judgment seriously, even though it was ambiguous. Both of them came out with a different, more complex view of knowledge. Kevin was told that the answer in the teacher's guide is not the only right answer in the public setting of the classroom, while Linda was told that the textbook answer has validity even though she sees things differently. Rita managed to deflect the vehement competition between these two students by issuing a more complex set of rules for judging one another's answers.

In my math class, I made it more difficult to draw the line between teaching that favored girls and teaching that favored boys. By muddying the waters with small-group instruction, I pushed the social conflicts that this dichotomy suggested further into the background. Rita did a similar thing in the area of instruction when she said Kevin and Linda were both right. She confused their ability to judge one another's knowledge and thereby mediated the conflict between them. As in my situation, she did not eliminate the original conflict; rather, she avoided it so as to avoid additional conflicts. This way of submerging the conflict below an improvised, workable, but superficial resolution is, of course, quite different from what many cognitive psychologists or curriculum experts would advocate.

IMAGES OF TEACHERS' WORK
AND THEIR IMPLICATIONS FOR IMPROVING IT

These two stories portray the teacher as an active negotiator, a broker of sorts, balancing a variety of interests that need to be satisfied in classrooms. The teacher in each story initiates actions as solutions to particular environmental problems and defines herself as the locus of various alternative perspectives on those actions. Conflicts among these perspectives arise in the teacher both presently within the classroom and in the way she interprets her own past experience. In order to do her job, the dilemma-managing teacher calls upon this conflicted "self" as a tool of her trade, building a working identity that is constructively ambiguous. While she works at solving society's problems and scholars' problems, she also works at coping with her own internal conflicts. She debates with herself about what to do, and instead of screening out responsibilities that contradict one another, she acknowledges them, embraces the conflict, and finds a way to manage.

What does this image of the teacher as a dilemma manager suggest about the nature of teachers' work and how to improve it? Images of teaching frame our construction of the tasks teachers perform; our sense of the work involved in successfully accomplishing these tasks forms the basis for designing improvements. Whether the actions of the two teachers I have described here should be thought of as typical strategies or be promoted as expedient practices will remain open to question. These stories are intended only to illustrate an image of teachers' work which can help us think about the nature of classroom practice. In order to learn something from the image about how to improve practice, it is necessary to compare it with other images of teachers in the literature and to examine the influence these images have had on the kind of help we give teachers when they face classroom problems.

Most commonly, *teachers are assumed to make choices among dichot-omous alternatives*: to promote equality *or* excellence; to build curriculum around children's interests *or* around subject matter; to foster indepen-dence and creativity *or* maintain standards and expect everyone to meet them.[17] These choices are thought to enable teachers to avoid dilemmas in their everyday practice. An example of this perspective can be found in the way Mary Haywood Metz analyzed the manner in which a group of teachers responded to the work tensions produced by the desegregation of their schools.[18] Metz defined keeping classroom order and promoting student learning as "contradictory imperatives" for teachers and concluded that those she observed could not both maintain standards of behavior in the classroom and nurture students' commitment to learning; instead, they divided themselves into opposing camps. Part of the work of these teach-ers, in this view, was to figure out whether classroom order or students' commitment was more important to their success as teachers, and then to choose between them. Thus it would seem appropriate that help from out-siders appear in the form of arguments to teachers about why they should pay more attention either to classroom order or to student commitment. Much preservice and inservice teacher education today takes this form. Professors and staff developers use evidence from research, rationales drawn from educational philosophy, or personal charisma to convince teachers that one approach is better than its opposite.

Another view of pedagogical work is illustrated by Gertrude McPher-son's picture of the "small town" teacher.[19] She describes teachers' conflicts entirely in terms of contradictory external pressures. In this image, *the teach-er is a person besieged by other people's expectations*. She cannot teach because of the need to defend herself against the inconsistencies in what students, administrators, colleagues, parents, and public officials expect her to do. Managing conflict is part of the teacher's job, in this view, but it is seen as a source of "unhappiness and frustration" rather than as a means by which the teacher defines herself. McPherson's view carries with it a sense of what must be done to improve teaching practice: There is very little worthwhile work that can be accomplished by the teacher "as long as the goals of our educational system are unclearly defined, . . . internally inconsistent, [and] inconsistent with dominant and often themselves inconsistent values in our larger society."[20] The more current literature on teacher stress takes a similar view: Unless the goals of the teacher's job are redefined, the only positive steps a practitioner can take to reduce the harmful effects of the tension produced by conflicting expectations are engaging in regular physical exer-cise and maintaining a healthy diet.[21] These attitudes toward teaching regard the contradictions in teaching as problems to be solved by altering the way education is organized and conceptualized by society. In this view, society needs to become more consistent about its own goals and what it expects of teachers, and, thus, conflict will be eliminated.

Yet another way of portraying teaching, one which might be thought of as a response to this abstract hope for unified goals, arises out of the work of social science researchers and government policymakers. These problem-solvers have teamed up to find ways to help teachers increase student achievement. They turn away from conflicts that might arise in the classroom and assume that *the teacher is a technical-production manager* who has the responsibility for monitoring the efficiency with which learning is being accomplished. In this view, teaching can be improved if practitioners use researchers' knowledge to solve classroom problems.[22] The teacher's work is to find out what researchers and policymakers say should be done with or to students and then to do it. How much time should be spent on direct instruction versus seatwork? How many new words should be in stories children are required to read? If the teacher does what she is told, students will learn. Taking this perspective suggests that practical conflicts can be avoided if researchers' solutions are correctly implemented by teachers.

Some educational scholars reject this image of the teacher as a "black box" through which researchers' knowledge passes into the classroom.[23] In their view, *the teacher has an active role in deciding how to teach*; she makes decisions by putting research findings together with the information available in the classroom environment to make choices about what process will produce the desired objectives. Because cognitive information processing has been used as the model in these studies of teacher decision making, however, a "decision" is seen only as a process of mathematically ordering one's choices on the basis of unequally weighted alternatives.[24] At each point in the thinking process, the decider is assumed to see clearly which of two alternative routes is preferred to reach a given goal.[25] Therefore, improving teaching involves simplifying alternatives by screening out contradictory concerns so that any reasonable person would make the same correct choice using the same information. The process is mechanical, not personal; it is the sort of thinking one can imagine would be done better by unbiased machines than by people.[26] This theory, therefore, cannot help teachers to figure out what to do about the sort of unsolvable conflicts in their work that I have described.[27]

These images of teachers—as cognitive information processors, as implementers of researchers' knowledge about how to produce learning, as stressed and neurotically defensive, and as members of opposing camps—portray the conflicts in teaching as resolvable in one way or another. In contrast, the image of the teacher as dilemma manager accepts conflict as a continuing condition with which persons can learn to cope. This latter view does not replace the idea that the teacher plays conflicting roles in society, or the idea that it is useful to note patterns in the relationship between behaviors and their outcomes in order to make productive decisions; but it puts the teacher in a different problem-solving relationship to the social conflicts and behavioral patterns in her work. It suggests that, in addition to defending against and choosing among conflicting expectations, she might also welcome their power to influence her working identity. The major difference, then, between the image of the teacher as dilemma manager and the other images I have described is that the dilemma manager accepts conflict as endemic and even useful to her work rather than seeing it as a burden that needs to be eliminated.

There are, of course, many incentives for teachers and scholars to want to eliminate conflict and to think of classroom problems as solvable. If pedagogical problems could be separated one from another rather than entangled in a web of contradictory goals, then they could be solved in some sort of linear progression—shot down like ducks coming up in a row at a penny arcade. Thinking of one's job as figuring out how to live with a web of related problems that cannot be solved seems like an admission of weakness. Sorting out problems and finding solutions that will make them go away is certainly a more highly valued endeavor in our society. Strategies which merely enable us to "cope" or "manage" go against our deep-seated hopes for making progress by gaining control over our interactions with one another. Many people—including teachers—believe that if only scholarship in psychology and the social sciences could come up to the levels achieved by the natural sciences, and if only, with the help of technology, individuals could achieve the ideal of control over the environment represented in such scholarship, then everyone could live happily ever after. The work of managing dilemmas, in contrast, requires admitting some essential limitations on our control over human problems. It suggests that some conflicts cannot be resolved and that the challenge is to find ways to keep them from erupting into more disruptive confrontations.

This connection of limitation with dilemma management needs to be clarified, because we have come to identify classroom management with the teacher's ability to control students' behavior and direct them in learning tasks. This common usage most closely parallels the nonschool definition of a manager as a person who controls or directs the affairs of others.

Such control is certainly an essential part of the teacher's job. I use the term *manage* in a different sense, however. To manage to do something can also mean to contrive to do it, implying that the capacity for invention or improvisation is a necessary part of the manager's repertoire. This usage suggests that a manager is one who is able to find a way to do something and that action and invention are fused together in the management process. We might also think of people as managing when they are able to continue to act or even to thrive in adverse circumstances. The teacher's work involves just this sort of invention and action in situations where potential adversity makes solving some kinds of problems inadvisable.

In order to do the work of teaching, as I have portrayed it, one needs to have the resources to cope with equally weighted alternatives when it is not appropriate to express a preference between them. One needs to be able to take advice from researchers but also to know what to do when that advice is contradictory, or when it contradicts knowledge that can only be gained in a particular context. One needs to hold at bay the conflicting expectations of those who have the power to determine whether one can succeed as a teacher or not and at the same time use those expectations as references in self-definition. One can be committed to a particular ideology or its opposite while recognizing the limitations of taking any single-minded view of such complicated process as teaching and learning in schools. One needs to be comfortable with a self that is complicated and sometimes inconsistent.

Perhaps it is our society's belief in the existence of a solution for every problem that has kept any significant discussion of the teacher's unsolvable problems out of both scholarly and professional conversations about the work of teaching. But there may be other explanations as well. It may be that many teachers are able to carry on with their work as if there were no conflicts in what they are expected to do, or that there are in fact no conflicts in the way they define their jobs. It also may be the case that the sorts of people who become teachers and stay in teaching do not have the intellectual capacity to recognize the complications in the work that I have described.[28] These possibilities certainly deserve our attention.

But if dilemma managing is a significant part of the work of teaching, there are several questions that deserve further examination. First, there are questions about *frequency*. I have argued only that it is possible for teachers to work in ways that suggest that some classroom problems are better managed than solved. How much of a role does this sort of work play in what teachers do? How often do dilemmas of the sort I have described arise in classrooms? How often are they "managed" rather than "resolved"? What are the characteristics of teachers who do more dilemma managing than others? What are the characteristics of classrooms in which dilemma management is common?

A second category of questions can be grouped around understanding and evaluating what teachers actually do when they manage dilemmas. My emphasis in this essay has not been on the particular strategies used by the teachers but on the more general elements of the work involved. What different kinds of *strategies* are used in classrooms to cope with unsolvable problems? How could they usefully be grouped? Are there better and worse ways of keeping classroom conflict under the surface? How do the strategies teachers use compare with those used by other professionals who face dilemmas?

We also need to know more about what kind of *resources* teachers have available to cope with contradictions within themselves and in their work. How do they learn to cope, or that it is an appropriate thing to do? What characteristics of their working environment make dilemma managing more or less possible? How can teachers who have trouble coping with conflict get better at it? What role do supervisors, formal course work, other life experiences, and colleagues play in the development of the teacher's capacity for actively tolerating ambiguity? How are the personal resources required to manage pedagogical dilemmas related to the skills that researchers and policymakers use to address educational problems or the knowledge that scholars use to analyze the tensions in the work of teaching? What resources besides skill and knowledge might teachers bring to this aspect of their work?

Our understanding of the work of teaching might be enhanced if we explored what teachers do when they choose to endure and make use of conflict. Such understanding will be difficult to acquire if we approach all of the problems in teaching as if they are solvable, and if we assume that what is needed to solve them is knowledge that can be produced outside the classroom. In order to pursue the questions I have listed here, we shall need to adopt an image of teaching which takes account of the possibility that the teacher herself is a resource in managing the problems of educational practice.

NOTES

1. My distinction between theory and practice here follows that developed by Joseph Schwab in his studies of curriculum development. Schwab has observed that

the particulars of time, place, person, and circumstance which surround questions of what and how to teach are incongruent with the order, system, economy, and generality required to build a good theory; see Schwab, "The Practical: Arts of Eclectic," in *Science, Curriculum, and Liberal Education: Selected Essays*, ed. Ian Westbury and Neil J. Wilkof (Chicago: University of Chicago Press, 1978), p. 322.

2. See, for example, Susan Florio and Martha Walsh, "The Teacher as a Colleague in Classroom Research," in *Culture and the Bilingual Classroom*, ed. Henry T. Trueba, Grace P. Guthrie, and Kathryn H. Au (Rowley, MA: Newbury House, 1981), pp. 87–101; Eliot Eisner, "Can Educational Research Inform Educational Practice?" *Phi Delta Kappan*, *65* (March 1984), 447–452; and Leslie L. Huling, Myron Trang, and Linda Cornell, "Interactive Research and Development: A Promising Strategy for Teacher Educators," *Journal of Teacher Education*, *32* (1981), 13–14.

Christopher Clark and Penelope L. Peterson have recently emphasized that descriptive research on how teachers make interactive decisions in the classroom should be done as a basis for further theory building about teacher thinking; see their "Teacher's Thought Processes," Occasional Paper No. 73, Institute for Research on Teaching (East Lansing, MI: Michigan State University, 1984), p. 76.

3. Schwab describes the value of such "deliberation" as a method for studying the teaching process in "The Practical 4: Something for Curriculum Professors to Do," *Curriculum Inquiry*, *13* (1983), 239–265. His notions are expanded, particularly with relation to deliberative exchanges among differing aspects of one's self, by Lee Shulman in "The Practical and the Eclectic: A Deliberation on Teaching and Educational Research," *Curriculum Inquiry*, *14* (1984), 183–200.

4. The "particularistic" nature of the teacher's perspective has been described by Arthur S. Bolster, "Toward a More Effective Model of Research on Teaching," *Harvard Educational Review*, *53* (1983), 294–308. The context-specific character of work in classrooms as it appears to practitioners has been examined by Walter Doyle in "Learning the Classroom Environment: An Ecological Analysis," *Journal of Teacher Education*, *28* (1977), 51–55, and "Paradigms for Research on Teacher Effectiveness," *Review of Research in Education*, Vol. 5, ed. Lee Shulman (Itasca, IL: Peacock, 1977), 163–198. Philip Jackson compared teachers' propensity for "anecdotal" descriptions of their work with the more abstract quality of academic writing about teaching. See Jackson, "The Way Teachers Think," in *Psychology and Educational Practice*, ed. Gerald S. Lesser (Glenview, IL: Scott, Foresman, 1971), pp. 10–34.

5. The personal quality of teachers' knowledge is emphasized by Sharon Feiman and Robert Floden. See their "Cultures of Teaching" in *Third Handbook*

of Research on Teaching, ed. Merlin C. Wittrock, in press. Gary Fenstermacher argues for considering the effect of the teacher's own concerns and personal history on the decisions she makes in the classroom in "A Philosophical Consideration of Recent Research on Teacher Effectiveness," in *Review of Research in Education*, 6, ed. Lee Shulman (Itasca, IL: Peacock, 1979), pp. 186–215.

6. I have chosen the feminine gender for pronouns which apply to teachers throughout this manuscript because the majority of teachers are women.

7. Schwab, "The Practical: A Language for Curriculum," in Westbury and Wilkof, p. 289.

8. See, for example, Bryan Wilson, "The Teacher's Role: A Sociological Analysis," *British Journal of Sociology, 13* (1962), 15–32; Charles Bidwell, "The School as a Formal Organization," in *Handbook of Organizations*, ed. James G. March (Chicago: Rand McNally, 1965), pp. 972–1022; and Ann Lieberman and Lynn Miller, "The Social Realities of Teaching," *Teachers College Record, 80* (1978), 54–68.

9. The language of "dilemmas" to describe classroom problems has also been used by Ann Berlak and Harold Berlak in *The Dilemmas of Schooling: Teaching and Social Change* (London: Methuen, 1981). However, their analysis focuses on cultural contradictions and opportunities for social change as they are manifest in teachers' dilemmas and gives less attention to the practical work involved in managing dilemmas in the classroom.

10. See Schwab, "The Practical: Arts of Eclectic," p. 318; for a comparison between the knowledge produced by social science research and the knowledge practitioners use in their work, see Charles E. Lindholm and David K. Cohen, *Usable Knowledge: Social Science and Social Problem Solving* (New Haven: Yale University Press, 1979); and also David K. Cohen, "Commitment and Uncertainty," Harvard University, unpublished manuscript, 1981.

11. Descriptions of teacher thinking have emphasized choice between alternative courses of action as the outcome of teacher decision making, based on models of cognitive information processing. See, for example, Richard J. Shavelson, "Teachers' Decision Making," in *The Psychology of Teaching Methods, The 75th Yearbook of the National Society for the Study of Education*, Part I, ed. Nathaniel L. Gage (Chicago: University of Chicago Press, 1976), pp. 143–165; John Eggleston, ed., *Teacher Decision Making in the Classroom* (London: Routledge & Kegan Paul, 1979); and Christopher Clark and Robert Yinger, "Research on Teacher Thinking," *Curriculum Inquiry* (1977), 279–304.

12. *Funk and Wagnalls' Standard College Dictionary* (New York: Harcourt Brace and World, 1963), p. 372. For a psychological description of the contradictory imperatives that can arise within the person of the teacher, see Angelika C. Wagner, "Conflicts in Consciousness: Imperative Cognitions Can Lead to Knots

in Thinking," paper presented at the First Symposium of the International Study Association on Teacher Training, Tilburg University, The Netherlands, 26–28 Oct. 1983.

13. For example, such dichotomous categories are used to examine teachers' work in Harry L. Gracey, *Curriculum or Craftsmanship: Elementary School Teachers in a Bureaucratic Setting* (Chicago: University of Chicago Press, 1972); George Spindler, "Education in a Transforming American Culture," *Harvard Educational Review*, 25 (1955), 145–156; and Mary Haywood Metz, *Classrooms and Corridors: The Crisis of Authority in Desegregated Secondary Schools* (Berkeley, CA: University of California Press, 1978). In contrast, views of the teacher derived from the social psychology of George Herbert Mead and others in "the Chicago School" present a more complex picture: for example, Willard Waller in *The Sociology of Teaching* (New York: Wiley, 1932); and Philip Jackson in *Life in Classrooms* (New York: Holt, Rinehart and Winston, 1968). The Berlaks in *The Dilemmas of Schooling*, p. 133, describe the teacher's job in the face of contradictions as "transformation," by which they mean the invention of a pedagogical process which joins opposing poles of a cultural contradiction; in their view, the teacher has the capacity to be a vehicle whereby "the contending presses of the culture at least for the moment are synthesized and thus overcome."

14. See Carl Bereiter, "Schools Without Education," *Harvard Educational Review*, 42 (1972), 390–414; see also John D. McNeil, "A Scientific Approach to Supervision," in *Supervision of Teaching*, ed. Thomas J. Sergiovanni (Alexandria, VA: Association for Supervision and Curriculum Development, 1982), pp. 18–34.

15. This position is characteristic of those educational reformers whose philosophy of learning is built on theories of individual cognitive development.

16. I had the opportunity to observe and work with Rita Cerone over 3 years as part of the Teacher Development Project in the Division for Study and Research in Education, Massachusetts Institute of Technology. This project is described in my "Teaching About Thinking and Thinking about Teaching," *Journal of Curriculum Studies*, 16 (1984), 1–18. Quotes of Rita's remarks are taken from transcripts of meetings of the teacher participants in that project and transcripts of my individual interviews with Rita, which occurred over a 3-year period. The name "Rita Cerone" is a pseudonym, as are all student names used in this manuscript.

17. See, for example, Gracey, *Curriculum or Craftsmanship*; Jackson, "The Way Teachers Think"; Bidwell, "The School as a Formal Organization"; and Spindler, "Education in a Transforming American Culture."

18. Metz, *Classrooms and Corridors*.

19. McPherson, *Small Town Teacher* (Cambridge: Harvard University Press, 1972).

20. McPherson, *Small Town Teacher*, p. 215.

21. Kathleen V. Hoover-Dempsey and Earline D. Kendell, "Stress and Coping in Teaching: An Integrative Review of the Literature," paper presented at the annual meeting of the American Educational Research Association, New Orleans, 25 April 1984.

22. See, for example, Nathaniel L. Gage, "An Analytic Approach to Research on Instructional Methods," in *The Social Psychology of Teaching*, ed. Arnold Morrison and Donald McIntyre (Hammondsworth, Eng.: Penguin Books, 1972); Robert E. Slavin, "Component Building: A Strategy for Research-Based Instructional Improvement," *Elementary School Journal*, *84* (1984), 255–269; John D. McNeil, "A Scientific Approach to Supervision"; and Jere Brophy and Thomas Good, *Teacher-Student Relationships: Causes and Consequences* (New York: Holt, Rinehart, and Winston, 1974).

23. Hilda Borko, Richard Cone, Nancy Russo, and Richard J. Shavelson, "Teachers' Decision Making," in *Research on Teaching: Concepts, Findings, and Implications*, ed. Penelope L. Peterson and Herbert T. Walberg (Berkeley, CA: McCutcheon, 1979).

24. See Shavelson, "Teachers' Decision Making" in Gage, *Psychology of Teaching Methods*; Eggleston, *Teacher Decision Making in the Classroom*; and Clark and Yinger, "Research on Teacher Thinking."

25. This model is outlined in Clark and Peterson, "Teacher's Thought Processes," pp. 63–69.

26. The problems with mechanical information processing as the ideal model for describing human decision making in situations fraught with conflict have been cogently outlined in David Braybrooke and Charles Lindblom, *A Strategy of Decision: Policy Evaluation as a Social Process* (New York: Free Press, 1963), pp. 246–247. More recently, Joseph Weizenbaum has argued against assuming that human judgment is comparable to even the most sophisticated computers, in *Computer Power and Human Reason: From Judgment to Calculation* (San Francisco: Freeman, 1976).

27. Richard Shavelson and Paula Stern, "Research on Teachers' Pedagogical Thoughts, Judgments, Decisions, and Behavior," *Review of Educational Research*, *51* (1981), 471.

28. Jackson proposes this possibility in *Life in Classrooms*, pp. 144–148.

About the Authors

Rebecca Akin, a K/1 teacher for 7 years in the San Francisco Bay Area, is now pursuing graduate studies in education. Her narrative was part of a larger study on student language use undertaken while she was a Carnegie Scholar.

Deborah Loewenberg Ball is professor of mathematics education and teacher education at the University of Michigan and an experienced elementary school teacher. Her chapter was written while she was teaching mathematics on a daily basis to third graders while she was also a faculty member at Michigan State University. It was the first article she wrote based on research using her own teaching.

Cynthia Ballenger has been teaching third and fourth grade in the Boston area and working with teachers of bilingual children through the Chèche Konnen Center at TERC. Her article was published as a part of a book she wrote called *Teaching Other People's Children: Literacy and Learning in a Bilingual Classroom* (Teachers College Press, 1999).

Ron Berger has been teaching fifth- and sixth-grade students for 25 years at the Shutesbury Elementary School in Shutesbury, a small rural community in western Massachusetts. He also consults with the Expeditionary Learning Outward Bound national school network and with Harvard's Project Zero; both these organizations have provided a rich professional community that contributed to the ideas embodied in his written piece here.

Timothy Boerst is a National Board–certified fifth-grade teacher at Jane Addams Elementary School in Redford, Michigan, and a Practitioner Scholar with the Center for Proficiency in Teaching Mathematics at the University of Michigan. He has been teaching for 12 years. His chapter stems from his early attempts to use ethnographic methods to capture an issue with salience to practitioners that would rarely be the subject of traditional educational scholarship.

Lois Brandts, who has been teaching for 30 years, currently teaches third grade at El Camino School in Goleta, California. As a member of the Santa

Barbara Research Group, she and her colleagues investigated issues of equity, access, and respect for all children. Her chapter was a result of her research over a 2-year period concerning the effectiveness of pullout programs in both first and second grades.

Vanessa Brown is a teacher on special assignment at the Philadelphia Writing Project at the Graduate School of Education, University of Pennsylvania in Philadelphia. She has been a teacher for almost 30 years. Her project is an outgrowth of an inquiry into practice that began shortly after she transferred to a new teaching position in a Philadelphia comprehensive high school.

Gerald Campano's contribution was the result of his work as a fifth-grade teacher-researcher at a neighborhood elementary school in California, where he investigated the school literacy practices of children from immigrant, migrant, and refugee backgrounds as part of his graduate studies. He is currently an assistant professor of education at Indiana University, Bloomington.

Marlene Carter has been an English teacher in the Los Angeles Unified School District for 26 years and is currently teaching English at Dorsey High School. Her article is based on teacher research she conducted with the support of the Carnegie Academy for the Scholarship of Teaching and Learning.

Joan Kernan Cone is an English teacher at El Cerrito High School in El Cerrito, California, and has been teaching for 40 years. Her chapter was written as a response to her growing concern over the damage of high-stakes testing and her longtime advocacy of untracking and of demanding and exciting curricula for all students.

Larry Copes is an independent consultant in educational mathematics, writing teaching materials for publishers and running workshops for teachers. His chapter is an amalgam of classroom experiences with this problem over 30 years of teaching college mathematics and preparing secondary teachers.

Griselle M. Diaz-Gemmati is a seventh- and eighth-grade language arts and social sciences teacher at Norwood Park School in Chicago. Her article, published as a chapter in *Inside City Schools* (Freedman et al., 1999), is the realization of her participation in the Multicultural Collaborative for Literacy and Secondary Schools (the M-CLASS Project), which motivated her to explore the underlying issues of race, ethnicity, and social justice in her classroom.

Yvonne Divans Hutchinson, a National Board–certified teacher and 38-year veteran, teaches 9th- and 10th-grade English at King Drew Magnet High School of Medicine and Science in Los Angeles. "A Friend of Their Minds" and "Thinking with Text" are part of her classroom research as a Carnegie Scholar.

Magdalene Lampert's chapter was written in 1984 while she was teaching fourth-, fifth-, and sixth-grade mathematics at Buckingham, Browne and Nichols School in Cambridge, Massachusetts. She then taught fifth-grade math for 7 years at Spartan Village School in East Lansing, Michigan. Both these teaching situations involved using her classroom as a site for teacher research and teacher education. She is currently on the faculty of the University of Michigan.

Steven Levy taught fourth grade at the Bowman School in Lexington, Massachusetts. After 28 years in the classroom, he now works as a school designer for Expeditionary Learning Outward Bound. He wrote his article as a chapter in his book, *Starting From Scratch*, to describe the power of a guiding question to motivate students and shape the scope of inquiry.

Heidi Lyne is one of the founding teachers at the Mission Hill School in Boston, where she now teaches middle school science and humanities. Her chapter was written for her Carnegie project on graduation by portfolio presentation.

A 23-year teaching veteran, **Jeffrey Maas** is currently teaching in a 2/3 classroom at Sandburg Elementary in Madison, Wisconsin. His ongoing inquiry into chaos theory and teaching began in the mid-1990s with his affiliation with the Wisconsin Alliance for Arts Education.

After teaching first grade in East Los Angeles for 6 years, **Ramón Martínez** taught English as a foreign language in the Czech Republic and Mexico. He wrote this article while he was actively involved in the Coalition for Educational Justice, a grassroots organization of parents, students, and teachers working to transform public education in Los Angeles.

Renee Moore, National Board–certified teacher and former Mississippi Teacher of the Year, is a 14-year veteran who currently teaches English and journalism at Broad Street High School in Shelby, Mississippi. Her chapter summarizes the action research process used in developing her work on teaching standard English to rural African American students.

Marsha R. Pincus is an English and drama teacher at J.R. Masterman Laboratory and Demonstration School. A teacher-scholar with Carnegie Academy for the Scholarship of Teaching and Learning and a Teacher Consultant with the Philadelphia Writing Project and the Philadelphia Young Playwrights Program, Marsha has been teaching in the School District of Philadelphia for 29 years.

Emily Wolk is a resource teacher at Pio Pico Elementary School in Santa Ana, California, and has been teaching for 16 years. Her chapter was based on her experience with her students, the Pio Pico Student Researchers, and their work to transform their world through participatory action research.

Index

Abdul, R., 265
Academic Performance Index (API), 268–269
Achievement
    African American male high achievement
        and, 202–208
    African American male underachievement
        and, 192–201, 207, 208–209, 210–213
Action-based project, Pio Pico Student
    Researchers and, 166–170
Act of Reading, The (Iser), 148
Adams, John, 171–172, 178–179
Adler, Mortimer, 185
Advanced Placement (AP) classes
    African American male high achievement
        and, 202–208
    African American male underachievement
        and, 192–201, 207, 208–209, 212–213
Affirmative action, 205–207, 228
African Americans. *See also* Haitians
    confronting racism in the classroom and,
        214–236
    culturally engaged instruction and, 77–90,
        196–197
    male, high achievement of, 202–208
    male, underachievement of, 192–201, 207,
        208–209, 210–213
    oral tradition among, 181–185
    social action and, 257–265
Akin, Rebecca, 6, 7, 9, 15, 67–69
Amato, M., 18
American Revolution, 171–180
    evaluating student learning on, 178–180
    grand question in study of, 171–172,
        178–179
    learning from history prior to, 172–178
Angelou, Maya, 186, 261
Applebee, A., 58
Aristotle, 173–176
Art, 46–48
    nature of "real art," 47–48
    project work and, 46, 48
    standards for, 47
Asian Americans, Hmong refugees, 237–241
Assessment, 40–43
    language of critique in, 41–42
    nature of, 40
    portfolios in, 40, 42–43
    preassessment in culturally engaged
        instruction, 87–88
    ranking versus, 40
    reporting test scores by race, 212
    self-assessment, 40–42, 43
    Stanford 9 exam and, 268–269
    of student learning in social studies,
        178–181
Athletics, African American male
    achievement and, 198–200, 208
Au, Kathryn H., 300 n. 2

Ball, Deborah Loewenberg, 6, 93, 95–132,
    111, 117
Ballenger, Cynthia, 187, 243–254
Barkley, Elizabeth, 7
Barr, R., 64
Barth, Roland, 56
Bass, R., 1
Beloved (Morrison), 161
Bereiter, Carl, 302 n. 14
Berger, Ron, 5, 15, 34–56
Berlak, Ann, 301 n. 9
Berlak, Harold, 301 n. 9
Berthoff, Ann, 81
Bidwell, Charles, 301 n. 8, 302 n. 17
Bilingualism
    Open Court reading program and, 269
    Proposition 227 and, 267–268
    Stanford 9 exam, 268–269
Boal, Augusto, 153
Boerst, Tim, 15, 17–33
Boggs, S., 244

Bolster, Arthur S., 300 n. 4
Boring, E. G., 100
Borko, Hilda, 303 n. 23
Brandts, Lois, 15, 57–66
Braybrooks, David, 303 n. 26
Bread Loaf School of English (Middlebury
    College), 80–86
Bread Loaf Teacher Network, 84
Brecht, Bertolt, 153
Briggs, J., 270, 278, 279
Broad Street High School (Shelby,
    Mississippi), 90 n. 1
Brookline Teacher-Researcher Seminar
    (BTRS), 244–246
Brooks, Gwendolyn, 261
Brophy, Jere, 303 n. 22
Brown, T., 20
Brown, Vanessa, 6, 9, 255, 257–266
Brown v. Board of Education, 229
Bruner, Jerome, 96–99, 111
Building model for addition and subtraction,
    103–107
Bush, George W., 154
Busing, 229–232
Butterfly effect, 272–273, 278–279

California
    California Learning Assessment System
        (CLAS), 184
    California State Department of Education,
        95
    Open Court reading program, 269
    Proposition 227, 267–268
    Stanford 9 exam, 268–269
Calkins, L. M., 265
Cambourne, B., 64
Campano, Gerald, 9, 187, 237–242
Carnegie Academy for the Scholarship of
    Teaching (CASTL)
    background and description of, 4
    The Laramie Project and, 149
    searching for models of scholarship of
        teaching, 5
Carnegie Foundation for the Advancement of
    Teaching, 4, 8–9, 190
Carter, Marlene, 187, 189–209
Casareno, A., 2
CASTL. *See* Carnegie Academy for the
    Scholarship of Teaching (CASTL)
Cerone, Rita, 289–294, 302 n. 16

Chaos theory, 270–280
    butterfly effect and, 272–273, 278–279
    first day of class and, 272–276
    fractals and, 279–280
    Halloween play and, 276–278
    nature of, 270, 272–273
    new definition of chaos and, 278
    principles of learning theory and, 271–272
Cisneros, Sandra, 261
Civil rights, 228, 229–232
Clark, Christopher, 300 n. 2, 301 n. 11, 303
    n. 25
Clinton, Bill, 154
Cochran-Smith, M., 2, 3, 152
Cohen, David K., 301 n. 10
College Board, 193–194, 197–198, 200, 204
Community
    building through journal writing, 261–264
    classroom violence and, 225–226, 233–236
    culturally engaged instruction and, 84–85
    in culture of quality, 55–56
    dilemmas of creating and using
        community in mathematics instruction,
        125–126
    first day of class and, 17–33, 272–276
    impact of pullout programs on community
        in schools, 57–66
    mathematics instruction and, 117–126, 129
    students' learning and, 123–125
Comprehensive School Mathematics Program
    (CSMP), 102–107
Cone, Joan Kernan, 6, 9, 187, 210–213
Cone, Richard, 303 n. 23
Contradictory imperatives (Metz), 295
Cook-Gumperz, J., 244
Copes, Larry, 93, 133–146
Cornell, Linda, 300 n. 2
Cromwell, Oliver, 177–178
Culturally engaged instruction (CEI), 77–90
    African American male achievement and,
        77–90, 196–197
    applying in the classroom, 87–88
    defining, 81–82
    expanding circle of involvement in, 82–85
    implications for teachers, 85–86
    lessons of, 88–90
    reading in, 80–81
    self-talk in, 78
    Stanford 9 exam and, 268–269
    talk with others in, 79–80

Culture of quality, 34–56
  art and, 46–48
  assessment and, 40–43
  details and, 49–51
  extending outside school, 53–55
  hard work and, 36–40
  negotiating standards and, 51–53
  non-curricular aspects of, 35–36
  peer pressure and, 44–46
  project-centered approach and, 37–38, 46, 48, 50–51
  student attitudes and, 35–36
  teacher training and, 55–56
  universal success and, 38–40
Culture of schools
  first day of fifth grade, 17–33
  Mission Hill School (website), 70–76
  pullout programs and, 57–66
  quality in, 34–56
  research on culturally engaged instruction, 77–90
Curriculum
  African American male achievement and, 193
  culturally engaged instruction (CEI) in English/language arts, 77–90
  drama and *The Laramie Project*, 93, 147–164
  first day of class and, 26, 27, 30–31, 32–33
  mathematics, 95–146
  Pio Pico Student Researchers and, 166–170
  social studies and American Revolution, 171–180
Curtis, Christopher Paul, 260, 261
Cziko, C., 263

Dahmer, Jeffrey, 233
Darling-Hammond, L., 3, 71–72
Davis, Gray, 268
Davis, S., 203
Deaf culture project, 52
Delpit, Lisa, 80
Desegregation, 229–232
Details, 49–51
  benefits of focus on, 50–51
  importance of, 49
Dewey, John, 3, 96, 101, 102, 112–113, 154, 156
Dialogue, in culturally engaged instruction, 79–80

Diaz-Gemmati, Griselle M., 187, 214–236
Dilemmas of teaching
  chaos theory of the classroom and, 270–280
  conflict between self and students in, 281–299
  conflict over contradictory social goals in classroom, 284–288
  conflict over nature and sources of knowledge in classroom, 288–294
  Open Court reading program (California) and English language learners, 269
  Proposition 227 (California) and English language learners, 267–268
  social action in the classroom and, 257–265
  Stanford 9 exam and English language learners, 268–269
Douglass, Frederick, 261
Doyle, Walter, 300 n. 4
Dreamkeepers, The (Ladson-Billings), 81

Early Academic Outreach Program, 205
Edmiston, Brian, 153, 163
Eggleston, John, 301 n. 11
Eisner, Eliot, 300 n. 2
Elementary School Journal, The, 6
Ellison, Ralph, 189
English/language arts
  African American male high achievement and, 202–208
  African American male underachievement and, 192–201, 207, 208–209, 210–213
  African American oral traditions, 181–185
  confronting racism in, 214–236
  drama and *The Laramie Project*, 93, 147–164
  grammar and culturally engaged instruction (CEI), 77–90
  Open Court reading program, 269
  Proposition 227 (California), 267–268
  Reader-response theory (Rosenblatt), 151–152, 155–162, 163
Epic Theatre, 159, 163–164

Faith in God, African American male achievement and, 202–203
Feiman, Sharon, 300–301 n. 5
Field trips, in culture of quality, 54
First day of class, 17–33
  chaos theory of the classroom and, 272–276
  classroom procedures and, 24, 25, 27

First day of class (cont'd)
  in-service days before, 23
  narrative analysis of, 19–33
  reasons to study, 19
  sense of urgency and, 18
  student knowledge of teacher and, 23–24,
    25, 31–32
  student participation in, 27, 28–32
  subject matter and, 26, 27, 30–31, 32–33
Floden, Robert, 300–301 n. 5
Florio, Susan, 300 n. 2
Fluty, Reggie, 161
Foster, Michele, 80
Fractals, and chaos theory of the classroom,
    279–280
Freedman, S. W., 2
*A Friend of Their Minds: Capitalizing on the
    Oral Tradition* (website), 182–185
Friends, dialogue with, 79–80
*From Classroom to Community:
    Transforming Teaching and Learning*
    (website), 166–170

Gage, Nathaniel L., 301 n. 11, 303 n. 22
Galileo, 173–176
Gallimore, R., 3
Gangs, African American male achievement
    and, 198
Gegeo, D., 244
Geology project, 48
Gilyard, Keith, 80
Good, Thomas, 303 n. 22
Goswami, Dixie, 81
Gracey, Harry L., 302 n. 13, 302 n. 17
Grammar, culturally engaged instruction and,
    77–90
Greenleaf, C., 263
Guthrie, Grace P., 300 n. 2

Haitians, 243–254
  disciplinary standards and methods for
    preschool, 243–253
  mainstream culture versus, 248, 254 n. 2
  socialization as children, 244
Hargreaves, A., 3
Harris, L. K., 147
Harvard Principals' Center, 56
Hatch, Thomas, 1–13, 170 n. 1, 185 n.
Hawkins, David, 96, 111–113

Heath, S. B., 248
Henderson, Russell, 154
Hiebert, J., 3
Hilliard, Asa, 80, 194
Hmong refugees, 237–241
Hollingsworth, S., 3
Homosexuality, drama and *The Laramie
    Project*, 93, 147–164
hooks, bell, 261
Hooray for Diffendoofer Day! (Dr. Seuss), 261
Hoover-Dempsey, Kathleen V., 303 n. 21
House on Mango Street, The (Cisneros), 261
Huling, Leslie L., 300 n. 2
Hunt, R., 203
Hurwitz, L., 263
Hutchings, P., 4
Hutchinson, Yvonne Divan, 6, 7–8, 93,
    181–186, 185 n.

Iiyoshi, T., 170 n. 1, 185 n.
I Know Why the Caged Bird Sings (Angelou),
    185
Improving Schools from Within (Barth), 56
Individual Education Programs (IEPs), 271
Inquiry, as central to learning, 3
Intellectual honesty (Bruner), 96–97, 127–130
Invention in mathematics, 111–117
  appreciating mathematics in children,
    113–116
  rationale for teaching, 111–113
  respecting children as thinkers, 117
  students' learning and, 116–117
Invisible Man (Ellison), 189
Iser, W., 148

Jackson, Philip, 127, 300 n. 4, 302 n. 13, 303
    n. 28
Japanese culture
  art in, 48
  importance of education in, 56
Jenkins, G., 203
Jenkins, Terrance, 148
Jewelry project, 50–51
Johannson, Mike, 204
Journal writing, 152, 261–264

Kalnin, J. S., 2
Kaufman, Moises, 147, 151–153, 155, 159
Kendell, Earline D., 303 n. 21

King, Martin Luther, Jr., 182
King, Rodney, 233
Kitcher, P., 98, 113
Kline, M., 109–110
Kunjufu, Jawnza, 194

Ladson-Billings, Gloria, 81
Lampert, Magdalene, 1, 9, 98, 99, 100–101, 117, 127–128, 255, 281–303
Langer, J., 58
Laramie Project, The, 93, 147–164
    background and context of, 148–151
    described, 151–152
    development of, 151, 152–153
    implications for practice, 162–164
    reader-response theory (Rosenblatt) and, 151–152, 155–162, 163
    student responses to, 155–162
    teacher-researcher development of, 152–154
Latinos, confronting racism in classroom and, 214–216
Learning theory, 271–272
Lee, H., 218
Lensmire, T., 128
Lesser, Gerald S., 300 n. 4
Levy, Steven, 93, 171–180
Lexington Public Schools (Massachusetts), 171–180
Lieberman, Ann, 2, 301 n. 8
Lindholm, Charles E., 301 n. 10, 303 n. 26
Literature circles
    described, 217–218
    for *Roll of Thunder, Hear My Cry* (Taylor), 218, 228–229, 232–233
    tension among students and, 225–226, 233–234
    for *To Kill a Mockingbird* (Lee), 218, 219–228, 229, 232–233
Little, J. W., 3
Lives on the Boundary (Rose), 243
Lortie, D., 127
Lubetkin, M. T., 169
Luther, Martin, 176–177
Lynchings, 229
Lyne, Heidi, 6, 7–8, 15, 70–76, 76 n. 1
Lytle, S. L., 2, 3, 152

Maas, Jeffrey, 255, 270–280
Mainstream culture (Heath), 248, 254 n. 2

Malcolm X, 261
March, James G., 301 n. 8
Martinez, Ramón, 6, 255, 267–269
Masterman High School (Philadelphia)
    described, 147–150
    The Laramie Project and, 147–164
Mathematically sacred ground (Hawkins), 112
Mathematics, 95–146
    classroom instruction based on standards in, 133–146
    community and, 117–126, 129
    contradictory goals of teachers of, 100–101
    intellectual honesty (Bruner) and, 96–97, 127–130
    invention in, 111–117
    pedagogical challenge of elementary, 99–101
    reform recommendations for, 93, 95
    research methodology for studying, 97–99
    standards for, 93, 95, 129, 133–146
    teaching negative numbers, 101–111
McIntyre, Donald, 303 n. 22
McKinney, Aaron, 154
McLaughlin, M., 3
McNeil, John D., 302 n. 14
McPherson, Gertrude, 295–296, 302–303 n. 19–20
Mead, George Herbert, 302 n. 13
Mentors, dialogue with, 79–80
Metz, Mary Haywood, 295, 302 n. 13, 302 n. 18
Michaels, S., 244
Miller, Lynn, 301 n. 8
Mission Hill School (website), 70–76
    portfolio work and, 70, 72–73
    reflection on, 73–76
    structure of, 70–71
Moeller, Victor, 185
Mohamed, J., 265
Mohanty, Satya P., 240, 241–242 n. 2
Money, in teaching negative numbers, 107–109
Moore, Renee, 9, 15, 77–91
Morrison, Arnold, 303 n. 22
Morrison, Toni, 161, 261
Moss, Beverly, 202

Narrative analysis
    of first day of class, 19–33
    future narrative, 32–33

Narrative analysis (cont'd)
  historical narrative, 21–32
  methodology and data for, 20–21
  multiple voices of teacher in, 67–69
National Council of Teachers of English
    (NCTE), 79
National Council of Teachers of Mathematics
    (NCTM), 93, 95, 133–146
National Research Council, 95
National Writing Project Urban Sites
    Network Conference, 192–193, 200–201
Negative numbers, 101–111
  analyzing content for teaching, 102–107
  Building model for teaching, 103–107
  community learning and, 118–123
  dilemmas of content and representation of,
    110–111
  money and, 107–109
  rationale for teaching integers, 102
  students' learning and, 109–110
Negotiation, 51–53
  earned power in, 53
  of types of support, 51–53
  of use of class time, 52–53
No Child Left Behind Act, 89
Nussbaum, Martha C., 237

O'Connor, M. C., 244
Open Court reading program (California),
    269
Operación Limpieza (Lubetkin), 169
Oral tradition
  African American, 181–185
  *A Friend of Their Minds: Capitalizing on
    the Oral Tradition* (website), 182–185
Outside resources
  African American male achievement and,
    205–207
  in culture of quality, 54–55

Page, L. F., 203
Palacco, Pat, 261
Palincsar, A., 99
Parents
  African American male achievement and,
    192, 193, 195–196, 203–204
  culturally engaged instruction and, 84–85
  in culture of quality, 54, 55
  reprimands by Haitian, 245–253
Parks, Rosa, 229

Patterson, N., 148
Peat, F. D., 270, 278, 279
Pedagogy
  conflict over contradictory social goals in
    classroom, 284–288
  conflict over nature and sources of
    knowledge in classroom, 288–294
  dilemma management and, 297–299
  pedagogical content knowledge and,
    101–102
Peer pressure, 44–46
  African American male achievement and,
    193, 200–201, 203, 207–208
  as negative, 44, 207–208
  as positive, 44–46
Perry, Theresa, 194
Personal learning plans, 88
Peterson, Penelope L., 98, 300 n. 2, 303 n.
    23, 303 n. 25
Phelps, Reverend, 157, 163
Philadelphia Writing Project, 262–263
Philadelphia Young Playwrights, 148, 149
Phillips, A., 244
Pincus, Marsha, 9, 93, 147–165
Pio Pico Student Researchers, 166–170
Pointer Mace, D., 170 n. 1, 185 n.
Portfolios
  in assessment process, 40, 42–43
  in culturally engaged instruction, 87–88
  Mission Hill School (website) and, 70,
    72–73
Power
  in negotiation process, 53
  Pio Pico Student Researchers and,
    166–170
Prejudice, confronting in English/language
    arts, 214–236
Presentations, art and, 46–48
Principals, Harvard Principals' Center and, 56
Prior preparation, African American male
    achievement and, 204
Project-centered approach
  art and, 46, 48
  community projects in, 55
  details and, 50–51
  negotiation and, 52
  portfolios and, 40, 42–43
  qualities of good project, 37–38
  universal success and, 39–40
Proposition 227 (California), 267–268

Pullout programs, 57–66
  changing, 63–64, 65–66, 271–280
  classroom chaos and elimination of,
    271–280
  impact on students, 59–61
  problems for teacher, 58
  reentry problems of students, 59–63
  research on, 64–65
  Ronnie (student) and, 60, 62–64
  student views of, 62
Putnam, R., 98

Quality. *See* Culture of quality

Racism, confronting in English/language arts,
    214–236
Reaching the Top (College Board), 193–194,
    197–198, 200, 204
Reader-response theory (Rosenblatt), 151–
    152, 155–162, 163
Reading
  in culturally engaged instruction, 80–81
  oral traditions versus, 181
  pullout programs for, 57–66
Reflection. *See also* Narrative analysis
  Mission Hill School (website) and, 73–76
Remillard, J., 102
Research for Action, 83
Richert, A., 101
Role models, African American male
    achievement and, 192, 196, 197
Roll of Thunder, Hear My Cry (Taylor), 218,
    228–229, 232–233
  prejudice in, 228–229, 232–233
  race as issue in, 228–229
Rose, Mike, 243
Rosenblatt, L., 151, 154, 156, 163
Royster, Jackie Jones, 79, 83
Rundquist, Sylvia, 97
Russo, Nancy, 303 n. 23

Sanchez, Sonia, 261
Sandburg, Carl, 184
Santa Barbara Classroom Discourse Group,
    64–65
Scarry, Elaine, 240
Schoenbach, R., 263
Schoenfeld, A., 98
Schwab, J. J., 96, 99, 100, 117, 299–300 n. 1,
    300 n. 3, 301 n. 7, 301 n. 10

Scott, Jerri Cobb, 79
Seating arrangements, 275–276
Self-advocacy, 52
Self-assessment, 40–42, 43
Self-determination, 265
Separate-but-equal practices, 229
Sergiovanni, Thomas J., 302 n. 14
Shavelson, Richard J., 301 n. 11, 303 n.
    23–24, 303 n. 27
Shepard, Matthew, 147, 152, 154, 163. *See
    also Laramie Project, The*
Shulman, Lee S., 3, 4, 101–102, 300–301 n.
    3–5
Siddle-Walker, Emilie, 80
Simons, E. R., 2
Slavin, Robert E., 303 n. 22
Smitherman, Geneva, 80
Social action, 257–265
  building community through journal
    writing, 261–264
  Pio Pico Student Researchers and,
    166–170
  student stories of, 259–264
  teacher beliefs about, 258
Social class, African American male
    achievement and, 193, 197–198
Social inquiry processes, 274–275
Socialization process, for Haitian
    preschoolers, 245–253
Social studies, American Revolution and,
    171–180
Sockett, H., 3
SooHoo, Suzanne, 169
Spindler, George, 302 n. 13
Split Open (theater performance), 150
Sports, African American male achievement
    and, 198–200, 208
Standards
  for art, 47
  for mathematics, 93, 95, 129, 133–146
  negotiating, 51–53
Stanford 9 exam, 268–269
Steele, C., 194
Stenhouse, L., 3
Stern, Paula, 303 n. 27
Stigler, J. W., 3
Strosser, M., 148
Student attitudes, culture of quality and, 35–36
Students with special needs. *See also* Pullout
    programs

Students with special needs (cont'd)
  detracking and, 211–213
  Hmong refugees, 237–241
  negotiating types of support for, 51–52
  remedial literacy programs and, 237
Systematic journal inquiry (Lytle & Cochran-
  Smith), 152

Taking Control (Jenkins), 148
Taylor, Mildred, 218, 228
Teacher attitudes
  African American male achievement and,
    192, 193–194, 196–197, 201, 208–209,
    210–213
  in confronting racism in the classroom,
    214–236
  detracking and, 211–212
  disciplinary standards and methods for
    Haitian preschoolers, 243–253
  toward social action, 258
Teaching. *See also* Dilemmas of teaching
  conventional assumptions about, 2–3
  general "problems" of, 1–2
  implications of culturally engaged
    instruction for, 85–86
  inquiry as central to learning and, 3
  narrative analysis in, 19–33, 67–69
  problems of pullout programs in, 57–66
  professional nature of, 10–11
  public nature of, 10–11
  representing complexities of, 2–3
  staff development in, 55–56
Teaching strategies, African American male
  achievement and, 193
Tectonic Theater Group, 151, 152–153, 163
Theater of the Oppressed (Boal), 153
To Kill a Mockingbird (Lee), 218, 219–228,
    229
  classroom violence and, 225–226, 233–236
  gender as issue in, 224–225
  prejudice in, 226–228, 232–233
  race as issue in, 220–224
Tracking
  impact of eliminating, 211–212
  reinstatement of, 212–213

Trueba, Henry T., 300 n. 2
Universal success, 38–40
University of California at Berkeley, 202
University of California at Los Angeles
  (UCLA), Career Based Outreach
  Program (CBOP), 205–207

Vacca, J. A. L., 184
Vacca, Richard T., 184
Violence
  African American male achievement and,
    198
  classroom, 225–226, 233–236

Wagner, Angelika C., 301–302 n. 12
Walberg, Herbert T., 303 n. 23
Waller, Willard, 302 n. 13
Walsh, Martha, 300 n. 2
Watson-Gegeo, K., 244
Watsons Go to Birmingham, The (Curtis),
    260, 264
Ways with Words (Heath), 248
Websites
  *A Friend of Their Minds: Capitalizing on
    the Oral Tradition*, 182–185
  Mission Hill School, 70–76
Weinstein, Rhona, 210
Weizenbaum, Joseph, 303 n. 26
Wilder, Laura Ingalls, 27
Wilson, Bryan, 301 n. 8
Wilson, S., 101, 128
Wineburg, S., 99
Wittrock, Merlin C., 300–301 n. 5
Wolk, Emily, 6, 7–8, 9, 93, 166–170, 170
    n. 1
Wong, H., 18
Wong, R., 18
Wood, D., 2
Worden, A., 147

Yinger, Robert, 301 n. 11
Young, Gifted, and Black (Perry et al.), 194

Zeichner, K. M., 3